Contents at a Glance

D1335913

Cloud Security

Cloud Security

A Comprehensive Guide to Secure Cloud Computing

Ronald L. Krutz
Russell Dean Vines

WILEY
Wiley Publishing, Inc.

Cloud Security: A Comprehensive Guide to Secure Cloud Computing

Published by
Wiley Publishing, Inc.
10475 Crosspoint Boulevard
Indianapolis, IN 46256
www.wiley.com

Copyright © 2010 by Wiley Publishing, Inc., Indianapolis, Indiana
Published simultaneously in Canada

ISBN: 978-0-470-58987-8

Manufactured in the United States of America

10 9 8 7 6 5 4 3 2 1

I thank God for His greatest gift of all—my family.

— Ronald L. Krutz

Dedicated to Elzy, for now and forever.

— Russell Dean Vines

About the Authors

 Ronald L. Krutz is a senior information system security consultant. He has over 30 years of experience in distributed computing systems, computer architectures, real-time systems, information assurance methodologies, and information security training. He holds B.S., M.S., and Ph.D. degrees in Electrical and Computer Engineering and is the author of best selling texts in the area of information system security.

He co-authored the *CISSP Prep Guide* for John Wiley and Sons and is co-author of the Wiley *Advanced CISSP Prep Guide*, the *CISSP Prep Guide, Gold Edition*, the *Security+Certification Guide*, the *CISM Prep Guide*, the *CISSP Prep Guide, 2nd Edition: Mastering CISSP and ISSEP*, the *Network Security Bible*, the *CISSP and CAP Prep Guide, Platinum Edition: Mastering CISSP and CAP*, the *Certified Ethical Hacker (CEH) Prep Guide*, and the *Certified Secure Software Lifecycle Prep Guide*. He is also the author of *Securing SCADA Systems* and of three textbooks in the areas of microcomputer system design, computer interfacing, and computer architecture. Dr. Krutz has seven patents in the area of digital systems and has published over 40 technical papers.

Dr. Krutz also serves as consulting Editor for John Wiley and Sons Information Security Certification Series, is a Distinguished Visiting Lecturer in the University of New Haven Henry C. Lee College of Criminal Justice and Forensic Sciences, and is an Adjunct Professor in Midway College, Kentucky.

Dr. Krutz is a Registered Professional Engineer in Pennsylvania.

Russell Dean Vines has been in the information systems industry for over 20 years, and has a unique ability to disseminate complex security issues to a wider audience, from CEOs to home Internet surfers.

He is also the author or co-author of 10 previous books, including the *CISSP Prep Guide*, which reached #25 on Amazon's best-sellers list. He co-authored the *Advanced CISSP Prep Guide*, the *CISSP Prep Guide, Gold Edition*, the *Security+Certification Guide*, the *CISM Prep Guide*, the *CISSP Prep Guide, 2nd Edition: Mastering CISSP and ISSEP*, the *CISSP and CAP Prep Guide, Platinum Edition: Mastering CISSP and CAP*, and the *Certified Ethical Hacker (CEH) Prep Guide*. He is also the author of *Wireless Security Essentials*, and *Composing Digital Music for Dummies*.

In addition to being a Certified Information Systems Security Professional (CISSP), Mr. Vines is a Certified Information Systems Manager (CISM), a Certified Ethical Hacker (CEH), certified in CompTIA's Security+ program, and is a Payment Card Industry (PCI) Qualified Security Assessor (QSA). Russ also has vendor security certifications from RSA, Websense, McAfee, Citrix, VMware, Microsoft, and Novell, and has been trained in the NSA's Information Assurance Methodology (IAM).

Mr. Vines is a frequent contributor to Web and trade publications; discusses Information Security Threats and Countermeasures as a member of SearchSecurityChannel.com's Ask the Experts panel, frequently speaks at industry events such as Comdex and Networld+Interop, and teaches CISSP, CEH, and Websense classes.

Credits

Executive Editor
Carol Long

Project Editor
Ed Connor

Technical Editor
David Chapa

Production Editor
Daniel Scribner

Editorial Director
Robyn B. Siesky

Editorial Manager
Mary Beth Wakefield

Marketing Manager
David Mayhew

Production Manager
Tim Tate

Vice President and Executive Group Publisher
Richard Swadley

Vice President and Executive Publisher
Barry Pruett

Associate Publisher
Jim Minatel

Project Coordinator, Cover
Lynsey Stanford

Proofreader
Nancy Bell

Indexer
Robert Swanson

Cover Designer
Ryan Sneed

Cover Image
© istockphoto.com/
GodfriedEdelman

Acknowledgments

I want to thank my wife, Hilda, for her support and encouragement during the writing of this text.

— Ronald L. Krutz

I'd like to give a big shout-out to the gang at Gotham Technology Group, in particular Ken Phelan, Joe Jessen, and Nancy Rand, for their assistance during this project. I'd also like to thank doctors Paul M. Pellicci and Lawrence Levin for the rare gift of health. But my greatest thanks is reserved for my wife, Elzy, for her continuous and unwavering support throughout my life.

— Russell Dean Vines

Both authors would like to express their gratitude to Carol Long and Ed Connor of John Wiley and Sons for their support and assistance in developing this text.

Contents

Foreword

Whenever we come upon something new, we try to understand it. A good way of understanding new things is to look for something from our experience that can serve as a metaphor. Sometimes this process works well, sometimes not.

Computer security has long labored under the metaphor of physical security. It stands to reason that we would assume that millennia of experience with keeping physical assets safe would serve us in keeping digital assets safe as well.

Much of our thinking in computer security has therefore been concerned with putting important things someplace "safe" and then controlling access to it. I distinctly recall a conversation with a security analyst at the beginning of the PC network era. When asked how to ensure the security of data on a PC, he said, "Simple. Put the data on the PC. Put the PC in a safe. Put the safe at the bottom of the ocean."

We have been challenged over the years with coming up with safe places that allowed access. We have been challenged with even figuring out what "safe" might mean in a world where risks could come from anywhere, including inside our own organizations.

In today's world, the physical security metaphor continues to deteriorate. We've all seen a movie or TV show where some critical piece of data becomes key to the plot. The location of the next terrorist attack is kept on a single USB that is subject to theft, deterioration, or any other number of physical ills designed to increase the drama. That is simply not the nature of data. Data is viral. Where did this data come from? It was never on a hard drive? No one ever emailed anybody about the attack? Can't somebody plug the damn key in and make a YouTube video about it so that everyone can see it?

As we move to this new era of cloud computing, the last vestiges of our physical world metaphors are swept way. We need to understand data access and validation in a new way — perhaps in the way they should have been understood all along. Data security needs to be understood as something new, requiring new and innovative solutions.

Security professionals are perhaps rightfully overwhelmed by this challenge. Despite increased spending, the average firm finds itself less secure than it was five years ago. Advancements in security tools and techniques have not kept pace with risks and attack vectors. How can the security community respond to these ever-increasing threats when the additional requirements of virtualization and agility drive data assets up into a nebulous "cloud"?

One thing we do know for sure: Security will not drive or control this change. Any business requirement for lower costs and increased agility of cloud computing will eventually rule the day. Security professionals have attempted to slow the growth of several technology initiatives over the years in an attempt to control the risks. E-mail, instant messaging, and web browsing are some that come to mind immediately. We know from past experience, however, that implementing appropriate controls generally works far better than attempting to simply stop these initiatives.

As security professionals, it is incumbent on us to generate innovations in our concepts of data security and integrity. We need tools and processes that recognize the ephemeral nature of data and the reality that physical locational controls simply will not work going forward. With a little hard work, we can achieve security models that minimize risk and enable this new method of computing. We don't need to give up on security; we simply need to abandon some of our metaphors.

This book serves as a guide for doing just that. As security professionals, we may not want to embrace the cloud, but we're certainly going to have to learn to live with it.

Ken Phelan
CTO Gotham Technology Group

Introduction

Cloud computing provides the capability to use computing and storage resources on a metered basis and reduce the investments in an organization's computing infrastructure. The spawning and deletion of virtual machines running on physical hardware and being controlled by hypervisors is a cost-efficient and flexible computing paradigm.

In addition, the integration and widespread availability of large amounts of "sanitized' information such as health care records can be of tremendous benefit to researchers and practitioners.

However, as with any technology, the full potential of the cloud cannot be achieved without understanding its capabilities, vulnerabilities, advantages, and trade-offs. This text provides insight into these areas and describes methods of achieving the maximum benefit from cloud computation with minimal risk.

Overview of the Book and Technology

With all its benefits, cloud computing also brings with it concerns about the security and privacy of information extant on the cloud as a result of its size, structure, and geographical dispersion. Such concerns involve the following issues:

- Leakage and unauthorized access of data among virtual machines running on the same server
- Failure of a cloud provider to properly handle and protect sensitive information

- Release of critical and sensitive data to law enforcement or government agencies without the approval and/or knowledge of the client

- Ability to meet compliance and regulatory requirements

- System crashes and failures that make the cloud service unavailable for extended periods of time

- Hackers breaking into client applications hosted on the cloud and acquiring and distributing sensitive information

- The robustness of the security protections instituted by the cloud provider

- The degree of interoperability available so that a client can easily move applications among different cloud providers and avoid "lock-in"

Cloud users should also be concerned about the continued availability of their data over long periods of time and whether or not a cloud provider might surreptitiously exploit sensitive data for its own gain.

One mitigation method that can be used to protect cloud data is encryption. Encrypting data can protect it from disclosure by the cloud provider or from hackers, but it makes it difficult to search or perform calculations on that data.

This book clarifies all these issues and provides comprehensive guidance on how to navigate the field of cloud computing to achieve the maximum return on cloud investments without compromising information security.

How This Book Is Organized

The text explores the principal characteristics of cloud computing, including scalability, flexibility, virtualization, automation, measured service, and ubiquitous network access, while showing their relationships to secure cloud computing.

The book chapters proceed from tracing the evolution of the cloud paradigm to developing architectural characteristics, security fundamentals, cloud computing risks and threats, and useful steps in implementing secure cloud computing.

Chapter 1 defines cloud computing and provides alternative views of its application and significance in the general world of computing. Following this introduction, the chapter presents the essential characteristics of cloud computing and traces the historical architectural, technical, and operational influences that converged to establish what is understand as cloud computing today.

Chapter 2 looks at the primary elements of the cloud computing architecture using various cloud-based computing architecture models. In this chapter we'll examine cloud delivery models (the SaaS, PaaS, and IaaS elements of the SPI framework), cloud deployment models (such as private, community, public, and hybrid clouds), and look at some alternative cloud architecture models, such as the Jericho Cloud Cube.

Chapter 3 explores the fundamental concepts of cloud computing software security, covering cloud security services, cloud security principles, secure software requirements, and testing concepts. It concludes by addressing cloud business continuity planning, disaster recovery, redundancy, and secure remote access.

Chapter 4 examines cloud computing risks and threats in more detail. We'll examine cloud computing risk to privacy assurance and compliance regulations, how cloud computing presents a unique risk to "traditional" concepts of data, identity, and access management (IAM) risks, and how those risks and threats may be unique to cloud service providers (CSPs).

Chapter 5 helps identify management challenges and opportunities. Security management must be able to determine what detective and preventative controls exist to clearly define the security posture of the organization, especially as it relates to the virtualization perimeter. We'll look at security policy and computer intrusion detection and response implementation techniques, and dive deeply into virtualization security management issues.

Chapter 6 addresses the important cloud computing security architectural issues, including trusted cloud computing, secure execution environments, and microarchitectures. It also expands on the critical cloud security principles of identity management and access control and develops the concepts of autonomic systems and autonomic protection mechanisms.

Chapter 7 presents cloud life cycle issues, together with significant standards efforts, incident response approaches, encryption topics, and considerations involving retirement of cloud virtual machines and applications.

Chapter 8 recaps the important cloud computing security concepts, and offers guidance on which services should be moved to the cloud and those that should not. It also reviews questions that a potential user should ask a cloud provider, and lists organizations that provide support and information exchange on cloud applications, standards, and interoperability. Chapter 8 concludes with advice on getting started in cloud computation and a "top ten" list of important related considerations.

Who Should Read This Book

Cloud Security: A Comprehensive Guide to Secure Cloud Computing is designed to be a valuable source of information for those who are contemplating using cloud computing as well as professionals with prior cloud computing experience and knowledge. It provides a background of the development of cloud computing and details critical approaches to cloud computing security that affect the types of applications that are best suited to the cloud.

We think that *Cloud Security: A Comprehensive Guide to Secure Cloud Computing* would be a useful reference for all of the following:

- Professionals working in the fields of information technology or information system security
- Information security audit professionals
- Information system IT professionals
- Computing or information systems management
- Senior management, seeking to understand the various elements of security as related to cloud computing
- Students attending information system security certification programs or studying computer security

Summary

We hope *Cloud Security: A Comprehensive Guide to Secure Cloud Computing* is a useful and readable reference for everyone concerned about the risk of cloud computing and involved with the protection of data.

Issues such as data ownership, privacy protections, data mobility, quality of service and service levels, bandwidth costs, data protection, and support have to be tackled in order to achieve the maximum benefit from cloud computation with minimal risk.

As you try to find your way through a maze of security minefields, this book is mandatory reading if you are involved in any aspect of cloud computing.

Cloud Computing Fundamentals

Out of intense complexities intense simplicities emerge.
—Winston Churchill

Cloud computing evokes different perceptions in different people. To some, it refers to accessing software and storing data in the "cloud" representation of the Internet or a network and using associated services. To others, it is seen as nothing new, but just a modernization of the time-sharing model that was widely employed in the 1960s before the advent of relatively lower-cost computing platforms. These developments eventually evolved to the client/server model and to the personal computer, which placed large amounts of computing power at people's desktops and spelled the demise of time-sharing systems.

In 1961, John McCarthy, a professor at MIT, presented the idea of computing as a utility much like electricity.[1] Another pioneer, who later developed the basis for the ARPANET, the Department of Defense's Advanced Research Projects Agency Network, and precursor to the Internet, was J.C.R. Licklider. In the 1960s, Licklider promulgated ideas at both ARPA and Bolt, Beranek and Newman (BBN), the high-technology research and development company, that envisioned networked computers at a time when punched card, batch computing was dominant. He stated, "If such a network as I envisage nebulously could be brought into operation, we could have at least four large computers, perhaps six or eight small computers, and a great assortment of disc files and magnetic tape units—not to mention remote consoles and teletype stations—all churning away."[2]

The conjunction of the concepts of utility computing and a ubiquitous world-wide network provided the basis for the future evolution of cloud computing.

What Is Cloud Computing?

In an October, 2009 presentation titled "Effectively and Securely Using the Cloud Computing Paradigm,"[3] by Peter Mell and Tim Grance of the National Institute of Standards and Technology (NIST) Information Technology Laboratory, cloud computing is defined as follows:

> *Cloud computing is a model for enabling convenient, on-demand network access to a shared pool of configurable and reliable computing resources (e.g., networks, servers, storage, applications, services) that can be rapidly provisioned and released with minimal consumer management effort or service provider interaction.*

This cloud model is composed of five essential characteristics, three service models, and four deployment models. The five essential characteristics are as follows:

- On-demand self-service
- Ubiquitous network access
- Resource pooling
- Location independence
- Rapid elasticity
- Measured service

The service models are as follows:

- Cloud Software as a Service (SaaS)—Use provider's applications over a network.
- Cloud Platform as a Service (PaaS)—Deploy customer-created applications to a cloud.
- Cloud Infrastructure as a Service (IaaS)—Rent processing, storage, network capacity, and other fundamental computing resources.

The deployment models, which can be either internally or externally implemented, are summarized in the NIST presentation as follows:

- Private cloud—Enterprise owned or leased
- Community cloud—Shared infrastructure for specific community
- Public cloud—Sold to the public, mega-scale infrastructure
- Hybrid cloud—Composition of two or more clouds

These characteristics and models are covered in detail in Chapter 2.

In 2009, the Open Cloud Manifesto was developed by a group of organizations including IBM, Intel, and Google to propose practices for use in the provision of cloud computing services. In the "Open Cloud Manifesto" (www.opencloudmanifesto.org), cloud computing is defined with a set of characteristics and value propositions. The characteristics outlined in the manifesto are as follows:

- The ability to scale and provision computing power dynamically in a cost-efficient way.

- The ability of the consumer (end user, organization, or IT staff) to make the most of that power without having to manage the underlying complexity of the technology.

- The cloud architecture itself can be private (hosted within an organization's firewall) or public (hosted on the Internet).

The value propositions listed in the manifesto are as follows:

- **Scalability on demand**—All organizations have to deal with changes in their environment. The ability of cloud computing solutions to scale up and down is a major benefit. If an organization has periods of time during which their computing resource needs are much higher or lower than normal, cloud technologies (both private and public) can deal with those changes.

- **Streamlining the data center**—An organization of any size will have a substantial investment in its data center. That includes buying and maintaining the hardware and software, providing the facilities in which the hardware is housed, and hiring the personnel who keep the data center running. An organization can streamline its data center by taking advantage of cloud technologies internally or by offloading workload into the public.

- **Improving business processes**—The cloud provides an infrastructure for improving business processes. An organization and its suppliers and partners can share data and applications in the cloud, enabling everyone involved to focus on the business process instead of the infrastructure that hosts it.

- **Minimizing startup costs**—For companies that are just starting out, organizations in emerging markets, or even advanced technology groups in larger organizations, cloud computing greatly reduces startup costs. The new organization starts with an infrastructure already in place, so the time and other resources that would be spent on building a data center are borne by the cloud provider, whether the cloud is private or public.

From a different perspective, in a ZDNet article titled "The Five Defining Characteristics of Cloud Computing" (http://news.zdnet.com/2100-9595_22-287001.html), Dave Malcolm Surgient proposes the following five defining characteristics of cloud computing:

- **Dynamic computing infrastructure**—A standardized, scalable, dynamic, virtualized, and secure physical infrastructure with levels of redundancy to ensure high levels of availability

- **IT service-centric approach**—As opposed to a server-centric model, the availability of an easily accessible, dedicated instance of an application or service

- **Self-service-based usage model**—The capability to upload, build, deploy, schedule, manage, and report on provided business services on demand

- **Minimally or self-managed platform**—Self-management via software automation employing the following:

  - A provisioning engine for deploying services and tearing them down, recovering resources for high levels of reuse

  - Mechanisms for scheduling and reserving resource capacity

  - Capabilities for configuring, managing, and reporting to ensure that resources can be allocated and reallocated to multiple groups of users

  - Tools for controlling access to resources, and policies for how resources can be used or operations can be performed

- **Consumption-based billing**—Payment for resources as they are used

---

IMPORTANT FACTORS IN THE DEVELOPMENT OF CLOUD COMPUTING

A number of dynamics such as software interoperability standards, virtualization technologies, high-bandwidth communications, the delivery of enterprise applications, and Web 2.0 contributed to the emergence of cloud computing.

Web 2.0 is a term that refers to Web design resulting in an interactive transport mechanism, rather than conventional static screens. Web 2.0 is viewed as a platform for running software applications instead of running them on desktop PCs. Tim O'Reilly of O'Reilly Media is generally acknowledged as coining the term "Web 2.0." Some of the characteristics commonly associated with Web 2.0 are as follows:

- Use of asynchronous JavaScript and XML (Ajax)

- Combination of services from a number of sources to create a new service (mashup)

- Free Web services

- Use of Really Simple Syndication (RSS)
- Social networking
- Interactive dictionaries and encyclopedias
- Blogging
- Collaborative applications
- Sophisticated gaming
- Wikipedia and other wikis
- Optimized search engines

In 1999, Salesforce.com was formed to deliver enterprise applications over the Internet. This capability was followed in 2002 by the provision of Amazon Web Services, and in 2006 by Amazon's Elastic Compute Cloud (EC2) commercial Web service for running customers' applications. In 2009, Google and Microsoft began offering enterprise application services.

Cloud computing developed from technologies and business approaches that emerged over a number of years. The major building blocks range from Internet technology to cloud service providers, as illustrated in Figure 1-1.

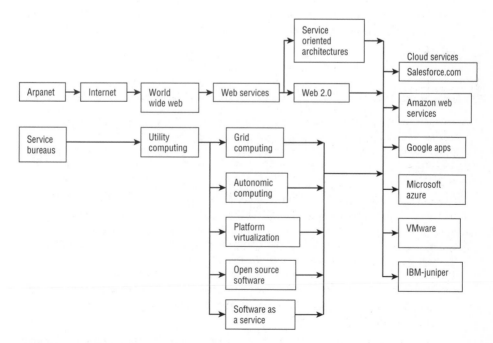

Figure 1-1: Origins of cloud computing

The important elements in the origination of cloud computing will be explored in detail in this book, but a few of the major items are summarized in Table 1-1 for background.

Table 1-1: Important Elements in the Origination of Cloud Computing

ITEM	DESCRIPTION
Utility Computing	The packaging and delivery of computing resources to a customer who pays for these resources as a metered service when needed. The objective is to use services effectively while reducing associated costs. The term "utility" is used to compare this type of computing resource utilization and payment to those of utilities such as providers of electricity or natural gas.
Grid Computing	The application of the processing power of multiple networked computing resources to solve a specific problem. It is a form of parallel processing conducted on a network of computers. In grid computing, servers, storage, and networks are combined to form powerful computing resource nodes that can be dynamically provisioned as needed.
Autonomic Computing	The functioning of a computer system without external control. The term is based on the autonomic nervous system of the human body, which controls breathing, heart functioning, and so on without conscious input from the individual. The objective of autonomic computing is to have the computer perform critical and complex functions without any major intervention by a user.
Platform Virtualization	The logical partitioning of physical computing resources into multiple execution environments, including servers, applications, and operating systems. Virtualization is based on the concept of a virtual machine running on a physical computing platform. Virtualization is controlled by a Virtual Machine Monitor (VMM), known as a *hypervisor*. Xen, an open-source hypervisor, is widely used for cloud computing.
Software as a Service (SaaS)	A software distribution and deployment model in which applications are provided to customers as a service. The applications can run on the users' computing systems or the provider's Web servers. SaaS provides for efficient patch management and promotes collaboration.
Service Oriented Architectures (SOA)	A set of services that communicate with each other, whose interfaces are known and described, whose functions are loosely coupled (the type of interface is not tied to the implementation), and whose use can be incorporated by multiple organizations. The SOA service interfaces are specified in XML and the services are expressed in WSDL. Applications can access services in a UDDI (Universal Description, Definition, and Integration) registration directory.

ITEM	DESCRIPTION
Cloud Services Examples	Salesforce.com provides enterprise cloud computing services in 1999.
	Cloud computing services provided by Amazon Web Services in 2002.
	Elastic Compute Cloud (EC2) commercial services offered by Amazon to small companies and individuals whereby computing resources can be rented.
	Google offers Google Apps, which include Web applications such as Gmail, Docs, and Calendar.
	Microsoft Azure Services Cloud Platform supports applications to be hosted and run at Microsoft data centers.
	VMware is a company that provides virtualization software for a variety of platforms.
	IBM and Juniper Networks formed a collaborative partnership in the delivery of cloud computing services.

What Cloud Computing Isn't

Even though cloud computing can incorporate some of the computing paradigms listed in Table 1-1, it is not synonymous with them. For example, cloud computing is not the same as utility computing. Cloud computing does not always employ the metered service pricing of utility computing, and cloud computing can use distributed, virtualized platforms instead of a centralized computing resource.

Is cloud computing the equivalent of grid computing? Grid computing does employ distributed virtual machines, but unlike cloud computing, these machines are usually focused on a single, very large task.

Sometimes client/server computing is viewed as cloud computing, with the cloud appearing in the server role. However, in the traditional client-server model, the server is a specific machine at a specific location. Computations running in the cloud can be based on computers anywhere, split among computers, and can use virtualized platforms, all unknown to the user. All the user knows is that he or she is accessing resources and using processing and storage somewhere to get results.

Cloud computing is not Software as a Service, which is software that an organization can purchase and manage; it is run on the user's hardware or someone else's machines.

Nor is cloud computing virtualization, although it can be used as an element to implement cloud computing. Operating system virtualization can be employed on an organization's local computers or in a data center, which is not cloud computing. However, virtualization can be employed in computing resources out in the cloud.

Cloud computing is not the same as service-oriented architecture (SOA), which supports the exchange of data among different applications engaged in business processes.

In short, although the preceding terms are not synonymous with cloud computing, depending on the implementation they can be a constituent of the cloud.

Alternative Views

A number of prominent people view cloud computing as pure hype and really nothing new. In an online video blog (`http://www.techcentral.ie/article.aspx?id=13775`), Oracle CEO Larry Ellison bluntly states, "What the hell is cloud computing? . . . When I read these articles on cloud computing, it is pure idiocy. . . . Some say it is a using a computer that is out there. . . . The people that are writing this are insane. . . . When is this idiocy going to stop?"

Noted information security expert Bruce Schneier, in his June 4, 2009 online newsletter *Schneier on Security* (`www.schneier.com/blog/archives/2009/06/cloud_computing.html`), says "This year's overhyped IT concept is cloud computing. . . . But, hype aside, cloud computing is nothing new. It's the modern version of the timesharing model from the 1960s, which was eventually killed by the rise of the personal computer. It's what Hotmail and Gmail have been doing all these years, and it's social networking sites, remote backup companies, and remote email filtering companies such as MessageLabs. Any IT outsourcing—network infrastructure, security monitoring, remote hosting—is a form of cloud computing."

In a February 10, 2009 *Information Week* article titled "HP on the Cloud: The World Is Cleaving in Two" (`http://www.informationweek.com/news/services/business/showArticle.jhtml?articleID=213402906`), Russ Daniels of Hewlett Packard states, "Virtually every enterprise will operate in hybrid mode," with some of its operations on the premises and some in the cloud, he predicted. Contrary to some theories put forth, he says that cloud computing is not a replacement for the data center. "The idea that we're going to one day throw a switch and move everything out to one of a small number of external data centers, located next to a low-cost power source, is nonsensical. It's not going to happen. Cloud computing is not the end of IT."

Another interesting view of cloud computing can be found at the hardware level. In an online article from EDN (Electronics Design, Strategy, News, at `www.edn.com/blog/1690000169/post/1490048349.html`), one mode of cloud computing is discussed as clusters of chips. The article reviews presentations from *Hot Chips 21, The Symposium on High-Performance Chips*, August 23–25, 2009 (`www.hotchips.org/hc21/main_page.htm`).

One of the conclusions that can be drawn from the symposium is that silicon designers have their own view of cloud computing that is related to chip architecture. Even though talking about cloud computing from the silicon chip level seems incongruous, it is valuable to understand their perspective.

According to the EDN article, silicon designers view cloud computing as a hierarchy of three elements, as follows:

1. Computing kernels—Processor cores or groups of cores enclosed within a secure perimeter and united by a single coherent address space. This definition is general enough that it could encompass a processor in a PC or a large multiprocessor system.

2. Clusters—Groups of kernels that are connected by a private local area network and whose respective tasks communicate among each other over low-bandwidth links.

3. Systems—Clusters connected through public networks and employing communications that cross security perimeter boundaries. These transactions are necessarily slower than intercluster communications.

Using these definitions, a conventional cloud would be viewed as large server farms that incorporate clusters and use kernels as server boards. An alternative approach broached at the symposium proposed the use of Sony PlayStation 3 (PS3) platforms containing the Cell Broadband processor as low-cost clusters and connecting these clusters through a public network to establish a robust cloud. The processors in this cluster would be powerful, with parallel floating-point hardware and high-speed internal communications. Using the PS3 or future equivalents, this type of cloud could be implemented at relatively low cost, be made widely available, and be amenable to open-source collaborations.

Essential Characteristics

The NIST definition of cloud computing[4] states that the cloud model comprises five essential characteristics. These characteristics are explored in the following sections.

On-Demand Self-Service

On-demand self-service enables users to use cloud computing resources as needed without human interaction between the user and the cloud service provider. With on-demand self-service, a consumer can schedule the use of cloud services such as computation and storage as needed, in addition to managing and deploying these services. In order to be effective and acceptable to the consumer, the self-service interface must be user-friendly and provide effective means to manage the service offerings. This ease of use and elimination of human interaction provides efficiencies and cost savings to both the user and the cloud service provider.

BroadNetwork Access

For cloud computing to be an effective alternative to in-house data centers, high-bandwidth communication links must be available to connect to the cloud services. One of the principal economic justifications for cloud computing is that the lowered cost of high-bandwidth network communication to the cloud provides access to a larger pool of IT resources that sustain a high level of utilization.

Many organizations use a three-tier architecture to connect a variety of computing platforms such as laptops, printers, mobile phones, and PDAs to the wide area network (WAN). This three-tier architecture comprises the following elements:

- Access switches that connect desktop devices to aggregation switches
- Aggregation switches that control flows
- Core routers and switches that provide connection to the WAN and traffic management

This three-tier approach results in latency times of 50 microseconds or more, which causes problematic delays when using cloud computing. For good performance, the switching environment should have a latency time of 10 microseconds or less. A two-tier approach that eliminates the aggregation layer can meet this requirement, using 10G (10 Gigabits/sec) Ethernet switches and the forthcoming 100G Ethernet switches.

Location-Independent Resource Pooling

The cloud must have a large and flexible resource pool to meet the consumer's needs, provide economies of scale, and meet service level requirements. Applications require resources for their execution, and these resources must be allocated efficiently for optimum performance. The resources can be physically located at many geographic locations and assigned as virtual components of the computation as needed. As stated by NIST,[5] "There is a sense of location independence in that the customer generally has no control or knowledge over the exact location of the provided resources but may be able to specify location at a higher level of abstraction (e.g., country, state, or datacenter)."

Rapid Elasticity

Rapid elasticity refers to the ability of the cloud to expand or reduce allocated resources quickly and efficiently to meet the requirements of the self-service characteristic of cloud computing. This allocation might be done automatically and appear to the user as a large pool of dynamic resources that can be paid for as needed and when needed.

One of the considerations in enabling rapid elasticity is the development and implementation of loosely coupled services that scale independently of other services and are not dependent on the elasticity of these other services.

Measured Service

Because of the service-oriented characteristics of cloud computing, the amount of cloud resources used by a consumer can be dynamically and automatically allocated and monitored. The customer can then be billed based on the measured usage of only the cloud resources that were allotted for the particular session.

The NIST view of measured service is "Cloud systems automatically control and optimize resource use by leveraging a metering capability at some level of abstraction appropriate to the type of service (e.g., storage, processing, bandwidth, and active user accounts). Resource usage can be monitored, controlled, and reported providing transparency for both the provider and consumer of the utilized service."[6]

Architectural Influences

The realization of cloud computing was affected by a number of architectural developments over the past decades. These influences range from advances in high-performance computing to scaling and parallelism advances. Some of the principal architectural developments that support cloud computing are summarized in the following sections.

High-Performance Computing

Because of the Internet and high-performance computers, an evolution is occurring in computing. This evolution is the movement from tasks that are computationally intensive to those problems that are data intensive. This evolution characterizes some types of cloud computing applications, which are practical to run because of high-performance computers. These computers play a key role in cloud computing, and some of the major milestones in their development are presented in this section.

The computers known as *supercomputers* evolved during the 1960s. In 1961, IBM developed the IBM 7030 "Stretch," which was the first transistor-based supercomputer. It was built for the Los Alamos National Laboratory and was specified at 1.2 MFLOPS (million floating-point operations per second.)

High-performance computing and supercomputing cannot be discussed without acknowledging Seymour Cray, who is credited with developing the first "real" supercomputers. While at Control Data Corporation (CDC), Cray developed the 3 MFLOP CDC 6600 in 1964 and the 36 MFLOP CDC 7600 in 1969. These were based on the relatively new silicon transistor technology. Cray left CDC in 1972 to form his own supercomputing company, Cray Research.

CDC continued on the supercomputer path and delivered the 100 MFLOP CDC STAR-100 in 1974. The STAR-100 was a vector processor, meaning it could operate on multiple arrays of data simultaneously.

Supercomputing technology developments accelerated during the next three decades with a variety of products. Detailing every one is beyond the scope of this text, but some of the key machines are summarized in Table 1-2. In the table, Gigaflops (GFLOPS) represent one billion (10^9) floating point operations per second, Teraflops (TFLOPS) refer to one trillion (10^{12}) floating point operations per second, and Petaflops (PFLOPS) represent are quadrillion (10^{15}) floating point operations per second.

An interesting milestone along the path of supercomputer development was the idea of connecting low-cost, commercially available personal computers in a network cluster to form a high-performance computing system. This idea was formulated in 1993 as the Beowulf computing cluster concept, developed by Thomas Sterling and Donald Becker of NASA. Beowulf uses open-source operating systems such as Solaris or Linux. One of the main characteristics of Beowulf is that all the connected machines appear as a powerful, single resource to the user.

The first prototype in the Beowulf project used 16 Intel DX4 processors connected by 10Mbit/second Ethernet. The DX4 processor is an Intel chip with triple clocking. Because the DX4 processor speed was too great for a single Ethernet bus, a "channel-bonded" Ethernet was developed by spreading the communications across two or more Ethernet buses. This approach is no longer necessary with the advent of Gigabit Ethernet. This initial cluster demonstrated the ability of COTS (commercial off the shelf) products to implement high-performance computing systems.

In general, a Beowulf architecture has the following characteristics:

- It is designed for parallel computing.

- Client nodes are usually diskless, dumb terminals.

- Client nodes are connected to a server node through a network, such as Ethernet and Ethernet switches.

- It uses Parallel Virtual Machine (PVM) software, which enables multiple networked computers to appear as a single parallel processor.

- It uses open-source operating systems such as Linux or Solaris.

- It incorporates the Message Passing Interface (MPI) API specification, which enables multiple computers to communicate to form a cluster.

Table 1-2: High-Performance Computing Evolution

COMPUTER	YEAR	PERFORMANCE	COMMENTS
Cray-1	1976	250 MFLOPS	Used integrated circuits and incorporated around 200,000 logic gates. The first Cray-1 was delivered to Los Alamos National Laboratories.
Cray X-MP	1983	941 MFLOPS	A Cray Research parallel vector processor supercomputer, which used multiple processors.
Cray-2	1985	1.9 GFLOPS	Successor to Cray X-MP; used an inert liquid cooling system.
Thinking Machines CM-5	1993	60 GFLOPS	A Connection Machine model (arrangement of thousands of connected microprocessors) using massively parallel processing and message-passing, distributed memory.
Intel Paragon XP/S	1993	143 GFLOPS	Incorporated the Intel i860 RISC microprocessor.
IBS ASCI White	2000	7.226 TFLOPS	A computer cluster comprising 512 interconnected IBM commercial RS/6000 SP computers.
NEC Earth Simulator	2002	35.86 TFLOPS	Comprises 640 supercomputers connected by a high-speed network. Each supercomputer contains eight vector processors with a peak performance of 8 GFLOPS.
IBM Blue Gene/L	2007	478.2 TFLOPS	Based on IBM Power Architecture; deployed at Lawrence Livermore National Laboratories.
IBM Roadrunner	2008	1.105 PFLOPS	The world's fastest computer, located at the Los Alamos National Laboratory. It incorporates both AMD 64 dual-core Opteron server processors and an IBM Cell accelerator processor that is connected to each Opteron core.

Some of the factors that have supported the acceptance and growth of Beowulf-type computers include the following:

- Increased demand for affordable, high-performance computing
- The availability of open-source software such as Linux
- Advances in the development of parallel algorithms
- The availability of low-cost, high-speed computer chips used for games, PCs, and entertainment systems
- The emergence of fully assembled subsystems for use in clusters
- Increased reliability of components and systems

The availability of high-performance computing platforms provides the basis for implementation of cloud computing.

Utility and Enterprise Grid Computing

According to the Grid Computing Info Centre's FAQ (`http://www.gridcomputing.com/gridfaq.html`), a computing *grid* is defined as "a type of parallel and distributed system that enables the sharing, selection, and aggregation of geographically distributed 'autonomous' resources dynamically at runtime depending on their availability, capability, performance, cost, and users' quality-of-service requirements."

The grid as a utility is based on SOA and provides resources using a "pay-as-you-go" utility model. According to *Grid Computing from Sun Microsystems* (`http://www.sun.com/servers/grid/`), "Grid Utility Computing is a pay-per-use service that lets users dynamically provision computing power, depending on application requirements."

An enterprise grid can serve a conventional or virtual organization. A virtual organization can use loosely coupled resources located in a number of geographic locations under different management.

An enterprise grid also provides use of a wide variety of IT services such as storage, printers, computers, applications, and databases as needed throughout the enterprise. The enterprise grid will register, manage, provision, provide security for, and bill for these types of services as needed.

Enterprise grid and utility computing are best implemented by employing standards and virtualization, which can provide the basis for offering SaaS services for customers. Some existing standard languages and protocols that support enterprise grid and utility computing are the Simple Object Access Protocol (SOAP), Extensible Markup Language (XML), Universal Description, Discovery, and Integration (UDDI), Web Services Description Language (WSDL), and the Open Grid Services Interface (OGSI).

Enterprise grid and utility computing, if implemented and managed properly, can result in the following benefits:

- Increased productivity
- Increased collaboration and improved communications
- Improved flexibility
- Virtual organizations that can share resources
- Ability to scale up and back
- Rapid and increased access to a variety of computing resources
- Reduction of effort required to manage multiple, non-integrated systems
- Increased resiliency and security

Autonomic Computing

The increasing complexity and connectivity of computing resources that are required to implement a cloud call for an innovative mechanism to manage, operate, and maintain the cloud infrastructure. *Autonomic computing* is one approach that holds great promise in helping to meet the expectations of cloud computing.

IBM developed the concept of autonomic computing, and on their autonomic computing website (`http://www.research.ibm.com/autonomic/overview/faqs .html#1`), they define it as "an approach to self-managed computing systems with a minimum of human interference. The term derives from the body's autonomic nervous system, which controls key functions without conscious awareness or involvement." The goal of autonomic computing is to provide complex, heterogeneous systems with self-diagnosis, self-healing, and self-optimizing capabilities.

Autonomic computing can be defined in architectural terms as follows:

- Managing systems to the specified requirements without extensive and detailed personnel involvement
- Extending and reducing system capabilities rapidly
- Managing systems of increasing complexity
- Managing complex systems at lower cost
- Adapting a system to new technologies
- Incorporating systems applications management drivers

Service Consolidation

Consolidation and sharing of services developed as a cost-effective tool to provide these services over a network, as needed. This capability depended on advances in standardization, optimization, service orientation, and virtualization. In particular, virtualization supports dynamic pools of resources such as servers and storage. Integration of services such as SaaS into the cloud paradigm on a pay-per-use basis provides organizations with attractive alternatives to in-house solutions. The decreasing costs of cloud computing hardware has made shared, consolidated services even more desirable today. This is particularly true when services can be delivered easily to such platforms as netbooks, IPods, and PDAs from either public, private, or hybrid clouds.

Service consolidation and utilization must also take into account the Quality of Service (QoS), compliance, security, governance, and exit strategy issues that arise with cloud computing. Also, at the enterprise level, the access of external cloud services should ensure their federation into the enterprise network.

Horizontal Scaling

In general, *scalability* is the property exhibited by a system or service wherein an increase of resources results in improved performance proportional to the additional amount of resources.

Scaling can be implemented in both centralized and distributed systems. In centralized systems, *vertical scaling*, or scaling up, is accomplished by increasing the size or capability of existing or fewer resources. In distributed systems, such as those used in cloud computing, *horizontal scaling* is the addition of more of the individual resource elements, such as servers. In addition to providing improved performance, horizontal scaling is used to implement redundancy and reliability of loosely coupled systems. Thus, distributed systems are more resilient and can tolerate failures of some resource units. This ability to reliably effect horizontal scaling is an important factor in the success of cloud computing.

Generally, vertical scaling is easier to implement, but it is more expensive. In addition, there is the possibility of a single point of failure. Horizontal scaling is usually less costly and more resilient, but it's relatively more difficult to implement than vertical scaling.

Horizontal scaling is particularly applicable to Web 2.0 in that, as applications expand, there is a corresponding decrease in performance. Because most applications are data intensive in cloud computing, significant improvements in performance can be achieved by horizontally scaling the database. This scaling involves replicating the database across multiple servers. Some Web 2.0 horizontal database scaling approaches include the following:

- **Caching**—Lowering application response times by performing memory caching of heavily accessed data using horizontally scaled, dedicated cache servers to reduce the load on application servers

- **Table-level partitioning**—Slicing data horizontally and distributing the data across database instances

- **Sharding**—Managing a growing number of applications by dividing datasets into smaller elements across many physical servers and segregating the transactional bandwidth across these servers

Web Services

The World Wide Web Consortium (W3C) (`http://www.w3.org/TR/ws-gloss/`) defines a *Web service* as "a software system designed to support interoperable machine-to-machine interaction over a network. It has an interface described in a machine-processable format (specifically WSDL). Other systems interact with the Web service in a manner prescribed by its description using SOAP-messages, typically conveyed using HTTP with an XML serialization in conjunction with other Web-related standards."

The *Web Services Descriptive Language* (WSDL), referred to in the Web service definition is "an XML format for describing network services as a set of endpoints operating on messages containing either document-oriented or procedure-oriented information. The operations and messages are described abstractly, and then bound to a concrete network protocol and message format to define an endpoint. Related concrete endpoints are combined into abstract endpoints (services). WSDL is extensible to allow description of endpoints and their messages regardless of what message formats or network protocols are used to communicate."

The *Simple Object Access Protocol* (SOAP), also cited in the Web service definition, is "a lightweight protocol for exchange of information in a decentralized, distributed environment. It is an XML-based protocol that consists of three parts: an envelope that defines a framework for describing what is in a message and how to process it, a set of encoding rules for expressing instances of application-defined data types, and a convention for representing remote procedure calls and responses. SOAP can potentially be used in combination with a variety of other protocols; however, the only bindings defined in this document describe how to use SOAP in combination with HTTP and the HTTP Extension Framework."

Copyright © 2000 DevelopMentor, International Business Machines Corporation, Lotus Development Corporation, Microsoft, UserLand Software (`http://www.w3.org/TR/2000/NOTE-SOAP-20000508/`).

NIST defines a Web service as "self-describing and stateless modules that perform discrete units of work and are available over the network."[6]

In summary, a Web service uses a standard interface that is described in WSDL to provide communication among computing platforms running different applications, with the SOAP XML-based protocol supporting this exchange of information over HTTP.

High-Scalability Architecture

As discussed in the previous section on horizontal scaling, the scalability of a cloud computing system ensures that the cloud can support increased load factors. Therefore, any cloud platform architecture should be designed with high scalability in mind, enabling increased capacity in a linear fashion in accordance with the corresponding workload. For example, Amazon's Provisioning Service exhibits high scalability by automatically scaling services in proportion to the load.

A number of options are available to promote high scalability. One approach, for example, would be to incorporate dynamically scalable CPUs and pipelining the processing of queued tasks. These options and additional possibilities are summarized in Figure 1-2.

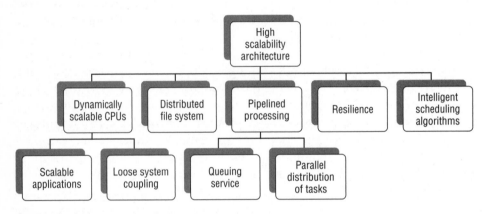

Figure 1-2: High-scalability architecture options

Technological Influences

As with architectural influences, advances in technology have obviously had an impact on the development and implementation of the cloud computing paradigm. Some of the key technological influences are presented in this section.

Universal Connectivity

Cloud computing requires universal access and connectivity to the Internet to thrive. In the United States, the economic stimulus bill of 2009 provided billions of dollars to expand and improve the nation's high-speed network infrastructure. Cloud computing serves consumers and organizations by ubiquitous connectivity among customers, businesses, and government organizations through avenues such as Web services, peer-to-peer exchanges, and Web 2.0. This universal connectivity should be accomplished through high-speed, broadband networks that do not provide different capabilities to different users on a selective basis.

It is estimated that the total number of broadband lines in the 40 biggest broadband countries in the world will grow to 635 million connections by 2013 (http://www.itfacts.biz/635-mln-broadband-users-in-40-countries-by-2013/12682). The continued expansion of broadband connections is vital to the expansion and worldwide growth of cloud computing.

An important issue related to universal connectivity is net neutrality. Net neutrality seeks to maintain the status quo of the Internet whereby users are in control of applications and content and all network traffic is treated equally. Users do not have to pay for different quality of service (QoS) levels. In some proposed models, broadband carriers would have the authority to provide "slow" or "fast" access to websites as a function of fees paid to the ISP by specific destinations.

Many Internet pioneers strongly oppose any changes to the current "neutral" Internet. For example, Tim Berners-Lee, inventor of the World Wide Web, has stated that "the neutral communications medium is essential to our society. It is the basis of a fair competitive market economy. It is the basis of democracy, by which a community should decide what to do. It is the basis of science, by which humankind should decide what is true. Let us protect the neutrality of the Net."

Commoditization

Prior to the 1980s, computer systems were proprietary and many had their own unique hardware, software, and protocols. With the rise of the PC in the 1980s, some software and hardware components became standardized and interchangeable among platforms. In the 1990s, the emphasis on local area networks (LANs) and wide area networks (WANs) led to commonality in communications protocols and eventually the Internet, which further accelerated commoditization. Organizations such as CompuServe and Prodigy with proprietary technologies gave way to the falling cost of bandwidth and the flexibility and accessibility provided by the World Wide Web. Strong drivers in the path toward commoditization are open-source software such as FireFox and OpenOffice, and the rapidly falling costs of servers, PCs, PDAs, and multifunction cellular products.

Commoditization usually follows the introduction of disruptive technologies. Entities that introduce a new technology are initially resistant to commoditization in order to control a large share of the marketplace and earn high profit margins. Two approaches to stalling commoditization are the bundling of a technology to a proprietary platform and attempting to file for patent protection. Eventually, if the new technology gains widespread acceptance and competitors arise, there is an impetus for exploring open-source possibilities, and ultimately commoditization of the technology. For example, the commoditization of music distribution was made possible by the Internet and freely available peer-to-peer software.

These commoditization issues also apply to cloud computing. As cloud computing usage becomes more popular and competition among vendors increases, costs will decrease and eventually commoditization is likely to occur. This trend will be accelerated by the expansion of cloud services and the wide availability of the technologies underlying cloud computing. In addition, there will be greater impetus for the adoption of standards.

In order to survive, cloud vendors will have to develop a competitive advantage over other vendors or exploit niche areas. Some of these viable organizations will be large vendors that are reliable, well known, have recognizable brand names, and offer a wide variety of services and applications for "one-stop" shopping. Another candidate for long-term success will be cloud suppliers that provide SaaS solutions to specific industries such as health care, defense, finance, and so on.

For users who are seeking cloud computing services, important differentiators among vendors include level of confidence in the security offered, the quality of customer support, and value-added features provided. Enterprise clients, in particular, will see high availability and failover provisions as important factors in choosing a cloud service.

On the way to cloud commoditization, if it does occur, the industry will coalesce around one or two standards that support interoperability and interchange of services among cloud vendors. These standards can be formal, de facto, or open. De facto standards might arise from their use by dominant vendors, such as Amazon or VMware, which promote the Elastic Compute Cloud (EC2) application programming interface (API) and the vCloud API, respectively.

An additional variable in the mix of cloud computing and the issue of commoditization would be the emergence of large cloud vendors in overseas markets such as India, China, or Europe. There are large organizations in these areas that have the capability and resources to enter the cloud computing market and offer strong competition to existing providers.

Excess Capacity

Excess capacity in the context of cloud computing has two interpretations. One refers to cloud-consuming organizations having to meet peak service demands on an intermittent basis, such as for a holiday season; the other denotes an organization offering cloud computing to generate revenue from its excess server, storage, or database capacity.

By using cloud computing to meet peak demands, an organization can invoke the "pay as you go" model and not have to incur the costs of unused capacity in local hardware, including depreciation, power, personnel, and software. This model is best executed if the excess capacity requirements in an organization are predictable and can be integrated into an organization's IT resource planning.

Conversely, excess capacity in the cloud can be considered an advantage for a cloud provider, and used to service many organizations, thus making the cloud environment more efficient by spreading costs over multiple consumers. Thus, fewer resources are required to serve a variety of clients, which results in the conservation of energy and capital. This reasoning would apply to both private and public clouds.

Organizations such as Amazon have chosen to use their large computing capabilities and excess capacity required for seasonal demand to offer cloud services and provide another income revenue stream. Amazon's cloud offering, Amazon Web Services, takes advantage of Amazon's years of experience in developing and operating large-scale e-commerce Web operations.

Open-Source Software

Open-source software has a place in cloud computing, but that place can take various forms and elicits different opinions. The use of open-source software in cloud computing can provide the following benefits:

- Availability and access to source code
- No license fees
- Ease of adoption for first-time users
- Ease of development and integration of new applications
- Ability to modify, extend, and redistribute software
- No payment for patches and upgrades
- Open file formats
- Avoidance of vendor lock-in
- Low barriers for new users to try the software

Some cloud providers are using open-source software such as Linux in order to access and sometimes modify the source code to provide customized services. This leads to proprietary technology in many instances.

An additional option for implementing cloud computing services is the use of open-source cloud computing platforms. Some of the popular platforms are summarized in Table 1-3.

Table 1-3: Open-Source Cloud Platforms

SOURCE	PLATFORM	COMMENT
University of Chicago (`http://workspace.globus.org`)	Globus Nimbus	Supports developing a computing cluster that supports an Infrastructure-as-a-Service (IaaS) cloud incorporating the Xen hypervisor
University of California, Santa Barbara; Eucalyptus Systems (`http://www.eucalyptus.com/`)	Eucalyptus	Supports the installation of on-premise private and hybrid clouds using the existing hardware and software
European Union/IBM (`http://www.reservoir-fp7.eu/`)	RESERVOIR (Resources and Services Virtualization without Barriers)	Provides for the large-scale deployment of IT services across multiple, different administrative domains
Enomoly (`www.enomaly.com/`)	Enomalism	Supports the creation of cloud capacity and management of virtual machines
Abiquo (`www.abiquo.com/`)	Abicloud	Infrastructure software for development and management of public and private clouds
Xen (`www.Xen.org`)	Xen Cloud Platform (XCP)	Cloud infrastructure platform for delivery of customizable, multi-tenant cloud services

For open-source cloud software to mature, open standards and protocols have to be developed to support interoperability of services. Toward this end, the independent nonprofit Open Web Foundation (`http://openwebfoundation .org/` was founded to support the development and protection of open, nonproprietary specifications for Web technologies.

Virtualization

Traditionally, server virtualization was viewed as a cost-saving measure. However, it has evolved to the point that it is now considered to have value both in providing flexibility in the utilization of resources and as an enabler of cloud computing. Some of the key benefits of virtualization that are indigenous to cloud computing are as follows:

- Billing based on usage (utility pricing) and not fixed hardware capacity
- Rapid deployment of additional servers
- Promotion of economies of scale
- Separation of the customer from physical server locations
- Usage based on service-level agreements
- Alternative sourcing supported
- Fault tolerance
- Application mobility among servers and data centers

Virtualization provides a level of freedom of choice for the customer, and efficiencies and cost savings for cloud providers. In many instances, the migration to virtualized clouds will be initially through hybrid clouds as customers test and evaluate the cloud paradigm in the context of their own business requirements. As users become accustomed to employing cloud computing, they will embrace the capability to have large numbers of servers available on demand; and, conversely, to rapidly reduce the number of servers they are using when they are not required. Additional benefits can be obtained by developing autonomic computing and integrating change management into the virtual machine model. Virtualization, if applied properly, can also result in minimal ramp-up times, reduction of time to develop and market applications, and rapid acquisition or reduction of resources, as requirements vary.

Virtualization also supports utility computing in that a cloud can enable a customer to open virtual machines on the cloud provider's resources as if the virtual instance were running on the customer's hardware. This capability can be extremely useful in meeting a customer's expected and unexpected peak demands.

Operational Influences

Operations considerations have a significant effect on the deployment, management, maintenance, and selection issues associated with cloud computing. The principal operational influences are explored in the following sections from the perspectives of both the customer and the provider of cloud computing services.

Consolidation

Traditionally, single applications were run on one or more servers. In many instances, the individual servers were not fully utilized and had spare processing capacity. In addition, an enterprise provided dedicated servers such as mail servers, print servers, Domain Name System (DNS) servers, and so on.

Virtualization offers a means to consolidate applications and servers, and changes the traditional relationship between software and hardware. Virtualization enables more than one application to run on a server and the capability to distribute multiple applications over multiple servers for resiliency. This consolidation increases resource utilization, boosts efficiency, lowers capital investment and maintenance costs, and provides the basis for increased security. Security can be enhanced because access control for an application running on its own virtual machine can be implemented simply and directly.

This form of consolidation is depicted in Figure 1-3.

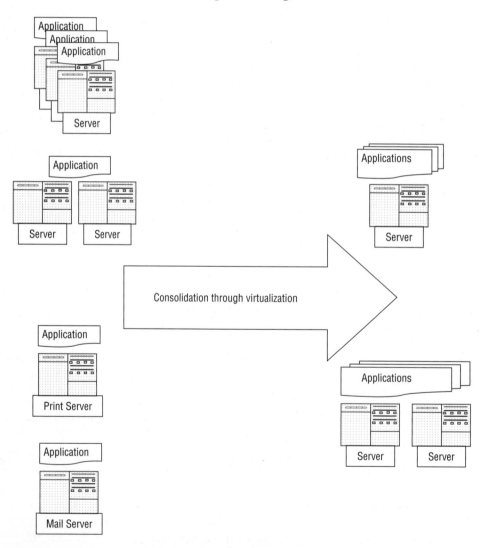

Figure 1-3: Server consolidation through virtualization

To achieve effective consolidation, it is important to understand the resources that are necessary to run the application over time. This data includes the application's usage characteristics, peak resource requirements, and performance when approaching or exceeding resource capacity. With this information, the virtual machines that will run the applications can be allocated across the physical computing and storage resources. Improper allocations can result in performance problems when applications' resource requirements vary widely over time. In instances where overloads do occur, applications can be migrated to additional servers using a number of available approaches.

One option is using MS Cluster Server software. According to Microsoft (`http://msdn.microsoft.com/en us/library/ms952401.aspx`), "a cluster connects two or more servers together so that they appear as a single computer to clients. Connecting servers in a cluster allows for workload sharing, enables a single point of operation/management, and provides a path for scaling to meet increased demand. Thus, clustering gives you the ability to produce high availability applications."

Another important factor in cloud computing consolidation is resource energy usage. Studies have shown that even when CPU utilization is running at 10%, power consumption is approximately at 50% of peak power usage.[7] Thus, it is important to take energy usage into consideration when viewing savings through consolidation.

When considering energy, the optimum savings in consolidation might not occur at very high resource utilization rates. Another metric that has to be considered is energy per unit service provided. In their paper addressing this subject, Srikantaiah, Kansal, and Zhao[8] state that the following factors should be considered to optimize energy usage:

- Design an effective consolidation strategy that takes into account the impact of consolidating applications on the key observable characteristics of execution, including resource utilization, performance, and energy consumption.

- Consolidation methods must carefully decide which workloads should be combined on a common physical server because workload resource usage, performance, and energy usages are not additive.

- There exists an optimal performance and energy point, which changes with acceptable degradation in performance and application mix.

- The optimal performance and energy point should be tracked as workloads change to improve energy-efficient consolidation.

The paper also states that "typical variation of energy per transaction with utilization (of a single resource) can be expected to result in a "U"-shaped curve. When the resource utilization is low, idle power is not amortized effectively and hence the energy per transaction is high. At high resource utilization, on the other hand, energy consumption is high due to performance degradation and longer execution time."

Outsourcing

Cloud computing offers opportunities for cost savings, increased efficiency, agility, and flexible billing options through outsourcing. The large investments of cloud providers in developing high-capability infrastructures eliminate the need for customers to make large initial or additional upfront expenditures for in-house IT systems. Some of the key benefits of outsourcing that can be provided by cloud offerings are as follows:

- Resiliency
- Disaster recovery
- Economy of scale
- Security
- Automatic and continuous hardware and software upgrades
- Libraries of applications
- Performance monitoring and management
- Rapid capability expansion
- Rapid capability downsizing
- Significant energy savings

An important activity that should accompany an outsourcing decision is the development and implementation of a long-term plan to improve business processes and the corresponding employment of computing platforms. This planning process should evaluate the impact of outsourcing on the organization.

Outsourcing Legal Issues

Organizations have to ensure that contracts with cloud vendors provide the protections and legal guarantees that are specific to the organization's mission and operations. The following list summarizes the critical areas that should be addressed:

- **Service-level agreements (SLAs)**—A SLA should be entered into with mutual understanding and commitment from both the customer and the cloud provider. The service provider should have a clear understanding of the customer's expectations and concerns. The following elements are typically included in a SLA:
    - Application security
    - Intellectual property protection

- Termination
- Compliance requirements
- Customer responsibilities
- Performance tracking
- Problem resolution
- Termination
- Lead time for implementation

- **Regulatory issues**—A contract between a cloud provider and customer should require the provider to adhere to the legal requirements of public privacy laws, including the following:
  - The Health Insurance Portability and Accountability Act (HIPAA)
  - The Fair Credit Reporting Act, as amended by the Fair and Accurate Credit Transactions Act of 2003
  - The Gramm-Leach-Bliley Act of 1999
  - The Payment Card Industry Data Security Standards

- **Customer privacy**—Customer information resident on a cloud provider's platforms can be subject to aggregation and data mining. Vendors must provide guarantees that personally identifiable information will be protected and not used for monetary gain, such as selling the information to advertisers. In addition, it is important to establish how long the vendor will maintain the customer's records and how those records will be deleted. There should be stipulations in any contract that the customer's data will be destroyed on an agreed upon date.

- **Termination**—The provisions for the customer or cloud provider to terminate the contractual agreement or temporarily halt usage should be specified, along with any required notification lead times.

- **Identity protection**—The cloud service customer should require the vendor to provide mutually agreed upon guarantees that the vendor will protect personally identifiable information from compromises that might result in the theft of an individual's identity for the purposes of credit fraud.

- **Patent issues**—The cloud vendor should warrant that they are the rightful and legal owners of the technologies they are providing and that they will indemnify the customer against any patent infringement situations that may arise.

- **Selection of jurisdiction**—The customer of the cloud provider usually specifies that the jurisdiction in the contract be that of the customer.

- **Export issues**—The cloud service provider should ensure that it complies with relevant export control laws that prohibit some types of encryption software to be stored or transmitted outside of a country. This situation might occur if a cloud provider has data centers located outside a nation's boundaries.

Business Process Outsourcing (BPO) Issues

In business process outsourcing, an organization outsources business activities such as finance, benefits, customer service, accounting, and payroll functions.

BUSINESS PROCESSING OUTSOURCING DEFINITION

SearchCIO.com (`http://searchcio.techtarget.com/sDefinition/0,, sid182_gci928308,00.html`) defines BPO as "the contracting of a specific business task, such as payroll, to a third-party service provider. Usually, BPO is implemented as a cost-saving measure for tasks that a company requires but does not depend upon to maintain their position in the marketplace. BPO is often divided into two categories: back office outsourcing, which includes internal business functions such as billing or purchasing, and front office outsourcing, which includes customer-related services such as marketing or tech support." This type of outsourcing is different from IT outsourcing, which involves applications, storage, and data center activities.

Business processes that are obtained in a user's country are known as *onshore outsourcing*, whereas those services that are contracted from a foreign country are described as *offshore outsourcing*. BPO widely employs vendors in nations such as India, China, and Malaysia.

The following are some typical BPO functions:

- **Financial services**—These services include expense processing, transaction processing, decision support, and capital equipment management.

- **Human resources (HR) functions**—HR functions include benefits, employee information management, recruiting, payroll, customer-service call centers, and application development.

- **Supply chain management (SCM)**—Management of the organization's supply chain involves coordinating among customers, partners, and suppliers, and includes procuring, managing payments, logistics support, operations management, and developing evaluation metrics.

An organization that is considering BPO must understand the following:

- What Web services are available
- Integration of data and services
- Possible reuse of existing applications
- Use of shared and/or open-source solutions
- Roles of IT staff in providing cloud engagement services

Figure 1-4 presents an example of the strategic aspects of embarking on a BPO endeavor.

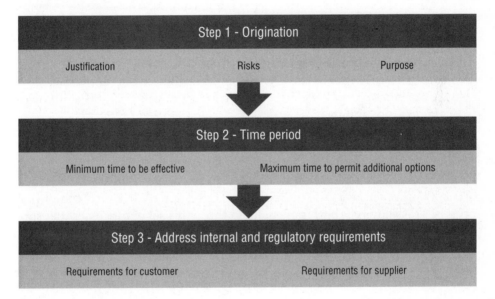

Figure 1-4: Typical steps in invoking BPO

Step 1 in Figure 1-4 emphasizes processes that involve determining the reasons and justifications for BPO, evaluating the risks associated with a possible outsourcing engagement, and analyzing the purpose and type of relationship expected with the vendor. Also, the processes to be outsourced and the processes to remain in house should be determined.

Step 2 requires a detailed analysis of the period of time that BPO should span. This step should develop both a lower limit, to allow expected benefits to be achieved; and an upper limit, to provide the flexibility to possibly engage another supplier.

Step 3 in the BPO strategic process should ensure that internal, legal, and regulatory requirements are met in the outsourced environment. This effort should define the requirements and actions to be performed by the customer and the vendor.

BPO, when implemented properly, can support more effective adherence to purchasing policies, increase productivity, and reduce capital expenditures. Some additional benefits of BPO are as follows:

- Market advantage from technology and process improvements
- Improved regulatory compliance
- Lowered procurement costs
- Enhanced integration of acquisitions
- Global perspectives

A category related to BPO is *knowledge processing outsourcing (KPO)*. KPO is a mode of outsourcing that requires special knowledge and expertise. KPO includes activities such as R&D and new product development that involves particular skills or abilities.

IT Service Management

From the perspective of the cloud provider, IT service management is the application of best practices to the oversight and operation of delivered computing services. This activity is best implemented through a set of processes that support the following functions:

- **Fault tolerance**—To provide availability of needed resources
- **Visibility**—To monitor performance and make required adjustments and improvements
- **Security**—To provide acceptable risk levels and meet compliance requirements
- **Control**—To manage virtualized resources across shared platforms
- **Automation**—To maintain performance and security and reduce costs of managing complex computing environments
- **Performance**—To meet committed requirements of customers and incorporate optimization to reduce operating costs

A cloud customer must also employ IT service management to evaluate the quality, effectiveness, and cost of contract services. The consumer organization should also develop processes to review operational reports and billings. It must follow up with the cloud provider to determine whether specified compliance requirements are being met and SLAs are satisfied.

One service management tool that can benefit both the cloud provider and the consumer is the use of a standard interface or API to deliver service monitoring data. Service performance information that is available through APIs can be analyzed and reviewed more effectively than conventional reports.

Automation

The ability to automatically manage and transport virtual applications dynamically is a key characteristic of effective cloud computing. Cloud automation provides the means to build processes that provision cloud services across virtual and physical cloud platforms. Cloud automation technologies should typically provide the following capabilities:

- Resiliency by automatic failover to other cloud platforms
- Triggers that respond to external occurrences to adjust cloud resource allocations to meet compliance and SLA requirements
- Management of the transition of development programs from prototype to test to commissioning across virtual platforms
- Provisioning to adjust to load demands and provide agility in assigning resources
- Management of resources based on SLAs and policies
- Monitoring of virtual machine–related data, such as storage usage, utilization history, owners, and file system access history
- General data collection and reporting, including change reporting
- Enforcement of security restrictions regarding directories and configuration elements
- Monitoring security and privacy violations

An emerging trend to support configuration of the automation requirements is the use of rule-based tools. These tools enable users to create rules that can specify triggers, set maximum and minimum windows for certain metrics, define SLA boundaries, and implement other runtime information-acquisition routines.

Summary

Cloud computing is becoming an increasingly attractive alternative to large, in-house data centers. Even though many managers and computing professionals have different views as to the composition and significance of cloud computing, it is clearly emerging as a major driver in the IT marketplace.

For cloud computing to mature, it is important that related standards are developed and adopted. This will not only make it more attractive to implement cloud systems, but also provide users with the flexibility to choose and move among vendors. It is significant that NIST has engaged in a cloud computing initiative to develop a common terminology and lay the foundation for the development of cloud standards.

Cloud computing was made possible by the confluence of a variety of architectural, technological, and operational influences. In the technological and architectural arenas, high-performance computing, grid computing, autonomic computing, Web services, virtualization, universal connectivity, and open-source software were some of the key drivers of cloud computing. Operationally, factors such as the growth of outsourcing, consolidation of resources, and IT service management provided the basis for organizations to migrate to the cloud computing paradigm.

Advanced technologies such as autonomic computing and developments such as the Beowulf-type, low-cost, high-performance computing clusters will provide further impetus and growth to the cloud computing market, providing economies of scale in terms of hardware and operational costs.

One aspect of the maturation of the cloud marketplace is the issue of commoditization. Commoditization will be driven by standards, competition both onshore and offshore, and the falling costs of platforms. On the one hand, this trend will be of great benefit to cloud customers; on the other hand, it might lead to the dominance of a small number of players in the cloud computing arena.

Notes

1. McCarthy, J., "Centennial Keynote Address," MIT, 1961.

2. Waldrop, M., "Computing's Johnny Appleseed." *Technology Review*, http://www.techreview.com/articles/jan00/waldrop.htm, Jan/Feb 2000.

3. csrc.nist.gov/groups/SNS/cloud-computing/cloud-computing-v25.ppt.

4. csrc.nist.gov/groups/SNS/cloud-computing/cloud-computing-v25.ppt.

5. csrc.nist.gov/groups/SNS/cloud-computing/cloud-computing-v25.ppt.

6. csrc.nist.gov/groups/SNS/cloud-computing/cloud-computing-v25.ppt.

7. Chen, G., He, W., Liu, J., Nath, S., Rigas, L., Xiao, L., and Zhao, F., "Energy-Aware Server Provisioning and Load Dispatching for Connection-Intensive Internet Services," Networked Systems Design and Implementation (NSDI), 2008.

8. Srikantaiah, S., Kansal, A., and Zhao, F., "Energy Aware Consolidation for Cloud Computing," USENIX HotPower '08: Workshop on Power Aware Computing and Systems at OSDI, USENIX, December 7, 2008.

Cloud Computing Architecture

*A man begins cutting his wisdom teeth
the first time he bites off more than he can chew.*
—**Herb Caen**

As shown in Chapter 1, cloud computing isn't as much a single technology as it is a combination of many existing technologies. Elements of cloud computing may resemble earlier computing eras, but advances in virtualization, storage, connectivity, and processing power are combining to create a new technical ecosystem for cloud computing, and the result is a fundamentally different and compelling phenomenon.

The adoption of cloud computing services is growing rapidly, and one of the reasons is because its architecture stresses the benefits of shared services over isolated products. This use of shared services helps an organization focus on its primary business drivers, and lets information system technology departments reduce the gap between available computing capacity (always-on high resource) and required systems demand (mostly low volume with occasional spikes). This results in a much more efficient usage-based cost model.

This chapter looks at the primary elements of the cloud computing architecture, using the NIST document described in Chapter 1 as a baseline (we'll also look at a couple of other accepted cloud based computing architecture models). Included in this chapter are the following:

- **Cloud delivery models** — The SaaS, PaaS, and IaaS elements of the SPI framework
- **Cloud deployment models (also called consumption modalities)** — Private, community, public, and hybrid clouds
- **Alternative cloud architecture models** — Such as the Jericho Cloud Cube

Cloud Delivery Models

Cloud computing architecture is still evolving, and will continue to evolve and change for a long time. As we begin to make sense of the various vendors' rush to brand everything as "cloud computing," it's important to try to weed out the purely marketing-related acronyms and concepts. The goal of this section is to describe the cloud concepts and terminology that appear to be able to stand the test of time. Then, later in this section, we'll examine the benefits of adopting these concepts, and how organizations are restructuring their information models to compete and thrive.

The SPI Framework

For some time now, the generally agreed upon classification scheme for cloud computing has been coined the *Software-Platform-Infrastructure (SPI) model*. This acronym represents the three major services provided through the cloud: SaaS, or Software as a Service; PaaS, Platform as a Service; and IaaS, Infrastructure as a Service.

Although there are a few other concepts circulating that suggest variations on this schema (we'll address some of these in the section "Alternative Deployment Models"), the SPI framework for cloud computing is currently the most widely accepted cloud computing classification. NIST follows this framework, and most CSPs (cloud service providers) support this concept.

SPI Evolution

To understand how the SPI framework evolved, perhaps it's helpful to place it in context with the development of Internet Service Providers (ISPs). A common way to look at how ISPs developed is through generational versions, as described in the following simplified list:

1.0 — As ISPs originally began to provide Internet services, dial-up modem service for homes and organizations proliferated, making the Internet a commercial commodity.

2.0 — During a period of merging and consolidation, ISPs began offering other services, such as e-mail and off-site data storage.

3.0 — The increasing demand for infrastructure to host their customers' applications and data led to the creation of data centers known as *collocation facilities*, where multiple customers could centralize their servers, storage, and communications systems on the ISP's premises.

4.0 — The commoditization of collocation facilities led to the development of *application service providers (ASPs)*. ASPs provided software applications tailored to an organization, owning both the application and the infrastructure.

5.0 — The ASP model eventually evolved into cloud computing, which brought new delivery models, such as the SPI framework, with its SaaS, PaaS, and IaaS service models, and various deployment models, such as private, community, public, and hybrid cloud models.

To better visualize this progression, Figure 2-1 shows data center evolution through basic virtualization into a full SPI framework, thereby increasing flexibility and lowering costs.

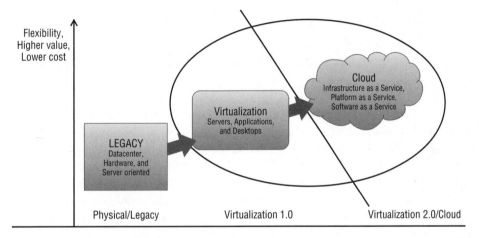

Figure 2-1: SPI evolution through virtualization

The SPI Framework vs. the Traditional IT Model

Although a lot of cloud computing infrastructure is based on existing technology, there are many differences between the SPI framework and the traditional IT model.

For instance, a traditional enterprise-wide application rollout requires resources and coordination from many parts of the organization. This rollout may require numerous new hardware (servers, perimeter network devices, workstations, backup systems), operating systems, communication link provisioning, and user and management training, for example.

One advantage of the traditional model is that software applications are more customizable, but even this advantage often comes at a high cost in resources and effort.

In the traditional IT model, software applications may require substantial licensing and support costs. These licensing costs may be based on formulae that don't translate well to the actual intended use of the application, such as hardware requirements (number of servers, processors, communication links) or other company characteristics unrelated to the original intent of the application (total number of employees in the organization, total number of remote offices, etc.).

In addition, changes in the original licensing structure due to usage increases (additional per-seat needs) may create substantial costs down the line, such as additional hardware, support SLAs, and IT resources.

In the traditional IT model, security is often owned "in-house," with security professionals and supporting security infrastructure (firewalls, intrusion detection/prevention systems, e-mail and web monitoring systems, etc.) under the direct control of the organization. This may make it easier to provide regulatory compliance for auditing purposes using the traditional model. However, the drawback of this security ownership is the infrastructure overhead, which requires considerable resources of manpower to secure properly.

Typically, organizations employing the SPI framework don't own the infrastructure that hosts the software application. They instead license application usage from the cloud provider, by employing either a subscription-based license or a consumption-oriented model. This enables companies to pay for only the resources they need and use, and to avoid paying for resources they don't need, thus helping them avoid a large capital expenditure for infrastructure.

The cloud service provider that delivers some or all of the SPI elements to the organization can also share infrastructure between multiple clients. This helps improve utilization rates dramatically by eliminating a lot of wasted server idle time. Also, the shared use of very high-speed bandwidth distributes costs, enables easier peak load management, often improves response times, and increases the pace of application development.

Another benefit of adopting the SPI framework for organizational computing is reduced startup costs. Eliminating the resource requirements mentioned above lowers the barrier to entry, and in many cases provides an organization much quicker access to computing power and software development than the traditional IT model did. Table 2-1 shows the three primary SPI framework services, paired with an example of the service the vendor supplies for that layer.

Table 2-1: SPI Services Delivery Vendors

SPI FRAMEWORK SERVICE	DESCRIPTION	VENDOR EXAMPLE
IaaS	Shared Internet infrastructure, such as servers and storage	Amazon EC2 and S3, Sun Microsystems Cloud Services, Terremark, Dropbox
PaaS	Application platform that provides developers with quick deployment	Google App Engine, force.com (from salesforce.com), Microsoft Azure
SaaS	Stateless cloud-enabled multiple-instance applications on a pay-per-use pricing model	Zoho Suite, Apple's MobileMe, Google Docs

The following sections take a closer look at these three primary cloud delivery models.

SECURITY VS. EXTENSIBILITY

According to the Cloud Security Alliance (see www.cloudsecurityalliance
.org/guidance/csaguide.pdf), it's important to continually "be aware of
the trade-offs between extensibility (openness) and security responsibility
within the three Cloud Service Delivery Models:

■ **SaaS (Software as a Service)** — Least extensibility and greatest amount
  of security responsibility taken on by the cloud provider

■ **IaaS (Infrastructure as a Service)** — Greatest extensibility and least
  amount of security responsibility taken on by the cloud provider

■ **PaaS (Platform as a Service)** — Lies somewhere in the middle, with
  extensibility and security features that must be leveraged by the
  customer."

Cloud Software as a Service (SaaS)

Simply stated, Software as a Service (SaaS) solutions deliver software applications over the Web. A SaaS provider deploys software to the user on demand, commonly through a licensing model. The provider may host the application on its own server infrastructure or use another vendor's hardware.

The application may be licensed directly to an organization, a user or group of users, or through a third party that manages multiple licenses between user organizations, such as an ASP. The user then accesses the application through any defined and authorized Internet device, most commonly a Web browser. A complete SaaS service should offer a full-featured application productivity suite as a service on demand, serving multiple organizations or individual users running from a single instance of the application on the cloud.

NIST defines Cloud Software as a Service (SaaS) as follows: "The capability provided to the consumer is to use the provider's applications running on a cloud infrastructure. The applications are accessible from various client devices through a thin client interface such as a web browser (e.g., web-based e-mail). The consumer does not manage or control the underlying cloud infrastructure, including network, servers, operating systems, storage, or even individual application capabilities, with the possible exception of limited user-specific application configuration settings."[1]

As shown earlier in the discussion of the SPI framework, there are vital and important differences between SaaS and the pure ASP delivery model. Unlike the traditional method of purchasing and installing software (usually involving a capital expense or a licensing charge), the SaaS customer rents the usage of the software using an operational expense model (a pay-per-use or subscription agreement). The pay-per-use licensing model is also known as *on-demand licensing*, as some applications delivered through the SaaS model are billed on a metered usage and time-period basis, rather than paying the common upfront costs of traditional licensing,

In the traditional model, the customer had a lot of areas to worry about that could easily become big headaches and drain resources:

- Compatibility with hardware, other software, and operating systems
- Licensing and compliance issues (unauthorized copies of the software floating around the organization)
- Maintenance, support, and patch revision processes

In some cases the software may be free to use, if the client is subscribing to a complete cloud hardware, software, and maintenance package.

ACRONYM CONFUSION

The acronym "SaaS" is used for both "Security as a Service" as well as the more common "Software as a Service." In this text, "SaaS" refers to "Software as a Service" unless "Security as a Service" is specifically noted.

Benefits of the SaaS Model

At a high level, SaaS provides several benefits throughout the organizational structure. First, it enables the organization to outsource the application hosting to an independent software vendor (ISV) or other software service provider. This almost always reduces the cost licensing, management hardware, and other resources required to internally host the app.

SaaS also benefits the application provider or ISV by increasing its control over the use of the software — by limiting the distribution of unlicensed copies and allowing the software vendor greater upgrade and patch management control. SaaS also enables the provider to create and control multiple revenue streams with a one-to-many model, thereby reducing duplication of software packages and overhead.

In addition, end users or remote/branch offices can access the application more readily through a browser, and rollout is greatly simplified. Other than modifications to perimeter devices (like firewalls) to allow specialized port references, for example, hardware requirements for the end user are minimal too.

SAAS AND THE ASP MODEL

At first glance, the ASP delivery concept may appear to be exactly like the SaaS delivery model. After all, the application is not hosted on the customer's premises, its development is probably outsourced, the application may not be owned by the customer, multiple clients may access the application, and the users most likely have to access the software through a cloud-like structure, perhaps the Internet.

However, there are important and fundamental differences between the two. One major difference is that the ASPs host the services through a dedicated infrastructure. Each organization usually has its private, dedicated server offering up its dedicated instances of the software, called *single-tenant* applications. True SaaS providers offer the application on shared infrastructure, offering a *multi-tenant* application infrastructure.

Another difference is that most ASP application development does not result in pure Internet-native software. The ASP applications are commonly typical premise-based client/server software applications with HTML-coded interfaces for remote access.

Conversely, SaaS applications are typically Internet-aware and optimized for the Internet, which typically results in better execution and response time, and helps facilitate upgrades and bug fixes.

As we described in Chapter 1, an example of SaaS is salesforce.com's Sales Cloud 2 CRM business solution. Although it actually pre-dated the cloud concept, salesforce.com is a very well-known example. It recently began offering a Platform as a Service (PaaS) model, called force.com. Another example of SaaS is the Google Apps suite of e-mail and word processing services, aimed at both businesses and individual users.

The Open Cloud Manifesto organization (`opencloudmanifesto.org`) describes Software as a Service as ". . . well-defined applications offering users online resources and storage. This differentiates SaaS from traditional websites or web applications which do not interface with user information (e.g., documents) or do so in a limited manner."[2]

Cloud Platform as a Service (PaaS)

As stated earlier, the "P" in the SPI framework represents "Platform as a Service (PaaS)." PaaS is similar to SaaS, but the service is an entire application development environment, not just the use of an application. PaaS solutions differ from SaaS solutions in that they provide a cloud-hosted virtual development platform, accessible via a Web browser.

PaaS solution providers deliver both the computing platform and the solution stack. This greatly accelerates development and deployment of software applications.

Using the concept of PaaS, software developers can build Web applications without having to install the software building tools on their own computer, and then distribute or deploy their apps to the cloud easily. PaaS encapsulates a layer of software and provides it as a service that can be used to build higher-level services.

NIST describes PaaS as follows: "The capability provided to the consumer is to deploy onto the cloud infrastructure consumer-created or acquired applications created using programming languages and tools supported by the provider. The consumer does not manage or control the underlying cloud infrastructure including network, servers, operating systems, or storage, but has control over the deployed applications and possibly application hosting environment configurations."

The PaaS vendor provides several services for application developers:

- A virtual development environment
- Application standards, usually based on the developers' requirements
- Toolkits configured for the virtual development environment
- A ready-made distribution channel for public application developers

The PaaS model provides a lower cost of entry for application designers and distributors, by supporting the complete software development life cycle (SDLC) of the Web app, thereby eliminating the need for the acquisition of hardware and software resources. A PaaS solution can comprise a complete end-to-end application solution for development, testing, and deployment of an application; or it can be a smaller, more specialized offering, focusing on a particular area such as content management.

In order for a software development platform to be considered a true PaaS solution, several elements need to be present:

- Baseline monitoring of application usage should be used to effect platform process improvement.
- The solution should provide seamless integration with other cloud resources, such as Web-based databases and other Web-based infrastructure components and services.
- Dynamic multi-tenancy must be achievable, and collaboration via the cloud between developers, clients, and users throughout the SDLC should be easily achievable.
- Security, privacy, and reliability must be maintained as a basic service.
- The development platform must be browser-based.

Creating a ready channel for sales and distribution is also a benefit of the PaaS model. Small or start-up software developers can use a PaaS provider to access development resources that would otherwise be unavailable to them.

Various types of PaaS vendor offerings can be extensive, and can include a complete application hosting, development, testing, and deployment environment, as well as extensive integrated services that include scalability, maintenance, and versioning.

The list of PaaS vendors is not as extensive as SaaS, largely because a PaaS offering has a smaller target market, developers rather than end users; but some SaaS vendors have begun to spin off PaaS offerings as a logical extension to their SaaS offerings. As mentioned previously, salesforce.com has begun a PaaS service at force.com.

Amazon Web Services (AWS) has instituted PaaS services for developers, largely through integration and partnering with AWS, to provide development platforms on top of AWS. For example, Pegasystems, Inc., a provider of business process management (BPM) software solutions, offers its SmartPass Platform as a Service running on AWS. Another example of a PaaS offering includes the Google App Engine, which serves applications on Google's infrastructure.

Sun Microsystems (`www.sun.com/featured-articles/CloudComputing.pdf`) describes two flavors of PaaS depending on the perspective of the producer or consumer of the services:

- Someone producing PaaS might produce a platform by integrating an OS, middleware, application software, and even a development environment that is then provided to a customer as a service.

- Someone using PaaS would see an encapsulated service that is presented to them through an API. The customer interacts with the platform through the API, and the platform does what is necessary to manage and scale itself to provide a given level of service.

Cloud Infrastructure as a Service (IaaS)

Infrastructure as a Service (IaaS) is the cloud model that most clearly demonstrates the difference between traditional IT infrastructure and the cloud-based infrastructure service. In the manner of the *aaS services mentioned previously, IaaS describes the delivery of the computing infrastructure as a service.

To return to the NIST cloud Infrastructure as a Service definition: "The capability provided to the consumer is to provision processing, storage, networks, and other fundamental computing resources where the consumer is able to deploy and run arbitrary software, which can include operating systems and applications. The consumer does not manage or control the underlying cloud infrastructure but has control over operating systems, storage, deployed applications, and possibly limited control of select networking components (e.g., host firewalls)."

IaaS benefits are similar to other *aaS models. Smaller shops now have access to a much higher level of IT talent and technology solutions, and dynamic infrastructure scalability enables IaaS consumers to tailor their requirements at a more granular level.

Organizational outlays for computing systems infrastructure has traditionally been a very large part of corporate expense. Leasing or purchasing dedicated hardware, software, and internal or consultative expertise consumes a major portion of any company's resources. Employing the IaaS model (often in conjunction with the SaaS or PaaS model) provides a level of scalability that can rapidly respond to demand in a way that traditional IT infrastructure acquisition, implementation, and maintenance cannot.

The spectrum of IaaS vendors is very wide, in that some offer large full data-center-style infrastructure replication (e.g., IBM, Oracle, Sun, Terremark, Joyent), while others offer more end-user-centric services, such as simple data storage (e.g., Amazon Simple Storage Service S3, Dropbox).

Again, Amazon is in the forefront of cloud computing, offering a large menu of cloud services, especially focused on IaaS:

- **Amazon Elastic Compute Cloud (Amazon EC2)** — Virtual computing environment, providing resizable compute capacity in the cloud

- **Amazon SimpleDB** — A Web service providing the core database functions of data indexing and querying in the cloud

- **Amazon Simple Storage Service (Amazon S3)** — A Web services interface that provides access to scalable and inexpensive data storage infrastructure

- **Amazon CloudFront** — Provides a Web service for content delivery

- **Amazon Simple Queue Service (Amazon SQS)** — Automated workflow service that provides a scalable queue for storing messages as they travel between computers

- **Amazon Elastic MapReduce** — Easily and cost-effectively processes vast amounts of data utilizing a hosted Hadoop framework (The Apache Hadoop project develops open-source software for reliable, scalable, distributed computing.)

- **Amazon Relational Database Service (Amazon RDS)** — A Web service that makes it easy to set up, operate, and scale a relational database in the cloud

IaaS can deliver either basic or complex storage capabilities as a service over the Internet. This enables the pooling and sharing of hardware resources, such as servers, storage (drives or sans), and perimeter devices (firewalls, routers). Figure 2-2 shows a virtualized infrastructure deployed as Infrastructure as a Service.

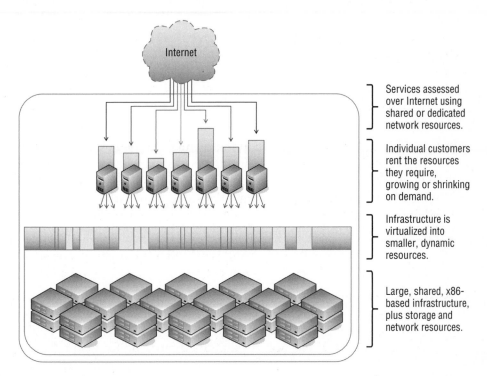

Internet

Services assessed over Internet using shared or dedicated network resources.

Individual customers rent the resources they require, growing or shrinking on demand.

Infrastructure is virtualized into smaller, dynamic resources.

Large, shared, x86-based infrastructure, plus storage and network resources.

Figure 2-2: IaaS example

Cloud Deployment Models

Within each of the three delivery models just described are multiple deployment models. For example, a SaaS delivery model can be presented to users in one of several deployment types, such as a private or public cloud. These deployment models are technically functionally unrelated to each of the delivery models — that is, any of the delivery models can exist in any of the deployment scenarios, although a specific delivery/deployment model pairing may be more common than others (e.g., SaaS/public).

Additionally, based upon the usage of the cloud by an organization and its relationship to the enterprise as a whole, these cloud deployment models are often referred to as external or internal clouds. Each of these models, however, must share the fundamental tenets of cloud computing:

- Each deployment model employs Internet-connected devices.

- Each model provides for dynamic scaling of virtual resources.

- Users of each model commonly don't have control over the technology being used.

Again using NIST as a baseline for our descriptions, NIST defines four cloud deployment models:[3]

- **Private cloud** — The cloud infrastructure is operated solely for an organization. It may be managed by the organization or a third party and may exist on premise or off premise.

- **Community cloud** — The cloud infrastructure is shared by several organizations and supports a specific community that has shared concerns (e.g., mission, security requirements, policy, and compliance considerations). It may be managed by the organizations or a third party and may exist on premise or off premise.

- **Public cloud** — The cloud infrastructure is made available to the general public or a large industry group and is owned by an organization selling cloud services.

- **Hybrid cloud** — The cloud infrastructure is a composition of two or more clouds (private, community, or public) that remain unique entities but are bound together by standardized or proprietary technology that enables data and application portability (e.g., cloud bursting for load-balancing between clouds).

An organization can implement one model or several different models, depending on which cloud model provides the best solution. For example, a critical app that has compliance or other security specifications may require a hybrid or private cloud model. Conversely, a general app that may be needed for a temporary project might be ideally suited for a public cloud.

It's important to remember that these four models do not specify the physical location of the infrastructure or application; a co-location facility could host both public and private clouds.

Public Clouds

A *public cloud* is a cloud computing deployment scheme that is generally open for use by the general public. The *general public* is defined in this case as either individual users or corporations. The public cloud infrastructure used is owned by a cloud services vendor organization; examples of public cloud deployment vendor offerings include Amazon Web Services, Google App Engine, Salesforce .com, and Microsoft Windows Azure.

Typically, the cloud is operated and managed at a data center owned by a service vendor that hosts multiple clients and uses dynamic provisioning. Implementation of a scalable services platform and pay-as-you-go licensing is also an attractive element of public cloud computing, as are the advantages of shared hardware infrastructure, software infrastructure, innovation and development, and maintenance and upgrades.

Economically, using a public cloud (sometimes referred to as an *external cloud*) can provide almost immediate cost savings to an organization. Shared infrastructure, remote hosting, and dynamic licensing and provisioning are strong enticements for a company. Public cloud implementation can be a big help in removing the crippling infrastructure maintenance burden on IT organizations.

A noteworthy example of a public cloud in action was a 2009 town hall meeting conducted by President Obama. By leveraging public cloud infrastructure, the White House was able to dynamically provision its servers to handle more than 3.5 million votes regarding which questions Obama should answer without having to provide a largely redundant system big enough to manage the increased traffic flow.

Depending on an organization's specific needs, such as customized configuration requirements and service-level agreements (SLAs) regarding up-time requirements, a company must carefully consider moving critical applications to a public cloud vendor. The most important of these requirements to consider is security. Of the four cloud deployment configurations discussed here, the public cloud configuration offloads the most management chores from the client, or user organization, to the third-party cloud service vendor.

In addition to daily operational tasks, this third-party management includes security tasks, such as logging, monitoring, and implementation of controls. This commonly relegates the user organization to a lower degree of control of sensitive or compliant data at both the physical and logical layers of the cloud.

Also, IT thinking has to evolve in order for an organization to use a public cloud efficiently. An example that Google uses is e-mail:

"There is limited value to running an Exchange Server in a virtual machine in the cloud. That server was never designed for the cloud, so you don't get additional scale. You'd also need to continue to maintain and monitor the mail server yourself, so the labor savings are marginal. But with cloud-based applications like Gmail, we take care of all of the hassle for you. We keep the application up and running, and have designed it to scale easily. All of this provides an application that is roughly less than 1/3 the cost of a privately hosted mail system, has 100x the typical storage, and innovates much faster."[4]

Figure 2-3 shows a simplified concept of a public cloud.

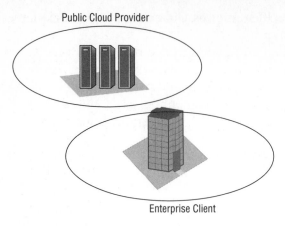

Public Cloud Provider

Enterprise Client

Figure 2-3: Public cloud example

Community Clouds

A cloud deployment model that is being rapidly implemented is called a *community cloud*. Conceptually residing somewhere between a private cloud and a public cloud, community cloud describes a shared infrastructure that is employed by and supported by multiple companies.

This shared cloud resource may be utilized by groups that have overlapping considerations, such as joint compliance requirements, noncompetitive business goals, or a need to pool high-level security resources.

Although the physical existence of the shared cloud may reside on any member's premises, or even on a third-party site, managing the community cloud may become complicated, due to unspecified or shifting ownership and responsibility, making it somewhat technically challenging to deal with concerns over resource management, privacy, resilience, latency, and security requirements.

In their paper "Digital Ecosystems in the Clouds: Towards Community Cloud Computing,"[5] Gerard Briscoe (Digital Ecosystems Lab, Department of Media and Communications, London School of Economics and Political Science), and Alexandros Marinos (Department of Computing, Faculty of Engineering and Physical Sciences, University of Surrey) have defined several elements that must be present in order for a cloud to properly defined as *community*. While some of these points also apply to other cloud types, they should all be present for a cloud to truly be called community:

- ▪ **Openness** — Removing the dependence on vendors makes the community cloud the open equivalent to vendor clouds, and therefore identifies a new dimension in the open versus proprietary struggle that has emerged in code, standards and data, but has not until now been expressed in the realm of hosted services.

- **Community** — The community cloud is as much a social structure as a technology paradigm, because of the community ownership of the infrastructure. This community ownership carries with it a degree of economic scalability, without which there would be diminished competition and potential stifling of innovation as risked in vendor clouds.

- **Graceful Failure** — The community cloud is not owned or controlled by any one organization, and therefore not dependent on the lifespan or failure of any one organization. It will be robust and resilient to failure, and immune to the system-wide cascade failures of vendor clouds, because of the diversity of its supporting nodes. When occasionally failing it will do so gracefully, non-destructively, and with minimal downtime, as the unaffected nodes compensate for the failure.

- **Convenience and Control** — The community cloud, unlike vendor clouds, has no inherent conflict between convenience and control, because its community ownership provides for democratic distributed control.

- **Environmental Sustainability** — The community cloud will have a significantly smaller carbon footprint than vendor clouds, because making use of underutilized user machines will require much less energy than the dedicated data centers required for vendor clouds. The server farms within data centers are an intensive form of computing resource provision, while the community cloud is more organic, growing and shrinking in a symbiotic relationship to support the demands of the community, which in turn supports it.

COMMUNITY CURRENCY

Briscoe and Marinos bring up an important point regarding community clouds, the idea that nodes can be contributors as well as consumers, and will therefore require a "community currency." A *community currency* is described by economists as a currency used by a community that is not the normally government backed currency recognized for exchange.

This community currency is redeemable against resources in the community and will allow for traditional cloud vendors to offer their resources to the community cloud to gather considerable community currency, which they can then monetize against participants who cannot contribute as much as they consume (i.e., running a community currency deficit). To avoid predicting or hard-coding the relative cost of resources (storage, computation, bandwidth), their prices can fluctuate based on market demand.

Private Clouds

Using virtualization, some companies are building private cloud computing environments intended to be used only by their employees or designated partners. Also referred to as *internal clouds*, private clouds can offer the benefits of public cloud computing, while still enabling the organization to retain greater control over the data and process.

NIST describes a *private cloud* as a cloud infrastructure operated solely for an organization, managed by the organization or a third party and existing either on premise or off-premise. The private cloud is typically hosted within the boundaries of the owner organization.

PRIVATE VS. PUBLIC CLOUD COMPUTING

Private cloud deployment appears to be spearheaded primarily by larger organizations and governmental agencies, rather than small companies or end users. The difference in startup costs is a major reason for this. A private cloud requires much of the same infrastructure outlay that traditional IT infrastructure requires, so an institution would need to be fairly large to get benefits from the private cloud model.

A larger company would also have the need for full control and access to the internal firewalls and virtualized environment required to build the private cloud. However, some smaller companies still have the need for such control, and they may need to subscribe to a private cloud vendor.

While the concept of a private cloud may create some cognitive dissonance (isn't the purpose of cloud infrastructure to be shared?), there are some specific characteristics of a private cloud that differentiate it from the traditional IT distributed infrastructure.

Firstly, private clouds differ from public clouds in that the infrastructure associated with a private cloud is commonly dedicated to a single enterprise and is not shared with any other enterprise. This infrastructure may include many corporate offices, business partners, intranet clients/vendors, resellers, or any other groups engaged in a business relationship with the enterprise.

Secondly, security is considered to be tighter in a private cloud deployment than it is in a public cloud. Obviously, a private cloud is not inherently more secure than a public cloud unless secure best practices are being followed, but an enterprise that has security, risk, or compliance concerns may want to exert the control a private cloud can offer, as the enterprise owns the infrastructure and has control over how applications are deployed on it.

Also, a private/hybrid cloud may help an enterprise prepare for the future, by leveraging existing infrastructure into a cloud. As the IT department begins to implement virtualization products into future data center plans, a private cloud may enable an organization to stick its collective toe in the water of cloud architecture without sacrificing control, corporate governance, or reliability.

Figure 2-4 shows an example of a private cloud.

Private cloud infrastructure

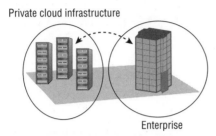

Enterprise

Figure 2-4: Private cloud example

Hybrid Clouds

Simply put, a *hybrid cloud* is any combination of the previous three cloud deployment models. More specifically, it's defined by NIST as "a composition of two or more clouds (private, community, or public) that remain unique entities but are bound together by standardized or proprietary technology that enables data and application portability (e.g., cloud bursting for load-balancing between clouds)."[6]

An example of hybrid cloud deployment may consist of an organization deploying noncritical software applications in the public cloud, while keeping critical or sensitive apps in a private cloud, on the premises. Hybrid clouds combine both public and private cloud models, and they can be particularly effective when both types of cloud are located in the same facility. Figure 2-5 shows a common hybrid cloud deployment combining public and private clouds.

One feature of hybrid clouds that makes them distinctive from the other cloud deployment types is the engagement of the "cloudburst." Most common hybrid clouds consist of a combination of both private and public cloud computing environments, which are deployed, utilized, and functioning continuously. These hybrid environments may employ multiple internal or external CSPs.

Some hybrid deployments, however, take advantage of the dynamic nature of the cloud and employ a "cloudburst" concept. A *cloudburst* generically refers to the dynamic deployment of an application that, while running predominantly on an organization's internal infrastructure, can also be deployed to the cloud in the event of a spike in demand.

Independent software vendors (ISVs) are beginning to offer virtual appliances that can provide a "cloudburst" self-service mechanism. A good source to check out many virtual appliance offerings is VMWare's Virtual Appliance Marketplace (www.vmware.com/appliances/directory/).

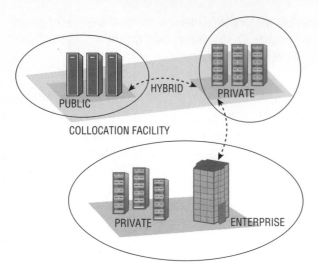

Figure 2-5: Hybrid cloud example

Alternative Deployment Models

As long as we're looking at the SPI framework, let's also take a quick peek at a couple of alternative deployment models, one that is based on SPI and extends it, the other a completely different view of the cloud computing architecture.

The Linthicum Model

David Linthicum, editor-in-chief of SYS-CON's *Virtualization Journal* (http://virtualizationjournal.com/),[7] is the proponent of a cloud computing model that enhances the SPI framework's maturity though the use of what he calls "stacks." He sees 10 major categories, or patterns, of cloud computing technology:

- **Storage as a Service** — The ability to leverage storage that physically exists remotely, but is logically a local storage resource to any application that requires storage.

- **Database as a Service** — The ability to leverage the services of a remotely hosted database, sharing it with other users, and having it logically function as if the database were local.

- **Information as a Service** — The ability to consume any type of information, remotely hosted, through a well-defined interface such as an API.

- **Process as a Service** — A remote resource that's able to bind many resources together, either hosted within the same cloud computing resource or remote, to create business processes.

- **Application as a Service** — (also referred to as SaaS) is any application delivered over the platform of the Web to an end user, typically leveraging the application through a browser.

- **Platform as a Service** — A complete platform, including application development, interface development, database development, storage, and testing, delivered through a remotely hosted platform to subscribers.

- **Integration as a Service** — The ability to deliver a complete integration stack from the cloud, including interfacing with applications, semantic mediation, flow control, and integration design.

- **Security as a Service** — The ability to deliver core security services remotely over the Internet.

- **Management/Governance as a Service** — Any on-demand service that provides the ability to manage one or more cloud services, typically simple things such as topology, resource utilization, virtualization, and uptime management.

- **Testing as a Service** — The ability to test local or cloud-delivered systems using testing software and services that are remotely hosted.

The Jericho Cloud Cube Model

In January 2004, an IT security association of companies, vendors, government groups, and academics "dedicated to advancing secure business in a global open-network environment" formed the Jericho Forum (www.jerichoforum .org),[8] under the auspices of The Open Group. Originally created to address network de-perimeterization (the erosion of the network perimeter), the forum has tackled the problem of securing business transactions through the Internet.

In Feb 2009, they delivered a practical framework geared toward creating the right collaboration-oriented architecture.

Then, in April 2009, the forum published the Jericho Cloud Cube Model[9] version 1.0. From their position paper, the purpose of the Cloud Cube Model is to:

- Point out that not everything is best implemented in clouds; it may be best to operate some business functions using a traditional non-cloud approach.

- Explain the different cloud formations that the Jericho Forum has identified.

- Describe key characteristics, benefits and risks of each cloud formation.

- Provide a framework for exploring in more detail the nature of different cloud formations and the issues that need answering to make them safe and secure places to work in.

The Jericho Cloud Cube Model describes the model for cloud computing as having four "dimensions":

- **Internal (I)/External (E)** — Defines the physical location of the data. If it is within your own physical boundary then it is Internal, if it is not within your own physical boundary then it is External.

- **Proprietary (P)/Open (O)** — Proprietary means that the organization providing the service is keeping the means of provision under their ownership. Clouds that are Open are using technology that is not proprietary, meaning that there are likely to be more suppliers.

- **Perimeterized (Per)/De-perimeterized (D-p) Architectures** — Inside your traditional IT perimeter or outside it? De-Perimeterization has always related to the gradual failure/removal/shrinking/collapse of the traditional silo-based IT perimeter.

- **Insourced/Outsourced** — Outsourced: the service is provided by a third party Insourced: the service is provided by your own staff under your control.

Figure 2-6 shows the Jericho Cloud Cube Model.

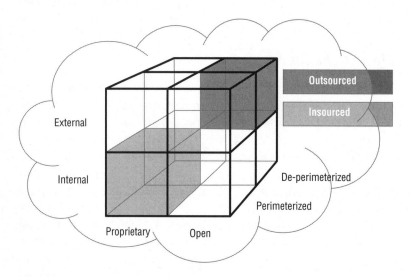

Figure 2-6: Jericho Cloud Cube Model

The following is taken verbatim from the Jericho Forum's file `cloud_cube_model_v1.0.pdf`. It provides a pretty concise description of the four dimensions of the model.

Internal (I)/External (E)

This is the dimension that defines the physical location of the data: where does the cloud form you want to use exist — inside or outside your organization's boundaries?

- If it is within your own physical boundary then it is Internal.
- If it is not within your own physical boundary then it is External.

For example, virtualized hard disks in an organization's data center would be internal, while Amazon SC3 would be external at some location "off-site."

Proprietary (P)/Open (O)

This is the dimension that defines the state of ownership of the cloud technology, services, interfaces, etc. It indicates the degree of interoperability, as well as enabling "data/application transportability" between your own systems and other cloud forms, and the ability to withdraw your data from a cloud form or to move it to another without constraint. It also indicates any constraints on being able to share applications.

Proprietary means that the organization providing the service is keeping the means of provision under their ownership. As a result, when operating in clouds that are proprietary, you may not be able to move to another cloud supplier without significant effort or investment. Often the more innovative technology advances occur in the proprietary domain. As such the proprietor may choose to enforce restrictions through patents and by keeping the technology involved a trade secret.

Clouds that are Open are using technology that is not proprietary, meaning that there are likely to be more suppliers, and you are not as constrained in being able to share your data and collaborate with selected parties using the same open technology. Open services tend to be those that are widespread and consumerized, and most likely a published open standard, for example email (SMTP).

Perimeterized (Per)/De-perimeterized (D-p) Architectures

The third dimension represents the "architectural mindset" — are you operating inside your traditional IT perimeter or outside it? De-perimeterization has always related to the gradual failure/removal/shrinking/collapse of the traditional silo-based IT perimeter.

Perimeterized implies continuing to operate within the traditional IT perimeter, often signaled by "network firewalls." As has been discussed in previous published Jericho Forum papers, this approach inhibits collaboration. In effect, when operating in the perimeterized areas, you may simply extend your own organization's perimeter into the external cloud computing domain using a VPN and operating the virtual server in your own IP domain, making use of your own directory services to control access. Then, when the computing task is completed you can withdraw your perimeter back to its original traditional position. We consider this type of system perimeter to be a traditional, though virtual, perimeter.

De-perimeterized assumes that the system perimeter is architected following the principles outlined in the Jericho Forum's Commandments and Collaboration Oriented Architectures Framework. The terms Micro-Perimeterization and Macro-Perimeterization will likely be in active use here — for example in a de-perimeterized frame the data would be encapsulated with meta-data and mechanisms that would protect the data from inappropriate usage. COA-enabled systems allow secure collaboration. In a de-perimeterized environment an organization can collaborate securely with selected parties (business partner, customer, supplier, outworker) globally over any COA capable network.

The de-perimeterized areas in our Cloud Cube Model use both internal and external domains but the collaboration or sharing of data should not be seen as internal or external — rather it is controlled by and limited to the parties that the using organizations select. For example, in the future frame, one organization will not feel uncomfortable about allowing data into the internal COA-compliant domain of a collaborating organization; rather, they will be confident that the data will be appropriately protected. This means:

- You can operate in any of the four cloud formations so far described (I/P, I/O, E/P, E/O) with either of two architectural mindsets — Perimeterized or De-perimeterized.

- The top-right E/O/D-p cloud formation is likely to be the "sweet spot" where optimum flexibility and collaboration can be achieved.

- A Proprietary cloud provider will likely want to keep you in the left side of the cube, achieved either by continuous innovation that adds value, or by limiting the means of migrating from the proprietary domain. The ability to move from that top-left cloud form to the "sweet-spot" top-right cloud form will require a rare interface because facilitating you making this move is going to be rarely in the cloud supplier's best business interests.

While the underlying intent remains the same, an added distinction in describing De-perimeterized cloud usage arises in that the detailed description changes based on the level of abstraction at which you choose to operate.

At the heart of all cloud forms is the concept of abstraction. Cloud models separate one layer of business from another, e.g., process from software, platform from infrastructure, etc. We show an example model here with four levels of abstraction; we can expect other models identifying different layers and abstraction levels to emerge to suit different business needs.

Most cloud computing activities today are occurring at the lower layers of the stack, so today we have more maturity at the lower level.

Insourced / Outsource

We define a fourth dimension that has two states in each of the eight cloud forms: Per(IP,IO,EP,EO) and D-p(IP,IO,EP,EO), that responds to the question "Who do you want running your Clouds?":

- Outsourced—The service is provided by a third party
- Insourced—The service is provided by your own staff under your control

These two states describe who is managing delivery of the cloud service(s) that you use. This is primarily a policy issue (i.e., a business decision, not a technical or architectural decision) which must be embodied in a contract with the cloud provider.

Given the ease with which a user within your business can procure cloud services — just by tendering a valid credit card — it is absolutely essential that your business develops the ability to rapidly set up legally binding collaboration agreements, and to close them equally rapidly as soon as they are no longer needed. Will it be possible in the future to design a cloud data capsulation approach that means if the cloud provider accepts the data capsule then they automatically accept the terms that the data came with –– for example "do not process outside the data owner's national boundary"?

A proponent of the Jericho Cloud Cube Model is Christopher Hoff, as is evident in his writings/postings at www.rationalsurvivability.com.[10]

Expected Benefits

There are many benefits of cloud computing but, also, some accompanying caveats. As with any physical system, cloud computation must operate within physical boundary parameters. The cloud offers the ability to provision massive amounts of computing power and storage, but these quantities are not infinite. Therefore, cloud users might have to fit their applications into one set of resource usage categories defined by the cloud provider.

Cloud computational resources can be scaled up and down on demand and paid for on a metered usage basis. This ability provides tremendous advantages for clients in that they do not have to maintain internal computing systems designed for peak loads that may occur only a small percentage of the time.

The cloud paradigm also supports innovation in that a variety of new, advanced applications can be used in an affordable manner while reducing the total cost of ownership.

Some applications that are of long duration and have stable computational requirements might be better served by in-house or leased computers and storage than by paying cloud fees over a long period of time. These options have to be evaluated on a case-by-case basis.

The major benefits of cloud computing can be summarized as follows:

- Means to move from operating in a capital expenditure environment to an operational expenditure environment
- Ability to rapidly deploy innovative business and research applications in a cost-effective manner
- Use of virtualization to detach business services from the underlying execution infrastructure
- Disaster recovery and business continuity capabilities are intrinsic in the cloud paradigm
- Ability of the cloud provider to apply security safeguards more effectively and efficiently in a centralized environment
- Ability to select among a variety of cloud suppliers that provide reliable scalable services, metered billing, and advanced development resources
- Scalable infrastructure that can rapidly provision and de-allocate substantial resources on an as-needed basis

The major benefits of the cloud paradigm can be distilled to its inherent flexibility and resiliency, the potential for reducing costs, availability of very large amounts of centralized data storage, means to rapidly deploy computing resources, and scalability.

Flexibility and Resiliency

A major benefit of cloud computing is the flexibility that is provided by the following:

- Freedom from concerns about updating servers
- Freedom from having to install software patches
- Automated provisioning of new services and technologies
- Acquiring increased resources on an as-needed basis
- Ability to focus on innovation instead of maintenance details
- Device independence

One factor that has to be considered, however, is that cloud providers cannot provide infinite configuration and provisioning flexibility and will seek to offer structured alternatives. They might offer a choice among a number of computing and storage resource configurations at different capabilities and costs, and the cloud customer will have to adjust his or her requirements to fit one of those models.

Resiliency is achieved through the availability of multiple redundant resources and locations. As autonomic computing becomes more mature, self-management and self-healing mechanisms can ensure the increased reliability and robustness of cloud resources. Also, disaster recovery and business continuity planning are inherent in using the provider's cloud computing platforms.

Reduced Costs

The cloud paradigm, in general, is a basis for cost savings because capability and resources can be paid for incrementally without the need for large investments in computing infrastructure. This model is especially true for adding storage costs for large database applications. Therefore, capital costs are reduced and replaced by manageable, scalable operating expenses.

Conversely, there might be some instances, particularly for long term, stable computing configuration usage, where cloud computation might not have a cost advantage over using one's internal resources or directly leasing equipment. For example, if the volume of data storage and computational resources required are essentially constant and there is no need for rapid provisioning and flexibility, an organization's local computational capabilities might be more cost effective than using a cloud.

Another factor to consider in choosing the cloud is that client organizational support and maintenance costs are reduced dramatically because these expenses are transferred to the cloud provider, including 24/7 support. The need for highly-trained and expensive IT personnel is also reduced. Resources are used more efficiently in cloud computing, resulting in substantial support and energy cost savings. According to IDC Worldwide and Regional Server 2009–2013 Forecast Update, December, 2009 (http://www.idc.com/research), server administrative expenses are now the largest data center costs and have increased approximately 400% in the last 15 years.

Energy costs are another consideration in moving to the cloud. 1E, a London-based consulting organization that helps clients reduce IT operational costs, published a survey that found approximately 4.7 million servers world-wide are idle most of the time and are wasting $25 billion per year in energy costs (http://www.1e.com/). In fact, they found that, in general, organizations spend twice as much on server energy costs as on hardware. Cloud computing offers an alternative to these expenses.

In general, cloud computing offers reductions in system administration, provisioning expenses, energy costs, software licensing fees, and hardware costs.

Centralization of Data Storage

The cloud offers larger amounts of data storage resources than are normally available in local, corporate computing systems. In addition, the cloud storage resources that are used can be decreased or increased as desired with corresponding operating cost adjustments. This centralization of storage infrastructure results in cost efficiencies in utilities, real-estate, and trained personnel. Also, data protections are much easier to implement and monitor in a centralized system than on large numbers of computing platforms that might be widely distributed geographically in different parts of an organization.

Many data centers are a conglomeration of legacy applications, operating systems, hardware, and software and are a support and maintenance nightmare. This situation requires more specialized maintenance personnel, increased costs because of lack of standardization, and a higher risk of crashes.

As with every advantage, there is a potential disadvantage in having large amounts of sensitive information stored in a centralized, albeit virtualized, environment. This storage might provide an attractive target for hackers or criminal organizations to gain access to critical information by focusing on a central repository. The counter argument is that, if implemented properly, information security can be made stronger and more safeguards employed and monitored in a central data store than in a distributed model.

Reduced Time to Deployment

In a competitive environment where rapid evaluation and development of new approaches is critical, the cloud offers the means to use powerful computational resources in a short time frame and large amounts of storage without requiring sizeable initial investments in hardware, software, and personnel. This rapid provisioning can be accomplished at relatively small cost and offers the client access to advanced technologies that are constantly being acquired by the cloud provider. Improved delivery of services obtained by rapid cloud provisioning improves time to market and market growth.

Scalability

Cloud computing provides the means, within limits, for a client to rapidly provision computational resources to meet increases or decreases in demand. In many instances, organizations require large amounts of storage capacity for critical data, and this need can be accommodated by the cloud provider. This approach provides an alternative to inefficient in-house systems that have to be designed for peak load but run at only partial capacity most of the time. Cloud scalability provides for remote optimization so that computing resources are organized for maximum cost-benefit.

Because the cloud provider operates on a utility model, the client organization has to pay only for the resources it is using at the time. However, the cloud provider must provide some type of resource limits on customers to protect against extreme demands and ensure that there is enough capacity to serve all of the cloud clients.

Summary

There are a number of choices that a client can use to take advantage of the benefits of cloud computing. These choices comprise the cloud delivery models SaaS, PaaS, and IaaS of the SPI framework and the private, community, public, and hybrid cloud deployment models. The combinations selected and their implementations are a function of the types of applications involved, storage needs, time criticality, scaling requirements, and the economics of the associated projects.

The benefits of using cloud computing are varied. They include a cloud's inherent flexibility and resiliency, the potential for reducing costs, availability of very large amounts of centralized data storage, means to rapidly deploy computing resources, and scalability. Cloud computing can also intrinsically provide for migration from operating in a capital expenditure environment to an operational expenditure environment, support disaster recovery and business continuity, and take advantage of centrally applied security safeguards. These security issues, associated principles, security testing, and cloud disaster recovery/business continuity planning are explored in detail in Chapter 3.

Notes

1. csrc.nist.gov/groups/SNS/cloud-computing/cloud-computing-v26.ppt

2. opencloudmanifesto.org/Cloud_Computing_Use_Cases_Whitepaper-2_0.pdf

3. http://csrc.nist.gov/groups/SNS/cloud-computing/index.html

4. http://googleenterprise.blogspot.com/2009/04/what-we-talk-about-when-we-talk-about.html

5. Digital Ecosystems in the Clouds: Towards Community Cloud Computing, community cloud computing.pdf

6. csrc.nist.gov/groups/SNS/cloud-computing/cloud-computing-v26.ppt

7. http://cloudcomputing.sys-con.com/node/811519

8. www.opengroup.org/jericho/publications.htm

9. www.jerichoforum.org cloud_cube_model_v1.0.pdf

10. www.rationalsurvivability.com/blog/?p=743

CHAPTER 3

Cloud Computing Software Security Fundamentals

People don't ever seem to realize that doing what's right is no guarantee against misfortune.

—William McFee

Security is a principal concern when entrusting an organization's critical information to geographically dispersed cloud platforms not under the direct control of that organization. In addition to the conventional IT information system security procedures, designing security into cloud software during the software development life cycle can greatly reduce the cloud attack surface.

In the document "Security Guidance for Critical Areas of Focus in Cloud Computing,"[1] the Cloud Security Alliance emphasizes the following points relative to the secure software life cycle in their listing of 15 cloud security domains:

- Domain 6, Information Life Cycle Management — "Understand cloud provider policies and processes for data retention and destruction and how they compare with internal organizational policy. Be aware that data retention assurance may be easier for the cloud provider to demonstrate, but data destruction may be very difficult. Perform regular backup and recovery tests to assure that logical segregation and controls are effective."

- Domain 11, Application Security — "IaaS, PaaS and SaaS create differing trust boundaries for the software development lifecycle, which must be accounted for during the development, testing and production deployment of applications."

- Domain 14, Storage — "Understand cloud provider storage retirement processes. Data destruction is extremely difficult in a multi-tenant environment and the cloud provider should be utilizing strong storage encryption that renders data unreadable when storage is recycled, disposed of, or accessed by any means outside of authorized applications."

With cloud computing providing SaaS, secure software is a critical issue. From the cloud consumer's point of view, using SaaS in the cloud reduces the need for secure software development by the customer. The requirement for secure software development is transferred to the cloud provider. However, the user might still find it necessary to develop custom code for the cloud. Whoever develops the software, this process requires a strong commitment to a formal, secure software development life cycle, including design, testing, secure deployment, patch management, and disposal. Yet, in many instances, software security is treated as an add-on to extant software and not as an important element of the development process.

These and other related issues in the secure software development life cycle for cloud computing are explored in detail in this chapter.

Cloud Information Security Objectives

Developing secure software is based on applying the secure software design principles that form the fundamental basis for software assurance. Software assurance has been given many definitions, and it is important to understand the concept. The Software Security Assurance Report[2] defines *software assurance* as "the basis for gaining justifiable confidence that software will consistently exhibit all properties required to ensure that the software, in operation, will continue to operate dependably despite the presence of sponsored (intentional) faults. In practical terms, such software must be able to resist most attacks, tolerate as many as possible of those attacks it cannot resist, and contain the damage and recover to a normal level of operation as soon as possible after any attacks it is unable to resist or tolerate."

The U.S. Department of Defense (DoD) Software Assurance Initiative[3] defines *software assurance* as "the level of confidence that software functions as intended and is free of vulnerabilities, either intentionally or unintentionally designed or inserted as part of the software."

The Data and Analysis Center for Software (DACS)[4] requires that software must exhibit the following three properties to be considered secure:

- **Dependability** — Software that executes predictably and operates correctly under a variety of conditions, including when under attack or running on a malicious host

- **Trustworthiness** — Software that contains a minimum number of vulnerabilities or no vulnerabilities or weaknesses that could sabotage the software's dependability. It must also be resistant to malicious logic.

- **Survivability (Resilience)** — Software that is resistant to or tolerant of attacks and has the ability to recover as quickly as possible with as little harm as possible

Seven complementary principles that support information assurance are confidentiality, integrity, availability, authentication, authorization, auditing, and accountability. These concepts are summarized in the following sections.

Confidentiality, Integrity, and Availability

Confidentiality, integrity, and availability are sometimes known as the *CIA triad* of information system security, and are important pillars of cloud software assurance.

Confidentiality

Confidentiality refers to the prevention of intentional or unintentional unauthorized disclosure of information. Confidentiality in cloud systems is related to the areas of intellectual property rights, covert channels, traffic analysis, encryption, and inference:

- **Intellectual property rights** — Intellectual property (IP) includes inventions, designs, and artistic, musical, and literary works. Rights to intellectual property are covered by copyright laws, which protect creations of the mind, and patents, which are granted for new inventions.

- **Covert channels** — A *covert channel* is an unauthorized and unintended communication path that enables the exchange of information. Covert channels can be accomplished through timing of messages or inappropriate use of storage mechanisms.

- **Traffic analysis** — *Traffic analysis* is a form of confidentiality breach that can be accomplished by analyzing the volume, rate, source, and destination of message traffic, even if it is encrypted. Increased message activity and high bursts of traffic can indicate a major event is occurring. Countermeasures to traffic analysis include maintaining a near-constant rate of message traffic and disguising the source and destination locations of the traffic.

- **Encryption** — *Encryption* involves scrambling messages so that they cannot be read by an unauthorized entity, even if they are intercepted. The amount of effort (*work factor*) required to decrypt the message is a function of the strength of the encryption key and the robustness and quality of the encryption algorithm.

- **Inference** — *Inference* is usually associated with database security. Inference is the ability of an entity to use and correlate information protected at one level of security to uncover information that is protected at a higher security level.

Integrity

The concept of cloud information *integrity* requires that the following three principles are met:

- Modifications are not made to data by unauthorized personnel or processes.
- Unauthorized modifications are not made to data by authorized personnel or processes.
- The data is internally and externally consistent — in other words, the internal information is consistent both among all sub-entities and with the real-world, external situation.

Availability

Availability ensures the reliable and timely access to cloud data or cloud computing resources by the appropriate personnel. Availability guarantees that the systems are functioning properly when needed. In addition, this concept guarantees that the security services of the cloud system are in working order. A denial-of-service attack is an example of a threat against availability.

The reverse of confidentiality, integrity, and availability is disclosure, alteration, and destruction (DAD).

Cloud Security Services

Additional factors that directly affect cloud software assurance include authentication, authorization, auditing, and accountability, as summarized in the following sections.

Authentication

Authentication is the testing or reconciliation of evidence of a user's identity. It establishes the user's identity and ensures that users are who they claim to be. For example, a user presents an identity (user ID) to a computer login screen and then has to provide a password. The computer system authenticates the user by verifying that the password corresponds to the individual presenting the ID.

Authorization

Authorization refers to rights and privileges granted to an individual or process that enable access to computer resources and information assets. Once a user's identity and authentication are established, authorization levels determine the extent of system rights a user can hold.

Auditing

To maintain operational assurance, organizations use two basic methods: system audits and monitoring. These methods can be employed by the cloud customer, the cloud provider, or both, depending on asset architecture and deployment.

- A *system audit* is a one-time or periodic event to evaluate security.
- *Monitoring* refers to an ongoing activity that examines either the system or the users, such as intrusion detection.

Information technology (IT) auditors are often divided into two types: internal and external. Internal auditors typically work for a given organization, whereas external auditors do not. External auditors are often certified public accountants (CPAs) or other audit professionals who are hired to perform an independent audit of an organization's financial statements. Internal auditors usually have a much broader mandate than external auditors, such as checking for compliance and standards of due care, auditing operational cost efficiencies, and recommending the appropriate controls.

IT auditors typically audit the following functions:

- System and transaction controls
- Systems development standards
- Backup controls
- Data library procedures
- Data center security
- Contingency plans

In addition, IT auditors might recommend improvements to controls, and they often participate in a system's development process to help an organization avoid costly reengineering after the system's implementation.

An *audit trail or log* is a set of records that collectively provide documentary evidence of processing, used to aid in tracing from original transactions forward to related records and reports, and/or backward from records and reports to their component source transactions. Audit trails may be limited to specific events or they may encompass all of the activities on a system.

Audit logs should record the following:

- The transaction's date and time
- Who processed the transaction

- At which terminal the transaction was processed
- Various security events relating to the transaction

In addition, an auditor should examine the audit logs for the following:

- Amendments to production jobs
- Production job reruns
- Computer operator practices
- All commands directly initiated by the user
- All identification and authentication attempts
- Files and resources accessed

Accountability

Accountability is the ability to determine the actions and behaviors of a single individual within a cloud system and to identify that particular individual. Audit trails and logs support accountability and can be used to conduct postmortem studies in order to analyze historical events and the individuals or processes associated with those events. Accountability is related to the concept of *nonrepudiation*, wherein an individual cannot successfully deny the performance of an action.

Relevant Cloud Security Design Principles

Historically, computer software was not written with security in mind; but because of the increasing frequency and sophistication of malicious attacks against information systems, modern software design methodologies include security as a primary objective. With cloud computing systems seeking to meet multiple objectives, such as cost, performance, reliability, maintainability, and security, trade-offs have to be made. A completely secure system will exhibit poor performance characteristics or might not function at all.

Technically competent hackers can usually find a way to break into a computer system, given enough time and resources. The goal is to have a system that is secure enough for everyday use while exhibiting reasonable performance and reliability characteristics.

In a 1974 paper that is still relevant today,[5] Saltzer and Schroeder of the University of Virginia addressed the protection of information stored in a computer system by focusing on hardware and software issues that are necessary to support information protection. The paper presented the following 11 security design principles:

- Least privilege
- Separation of duties

- Defense in depth
- Fail safe
- Economy of mechanism
- Complete mediation
- Open design
- Least common mechanism
- Psychological acceptability
- Weakest link
- Leveraging existing components

The fundamental characteristics of these principles are summarized in the following sections.

Least Privilege

The principle of *least privilege* maintains that an individual, process, or other type of entity should be given the minimum privileges and resources for the minimum period of time required to complete a task. This approach reduces the opportunity for unauthorized access to sensitive information.

Separation of Duties

Separation of duties requires that completion of a specified sensitive activity or access to sensitive objects is dependent on the satisfaction of a plurality of conditions. For example, an authorization would require signatures of more than one individual, or the arming of a weapons system would require two individuals with different keys. Thus, separation of duties forces collusion among entities in order to compromise the system.

Defense in Depth

Defense in depth is the application of multiple layers of protection wherein a subsequent layer will provide protection if a previous layer is breached.

The Information Assurance Technical Framework Forum (IATFF), an organization sponsored by the National Security Agency (NSA), has produced a document titled the "Information Assurance Technical Framework" (IATF) that provides excellent guidance on the concepts of defense in depth.

The IATFF encourages and supports technical interchanges on the topic of information assurance among U.S. industry, U.S. academic institutions, and U.S. government agencies. Information on the IATFF document can be found at www.niap-ccevs.org/cc-scheme/IATF_3.1-Chapter_03-ISSEP.pdf.

The IATF document 3.1[6] stresses the importance of the *people* involved, the *operations* required, and the *technology* needed to provide information assurance and to meet the organization's mission.

The defense-in-depth strategy as defined in IATF document 3.1 promotes application of the following information assurance principles:

- **Defense in multiple places** — Information protection mechanisms placed in a number of locations to protect against internal and external threats

- **Layered defenses** — A plurality of information protection and detection mechanisms employed so that an adversary or threat must negotiate a series of barriers to gain access to critical information

- **Security robustness** — An estimate of the robustness of information assurance elements based on the value of the information system component to be protected and the anticipated threats

- **Deploy KMI/PKI** — Use of robust key management infrastructures (KMI) and public key infrastructures (PKI)

- **Deploy intrusion detection systems** — Application of intrusion detection mechanisms to detect intrusions, evaluate information, examine results, and, if necessary, take action

Fail Safe

Fail safe means that if a cloud system fails it should fail to a state in which the security of the system and its data are not compromised. One implementation of this philosophy would be to make a system default to a state in which a user or process is denied access to the system. A complementary rule would be to ensure that when the system recovers, it should recover to a secure state and not permit unauthorized access to sensitive information. This approach is based on using permissions instead of exclusions.

In the situation where system recovery is not done automatically, the failed system should permit access only by the system administrator and not by other users, until security controls are reestablished.

Economy of Mechanism

Economy of mechanism promotes simple and comprehensible design and implementation of protection mechanisms, so that unintended access paths do not exist or can be readily identified and eliminated.

Complete Mediation

In complete meditation, every request by a subject to access an object in a computer system must undergo a valid and effective authorization procedure.

This mediation must not be suspended or become capable of being bypassed, even when the information system is being initialized, undergoing shutdown, being restarted, or is in maintenance mode. Complete mediation entails the following:

1. Identification of the entity making the access request
2. Verification that the request has not changed since its initiation
3. Application of the appropriate authorization procedures
4. Reexamination of previously authorized requests by the same entity

Open Design

There has always been an ongoing discussion about the merits and strengths of security designs that are kept secret versus designs that are open to scrutiny and evaluation by the community at large. A good example is an encryption system. Some feel that keeping the encryption algorithm secret makes it more difficult to break. The opposing philosophy believes that exposing the algorithm to review and study by experts at large while keeping the encryption key secret leads to a stronger algorithm because the experts have a higher probability of discovering weaknesses in it. In general, the latter approach has proven more effective, except in the case of organizations such as the National Security Agency (NSA), which employs some of the world's best cryptographers and mathematicians.

For most purposes, an open-access cloud system design that has been evaluated and tested by a myriad of experts provides a more secure authentication method than one that has not been widely assessed. Security of such mechanisms depends on protecting passwords or keys.

Least Common Mechanism

This principle states that a minimum number of protection mechanisms should be common to multiple users, as shared access paths can be sources of unauthorized information exchange. Shared access paths that provide unintentional data transfers are known as *covert channels*. Thus, the *least common mechanism* promotes the least possible sharing of common security mechanisms.

Psychological Acceptability

Psychological acceptability refers to the ease of use and intuitiveness of the user interface that controls and interacts with the cloud access control mechanisms. Users must be able to understand the user interface and use it without having to interpret complex instructions.

Weakest Link

As in the old saying "A chain is only as strong as its weakest link," the security of a cloud system is only as good as its weakest component. Thus, it is important to identify the weakest mechanisms in the security chain and layers of defense, and improve them so that risks to the system are mitigated to an acceptable level.

Leveraging Existing Components

In many instances, the security mechanisms of a cloud implementation might not be configured properly or used to their maximum capability. Reviewing the state and settings of the extant security mechanisms and ensuring that they are operating at their optimum design points will greatly improve the security posture of an information system.

Another approach that can be used to increase cloud system security by leveraging existing components is to partition the system into defended sub-units. Then, if a security mechanism is penetrated for one sub-unit, it will not affect the other sub-units, and damage to the computing resources will be minimized.

Secure Cloud Software Requirements

The requirements for secure cloud software are concerned with nonfunctional issues such as minimizing or eliminating vulnerabilities and ensuring that the software will perform as required, even under attack. This goal is distinct from security functionality in software, which addresses areas that derive from the information security policy, such as identification, authentication, and authorization.

Software requirements engineering is the process of determining customer software expectations and needs, and it is conducted before the software design phase. The requirements have to be unambiguous, correct, quantifiable, and detailed.

Karen Goertzel, Theodore Winograd, and their contributors in "Enhancing the Development Life Cycle to Produce Secure Software"[7] from the United States Department of Defense Data and Analysis Center for Software (DACS) state that all software shares the following three security needs:

- It must be dependable under anticipated operating conditions, and remain dependable under hostile operating conditions.

- It must be trustworthy in its own behavior, and in its inability to be compromised by an attacker through exploitation of vulnerabilities or insertion of malicious code.

■ It must be resilient enough to recover quickly to full operational capability with a minimum of damage to itself, the resources and data it handles, and the external components with which it interacts.

In the following sections, cloud software considerations related to functional security and secure properties are explored in the context of software requirements engineering. Secure requirements for security-related cloud software functions generally define what the software has to accomplish to perform a task securely.

Secure Development Practices

There are many methods for developing code. Any of them can be used to develop a secure cloud application. Every development model must have both requirements and testing. In some models, the requirements may emerge over time. It is very important that security requirements are established early in the development process.

Security in a cloud application tends to be subtle and invisible. Security is prominent at only two times in the development life cycle: requirements definition and testing. At other times, deadlines, capabilities, performance, the look and feel, and dozens of other issues tend to push security to the back. This is why it is important to ensure that security requirements are prominent at the beginning of the software development life cycle.

In many respects, the tools and techniques used to design and develop clean, efficient cloud applications will support the development of secure code as well. Special attention, however, should be shown in the following areas:

■ **Handling data** — Some data is more sensitive and requires special handling.

■ **Code practices** — Care must be taken not to expose too much information to a would-be attacker.

■ **Language options** — Consider the strengths and weakness of the language used.

■ **Input validation and content injection** — Data (content) entered by a user should never have direct access to a command or a query.

■ **Physical security of the system** — Physical access to the cloud servers should be restricted.

Handling Data

As the Internet continues to be a driving force in most of our everyday lives, more and more personal and sensitive information will be put on cloud servers. Requirements for handling this private information did not exist five years ago, while other data, such as passwords, has always required special handling. Following are some special cases for the handling of sensitive or critical data:

- Passwords should never be transmitted in the clear. They should always be encrypted.

- Passwords should never be viewable on the user's screen as they are entered into the computer. Even though asterisks (*) are being displayed, care must be taken to ensure that it is not just because the font is all asterisks. If that is the case, someone could steal the password by copying and pasting the password from the screen.

- If possible, passwords should always be encrypted with one-way hashes. This will ensure that no one (not even a system administrator) can extract the password from the server. The only way to break the password would be through brute-force cracking. With one-way hashing, the actual passwords are not compared to authenticate the user; rather, the hashed value is stored on the server and is compared with the hashed value sent by the user. If the passwords cannot be decrypted, users cannot be provided their passwords when they forget them. In such cases, the system administrator must enter a new password for the user, which the user can change upon re-entering the application.

- Credit card and other financial information should never be sent in the clear.

- Cloud servers should minimize the transmissions and printing of credit card information. This includes all reports that may be used for internal use, such as troubleshooting, status, and progress reports.

- Sensitive data should not be passed to the cloud server as part of the query string, as the query string may be recorded in logs and accessed by persons not authorized to see the credit card information. For example, the following query string includes a credit card number:

```
http://www.server site.com/process_card.asp?cardnumber=1234567890123456
```

Code Practices

The minimum necessary information should be included in cloud server code. Attackers will spend countless hours examining HTML and scripts for information that can be used to make their intrusions easier to accomplish.

Comments should be stripped from operational code, and names and other personal information should be avoided. HTML comment fields should not reveal exploitable information about the developers or the organization. Comments are not bad per se, but those embedded in the HTML or client script and which may contain private information can be very dangerous in the hands of an attacker.

Third-party software packages, such as Web servers and FTP servers, often provide banners that indicate the version of the software that is running. Attackers can use this information to narrow their search of exploits to apply to these targets. In most cases, these banners can be suppressed or altered.

Language Options

One of the most frequently discovered vulnerabilities in cloud server applications is a direct result of the use of C and C++. The C language is unable to detect and prevent improper memory allocation, which can result in buffer overflows.

Because the C language cannot prevent buffer overflows, it is left to the programmer to implement safe programming techniques. Good coding practices will check for boundary limits and ensure that functions are properly called. This requires a great deal of discipline from the programmer; and in practice even the most experienced developers can overlook these checks occasionally.

One of the reasons Java is so popular is because of its intrinsic security mechanisms. Malicious language constructs should not be possible in Java. The Java Virtual Machine (JVM) is responsible for stopping buffer overflows, the use of uninitialized variables, and the use of invalid opcodes.

Input Validation and Content Injection

All user input that cannot be trusted must be verified and validated. Content injection occurs when the cloud server takes input from the user and applies the content of that input into commands or SQL statements. Essentially, the user's input is injected into a command that is executed by the server. Content injection can occur when the server does not have a clear distinction and separation between the data input and the commands executed.

Physical Security of the System

Any cloud server is vulnerable to an attacker with unlimited time and physical access to the server. Additionally, physical problems could cause the server to have down time. This would be a loss of availability, which you may recall is one of the key principles of the security triad — confidentiality, integrity, and availability (CIA). The following items should be provided to ensure server availability:

- Provide an uninterruptible power supply (UPS) unit with surge protection.
- Provide fire protection to minimize the loss of personnel and equipment.
- Provide adequate cooling and ventilation.
- Provide adequate lighting and workspace for maintaining and upgrading the system.

- Restrict physical access to the server. Unauthorized persons should not get near the server. Even casual contact can lead to outages. The server space should be locked and alarmed. Any access to the space should be recorded for later evaluation should a problem occur. Inventory should be tightly controlled and monitored.

- The physical protections listed here should extend to the network cables and other devices (such as routers) that are critical to the cloud server's operation.

Approaches to Cloud Software Requirements Engineering

Cloud system software requirements engineering demands extensive interaction with the user, and the product of the process includes both nonfunctional and functional software performance characteristics. Figure 3-1 illustrates the major elements of the software requirements engineering process.

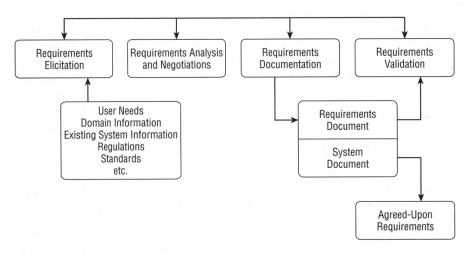

Figure 3-1: Software requirements engineering components

Source: Information Assurance Technology Analysis Center (IATC), Data and Analysis Center for Software (DACS), "State-of-the-Art Report," July 31, 2007.

Figure 3-2 illustrates additional elements that can be used to augment traditional software requirements engineering to increase cloud software security.

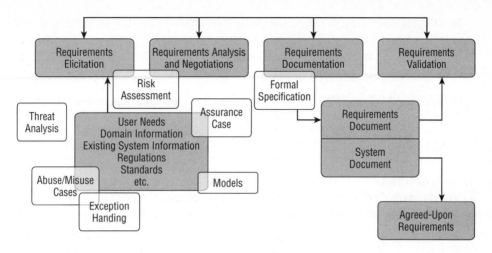

Figure 3-2: Additions to the software requirements engineering process to promote secure software

Source: Information Assurance Technology Analysis Center (IATC), Data and Analysis Center for Software (DACS), "State-of-the-Art Report," July 31, 2007.

A Resource Perspective on Cloud Software Security Requirements

Approaching software security requirements derivation from a resource perspective provides an effective method for addressing cloud software security requirements. In their April 1995 paper "SMART Requirements" (`www.win .tue.nl/~wstomv/edu/2ip30/references/smart-requirements.pdf`), Mike Mannion and Barry Keepence of Napier University, Edinburgh, U.K., take this approach by defining the following SMART basic properties that requirements should possess:

- **Specific** — The requirement should be unambiguous and direct. Mannion and Keepence define this characteristic as being clear, consistent, and simple.

- **Measurable** — The requirement should be measurable to ensure that it has been met.

- **Attainable** — The system must be able to exhibit the requirement under the specified conditions.

- **Realizable** — The requirement must be achievable under the system and project development constraints.

- **Traceable** — The requirement should be traceable both forward and backward throughout the development life cycle from conception through design, implementation, and test.

The Open Web Application Security Project (OWASP) has modified the SMART acronym (`www.owasp.org/index.php/Document_security-relevant_requirements`) to be SMART+ requirements. These requirements, taken from the OWASP website, are as follows:

- **Specific** — Requirements should be as detailed as necessary so there are no ambiguities.

- **Measurable** — It should be possible to determine whether the requirement has been met, through analysis, testing, or both.

- **Appropriate** — Requirements should be validated, thereby ensuring both that they derive from a real need or demand and that different requirements would not be more appropriate.

- **Reasonable** — While the mechanism or mechanisms for implementing a requirement need not be solidified, one should conduct some validation to determine whether meeting the requirement is physically possible, and possible given other likely project constraints.

- **Traceable** — Requirements should also be isolated to make them easy to track/validate throughout the development life cycle.

Goal-Oriented Software Security Requirements

Another complementary method for performing cloud software security requirements engineering is a *goal-oriented* paradigm in which a goal is a software objective. The types of goals that are targeted are functional goals, nonfunctional goals, security robustness, and code correctness. As Axel van Lamsweerde, Simon Brohez, Renaud De Landtsheer, and David Janssens write in "From System Goals to Intruder Anti-Goals: Attack Generation and Resolution for Security Requirements Engineering," "A goal is a prescriptive statement of intent about some system (existing or to-be) whose satisfaction in general requires the cooperation of some of the agents forming that system. Agents are active components such as humans, devices, legacy software or software-to-be components that play some role towards goal satisfaction. Goals may refer to services to be provided (functional goals) or to quality of service (nonfunctional goals)."[8]

One implementation of goal-oriented requirements engineering is the *nonfunctional requirements (NFR) framework,*[9] which provides a basis for determining if a goal has been satisfied through meeting lower-level goals.

Nonfunctional requirements include characteristics of a software system such as reliability, performance, security, accuracy, costs, reliability, and maintainability. According to Goertzel and Winograd et al., these requirements should specify the following:[10]

- Properties the software must exhibit (e.g., its behavior must be correct and predictable; it must remain resilient in the face of attacks)

- Required level of assurance or risk-avoidance of individual security functions and constraints

- Controls and rules governing the processes by which the software will be built, deployed, and operated (e.g., it must be designed to operate within a virtual machine, and its source code must not contain certain function calls)

Goertzel and Winograd et al. also provide an example of a negative nonfunctional requirement as follows: "The software must validate all input to ensure it does not exceed the size specified for that type of input."

A related goal-oriented requirements engineering approach is the MILOS[11] project methodology for goal-oriented security requirements engineering. The MILOS security model uses generic specification patterns that map to the information system's properties of confidentiality, integrity, availability, privacy, authentication, authorization, and nonrepudiation. The security patterns are transformed into goals that are used to develop a correlated "anti-model" that comprises a pattern of "anti-goals" an attacker would use to prevent meeting the specified system security goals.

> **NOTE** Cloud software security requirements address necessary attributes for software behavior and limitations on software functionality, whereas cloud software requirements are concerned with necessary software functionality and performance specifications.

Monitoring Internal and External Requirements

The requirements of the information system security policy relative to software assurance should be analyzed to ensure their consistency and correctness. Two types of secure software requirements analysis should be performed:

- **Internal** — Necessary in order to ascertain that the requirements are complete, correct, and consistent with the related specification requirements. The analysis should address the following:
  - Security constraints
  - The software's nonfunctional properties
  - The software's positive functional requirements

- **External** — Necessary to determine the following:
  - The software assurance requirements address the legal regulatory and required policy issues.

- The nonfunctional security requirements represent a proper decomposition of the system security goals.
- Software assurance requirements don't conflict with system security goals.
- The software is resilient.

Also, in the context of internal and external access to information systems, the issues in Table 3-1 should be considered.

Table 3-1: Internal and External Security Requirements

INTERNAL	EXTERNAL
Maintain identity of active users	External connections must incorporate adequate controls to safeguard IT resources.
Implement internal access controls	At a minimum, all external connections must incorporate a firewall.
Use secure gateways to allow internal users to connect to external networks	If the user access originates from outside the protected network, user must be identified and authenticated at the gateway.
Hide internal Domain Name Systems (DNSs)	Use external authentication databases, such as RADIUS.
Dial-up modems should not be connected to computers that are connected to the internal network.	Employ content filtering to permit or deny services to specific external hosts.
E-mail messages flowing through the information systems should be monitored for internal policy compliance.	Accredit external connections prior to use.
	External connections should be periodically reviewed by an independent organization.

Source: National Institute of Standards and Technology, "An Introduction to Computer Security: The NIST Handbook, Special Publication 800-12," October 1995.

Cloud Security Policy Implementation and Decomposition

Cloud software security requirements are a function of policies such as system security policies, software policies, and information system policies. Cloud providers also have to satisfy regulations and directives such as FISMA, Gramm-Leach-Bliley, Sarbanes-Oxley, and HIPAA. For proper secure cloud software implementation, these issues have to be accounted for during the software development life cycle and through an effective cloud software security policy.

Implementation Issues

Important areas addressed by a software system's cloud security policy include the following:

- Access controls
- Data protection
- Confidentiality
- Integrity
- Identification and authentication
- Communication security
- Accountability

In the context of secure software, a requirement should follow from the general policy statements. An example of such a process is provided by Goertzel and Winograd et al.,[12] for the high-level policy functional requirement: "The server should store both public-access and restricted Web pages." From this high-level statement, the following activities should result as presented by Goertzel, Winograd, et al:

- Derive the detailed functional requirements, e.g., "The server should return public-access Web pages to any browser that requests those pages."
- Identify the related constraint requirements, e.g., "The server should return restricted Web pages only to browsers that are acting as proxies for users with authorized privileges sufficient to access those Web pages."
- Derive the functional security requirements, e.g., "The server must authenticate every browser that requests access to a restricted Web page."
- Identify the related negative requirements, e.g., "The server must not return a restricted Web page to any browser that it cannot authenticate."

The security requirements in a software security policy can also be specified in terms of functionality properties, such as restrictions on system states and information flows.

Goertzel and Winograd et al. list the following common sources of security requirements:

- Stakeholders' expressed security concerns
- Security implications of the functional specification
- Requirements for security functions
- Compliance and conformance mandates
- Secure development and deployment standards, guidelines, and best practices

- Attack models and environment risk analysis

- Known and likely vulnerabilities in the technologies and commercial-off-the-shelf (COTS) and open-source software (OSS) components that, due to preexisting commitments, must be used

An additional source of inputs to secure software policies is NIST FIPS Publication 200,[13] which specifies the following items:

- **System and Services Acquisition** — "Organizations must . . . (ii) employ system development life cycle processes that incorporate information security considerations; (iii) employ software usage and installation restrictions; and (iv) ensure that third-party providers employ adequate security measures to protect information, applications, and/or services outsourced from the organization."

- **System and Communications Protection** — "Organizations must . . . (ii) employ architectural designs, software development techniques, and systems engineering principles that promote effective information security within organizational information systems."

- **System and Information Integrity** — "Organizations must: (i) identify, report, and correct information and information system flaws in a timely manner; (ii) provide protection from malicious code at appropriate locations within organizational information systems."

Security policies are the foundation of a sound cloud system security implementation. Often organizations will implement technical security solutions without first creating this foundation of policies, standards, guidelines, and procedures, unintentionally creating unfocused and ineffective security controls.

According to the Data and Analysis Center for Software (DACS), "Information security policy is concerned, in large part, with defining the set of rules by which system subjects are allowed to change the states of data objects in the system. In practical terms, this means defining for every system subject whether, and if so how, it may store, transmit, create, modify, or delete a given data object (or type of data object)."[14]

The same document also lists three main objectives common to all system security policies and the mechanisms and countermeasures used to enforce those policies:

- They must allow authorized access and connections to the system while preventing unauthorized access or connections, especially by unknown or suspicious actors.

- They must enable allowable reading, modification, destruction, and deletion of data while preventing unauthorized reading (data leakage), modification (data tampering), destruction (denial of service), or deletion (denial of service).

- They must block the entry of content (user input, executable code, system commands, etc.) suspected of containing attack patterns or malicious logic that could threaten the system's ability to operate according to its security policy and its ability to protect the information.

Decomposing Critical Security Issues into Secure Cloud Software Requirements

An information system security policy addresses the critical issues of confidentiality, integrity, availability, identification, authentication, authorization, and auditing; and decomposes their elements into the following secure software requirements.

Confidentiality

Confidentiality in a cloud system policy is concerned with protecting data during transfers between entities. A policy defines the requirements for ensuring the confidentiality of data by preventing the unauthorized disclosure of information being sent between two end points. The policy should specify who can exchange information and what type of data can be exchanged. Related issues include intellectual property rights, access control, encryption, inference, anonymity, and covert channels. These policy statements should translate into requirements that address the following:

- Mechanisms that should be applied to enforce authorization
- What form of information is provided to the user and what the user can view
- The means of identity establishment
- What other types of confidentiality utilities should be used

Integrity

A cloud policy has to provide the requirements for ensuring the integrity of data both in transit and in storage. It should also specify means to recover from detectable errors, such as deletions, insertions, and modifications. The means to protect the integrity of information include access control policies and decisions regarding who can transmit and receive data and which information can be exchanged. Derived requirements for integrity should address the following:

- Validating the data origin
- Detecting the alteration of data
- Determining whether the data origin has changed

The policy should also provide for the integrity of data stored on media through monitoring for errors. Consideration should be given to determining the attributes and means that will be used as the basis for the monitoring and the actions that need to be taken should an integrity error occur. One type of integrity can also be described as maintaining a software system in a predefined "legitimate" state.

Availability

Cloud policy requirements for availability are concerned with denying illegitimate access to computing resources and preventing external attacks such as denial-of-service attacks. Additional issues to address include attempts by malicious entities to control, destroy, or damage computing resources and deny legitimate access to systems. While availability is being preserved, confidentiality and integrity have to be maintained. Requirements for this category should address how to ensure that computing resources are available to authorized users when needed.

Authentication and Identification

A cloud system policy should specify the means of authenticating a user when the user is requesting service on a cloud resource and presenting his or her identity. The authentication must be performed in a secure manner. Strong authentication using a public key certificate should be employed to bind a user to an identity. Exchanged information should not be alterable. This safeguard can be accomplished using a certificate-based digital signature. Some corresponding requirements include the following:

- Mechanisms for determining identity
- Binding of a resource to an identity
- Identification of communication origins
- Management of out-of-band authentication means
- Reaffirmations of identities

Authorization

After authentication, the cloud system policy must address authorization to allow access to resources, including the following areas:

- A user requesting that specified services not be applied to his or her message traffic
- Bases for negative or positive responses
- Specifying responses to requests for services in a simple and clear manner

- Including the type of service and the identity of the user in an authorization to access services
- Identification of entities that have the authority to set authorization rules between users and services
- Means for the provider of services to identify the user and associated traffic
- Means for the user to acquire information concerning the service profile kept by the service provider on the user

These policy issues should generate requirements that address the following:

- Specific mechanisms to provide for access control
- Privileges assigned to subjects during the system's life
- Management of access control subsystems

Auditing

The auditing of a cloud system has characteristics similar to auditing in the software development life cycle (SDLC) in that the auditing plan must address the following:

- Determination of the audit's scope
- Determination of the audit's objectives
- Validation of the audit plan
- Identification of necessary resources
- Conduct of the audit
- Documentation of the audit
- Validation of the audit results
- Report of final results

The Information Systems Audit and Control Association (ISACA) has developed information systems (IS) audit standards, guidelines, and a code of ethics for auditors that are directly applicable to cloud platforms. This information can be found on the ISACA website at www.isaca.org. The cloud system security policy should decompose the audit requirements to risk-based elements that consider the following three types of audit-related risks:

- **Inherent risk** — The susceptibility of a process to perform erroneously, assuming that no internal controls exist
- **Detection risk** — The probability that an auditor's methods will not detect a material error
- **Control risk** — The probability that extant controls will not prevent or detect errors in a timely fashion

The cloud system security policy decomposition for auditing should also consider organizational characteristics such as supervisory issues, institutional ethics, compensation policies, organizational history, and the business environment. In particular, the following elements of the cloud system organizational structure and management should be taken into account:

- Organizational roles and responsibilities
- Separation of duties
- IS management
- IS training
- Qualifications of IS staff
- Database administration
- Third party–provided services
- Managing of contracts
- Service-level agreements (SLAs)
- Quality management and assurance standards
- Change management
- Problem management
- Project management
- Performance management and indicators
- Capacity management
- Economic performance

    - Application of SOP 98-1,[15] which is an accounting statement of position that defines how information technology software development or acquisition costs are to be expended or capitalized
    - Expense management and monitoring

- Information system security management
- Business continuity management

The cloud policy decomposition for the audit component is recursive in that the audit has to address the cloud system security policy, standards, guidelines, and procedures. It should also delineate the three basic types of controls, which are preventive, detective, and corrective; and it should provide the basis for a qualitative audit risk assessment that includes the following:

- Identification of all relevant assets
- Valuation of the assets

- Identification of threats
- Identification of regulatory requirements
- Identification of organizational risk requirements
- Identification of the likelihood of threat occurrence
- Definition of organizational entities or subgroupings
- Review of previous audits
- Determination of audit budget constraints

The cloud policy should ensure that auditing can pass a test of *due care*, which is defined by the ISACA as "the level of diligence that a prudent and competent person would exercise under a given set of circumstances."[16]

In the event that it is necessary to conduct forensic investigations in cloud systems, the confidentiality and integrity of audit information must be protected at the highest level of security.

In 1996, the ISACA introduced a valuable audit planning and execution tool, the "Control Objectives for Information and Related Technology (COBIT)" document. As of this writing, COBIT is now in version 4.1. It is divided into four domains comprising 34 high-level control objectives. These 34 control objectives are further divided into 318 specific control objectives. COBIT defines a *control objective* that is a goal aimed at preventing a set of risks from occurring . The four COBIT domains are as follows:

- **Planning and organization (PO)** — Provides direction to solution delivery (AI) and service delivery (DS)

- **Acquisition and implementation (AI)** — Provides the solutions and passes them to be turned into services

- **Deliver and support (DS)** — Receives the solutions and makes them available for end users

- **Monitor and evaluate (ME)** — Monitors all processes to ensure that the direction provided is followed

NIST 33 Security Principles

In June 2001, the National Institute of Standards and Technology's Information Technology Laboratory (ITL) published NIST Special Publication 800-27, "Engineering Principles for Information Technology Security (EP-ITS)," to assist in the secure design, development, deployment, and life cycle of information systems. The document was revised (Revision A) in 2004. It presents 33 security principles that begin at the design phase of the information system or application and continue until the system's retirement and secure disposal.

Some of the 33 principles that are most applicable to cloud security policies and management are as follows:

- Principle 1 — Establish a sound security policy as the "foundation" for design.
- Principle 2 — Treat security as an integral part of the overall system design.
- Principle 3 — Clearly delineate the physical and logical security boundaries governed by associated security policies.
- Principle 6 — Assume that external systems are insecure.
- Principle 7 — Identify potential trade-offs between reducing risk and increased costs and decreases in other aspects of operational effectiveness.
- Principle 16 — Implement layered security; ensure there is no single point of vulnerability.
- Principle 20 — Isolate public access systems from mission-critical resources (e.g., data, processes, etc.).
- Principle 21 — Use boundary mechanisms to separate computing systems and network infrastructures.
- Principle 25 — Minimize the system elements to be trusted.
- Principle 26 — Implement least privilege.
- Principle 32 — Authenticate users and processes to ensure appropriate access control decisions both within and across domains.
- Principle 33 — Use unique identities to ensure accountability.

Secure Cloud Software Testing

Secure cloud software testing involves a number of activities. Each activity is based on a formal standard or methodology and adds unique value to the overall secure software testing process. An organization typically selects testing activities based on a number of factors, including secure cloud software requirements and available resources.

Analyses of test results form the basis for assessing risk to cloud information and means of remediation. Standards and methodologies such as the International Organization for Standardization (ISO) 9126 Standard for Software Engineering/Product Quality, the Systems Security Engineering Capability Maturity Model (SSE-CMM) and the Open Source Security Testing Methodology Manual (OSSTMM) provide additional guidance for secure software evaluation and mitigation. After software has been modified, regression testing provides assurance that the original software system functionality and security characteristics are not negatively affected by the respective changes.

Testing for Security Quality Assurance

Secure software testing has considerations in common with quality assurance testing. For example, the correct version of the software should always be tested. However, secure software testing must also measure the quality of the software's security properties. For example, software should be tested to ensure that it meets its functional specifications, and does nothing else. Testing that software does nothing else — that is, does not contain any unintended functionality — is a measure of security quality.

There is a lack of commonly agreed-upon definitions for software quality, but it is possible to refer to software quality by its common attributes. One well-known characterization of software quality is the International Organization for Standardization (ISO) 9126 standard. The ISO 9126 standard characterizes software quality with six main attributes and 21 subcharacteristics, as shown in Table 3-2.

Table 3-2: The ISO 9126 Software Quality Standards

ATTRIBUTES	SUBCHARACTERISTICS	DEFINITION
Functionality	Suitability	Attributes of software that bear on the presence and appropriateness of a set of functions for specified tasks
	Accurateness	Attributes of software that bear on the provision of right or agreed upon results or effects
	Interoperability	Attributes of software that bear on its ability to interact with specified systems
	Compliance	Attributes of software that make the software adhere to application-related standards or conventions or regulations in laws and similar prescriptions
	Security	Attributes of software that bear on its ability to prevent unauthorized access, whether accidental or deliberate, to programs or data
Reliability	Maturity	Attributes of software that bear on the frequency of failure by faults in the software
	Fault tolerance	Attributes of software that bear on its ability to maintain a specified level of performance in case of software faults or infringement of its specified interface

Continued

Table 3-2 *(continued)*

ATTRIBUTES	SUBCHARACTERISTICS	DEFINITION
	Recoverability	Attributes of software that bear on the capability to re-establish its level of performance and recover the data directly affected in case of a failure and on the time and effort needed for it
Usability	Understandability	Attributes of software that bear on the users' effort for recognizing the logical concept and its applicability
	Learnability	Attributes of software that bear on the users' effort for learning its application
	Operability	Attributes of software that bear on the users' effort for operation and operation control
Efficiency	Time behavior	Attributes of software that bear on response and processing times and on throughput rates in performing its function
	Resource behavior	Attributes of software that bear on the amount of resources used and the duration of such use in performing its function
Maintainability	Analyzability	Attributes of software that bear on the effort needed for diagnosis of deficiencies or causes of failures or for identification of parts to be modified
	Changeability	Attributes of software that bear on the effort needed for modification, fault removal, or environmental change
	Stability	Attributes of software that bear on the risk of unexpected effect of modifications
	Testability	Attributes of software that bear on the effort needed for validating the modified software

ATTRIBUTES	SUBCHARACTERISTICS	DEFINITION
Portability	Adaptability	Attributes of software that bear on the opportunity for its adaptation to different specified environments without applying other actions or means than those provided for this purpose for the software considered
	Installability	Attributes of software that bear on the effort needed to install the software in a specified environment
	Conformance	Attributes of software that make the software adhere to standards or conventions relating to portability
	Replaceability	Attributes of software that bear on opportunity and effort using it in the place of specified other software in the environment of that software

Conformance Testing

The National Institute of Standards and Technology (NIST) states that "conformance testing activities assess whether a software product meets the requirements of a particular specification or standard."[17] These standards are typically well regarded and widely accepted, such as those from the International Organization for Standardization (ISO), the Institute of Electrical and Electronics Engineers, Inc. (IEEE), or the American National Standards Institute (ANSI). They reflect a commonly accepted "reference system" whose standards recommendations are sufficiently defined and tested by certifiable test methods. They are used to evaluate whether the software product implements each of the specific requirements of the standard or specification.

Conformance testing methodologies applicable to cloud services have been developed for operating system interfaces, computer graphics, documented interchange formats, computer networks, and programming language processors. Most testing methodologies use test case scenarios (e.g., abstract test suites, test assertions, test cases), which themselves must be tested.

Standardization is an important component of conformance testing. It usually includes developing the functional description and language specification, creating the testing methodology, and "testing" the test case scenarios.

A major benefit of conformance testing is that it facilitates interoperability between various cloud software products by confirming that each software product meets an agreed-upon standard or specification.

One type of conformance testing, protocol-based testing, uses an application's communication protocol as a direct basis for testing the application. This method is useful for cloud-based applications. Protocol-based testing is especially important for security testing in Web-based applications, because Web protocols provide the easiest way for remote attackers to access such applications.[18]

Functional Testing

In functional testing, a cloud software application is tested at runtime to determine whether it conforms to its functional requirements. Requirements that state how the application should respond when a specific event occurs are referred to as *positive requirements*. Typically, a positive requirement is mapped to a specific software artifact meant to implement that requirement. This provides traceability from requirements to implementation and informs the tester of which code artifact to test to validate the expected functionality.

An example of a positive requirement is "the application should lock the user account after three failed login attempts." A tester can validate the expected functionality (the lockout) by attempting to log in to the application three times with the same username and incorrect passwords. This type of test can be easily automated with a functional testing tool suite, such as the open-source Canoo WebTest (`http://webtest.canoo.com`).

Functional testing also includes *negative requirements*, which specify what software should *not* do. An example of a negative requirement is "the cloud application should not allow for the stored data to be disclosed." This type of requirement is more difficult to test because the expected behavior is not implemented in a specific software artifact. Testing this requirement properly would require the tester to anticipate every anomalous input, condition, cause, and effect. Instead, the testing should be driven by risk analysis and threat modeling. This enables the negative requirement to be documented as a threat scenario, and the functionality of the countermeasure as a factor to mitigate the threat. The following steps summarize this approach from the Open Web Application Security Project (OWASP) Testing Guide (`www.owasp.org/index.php/Category:OWASP_Testing_Project`).

First, the security requirements are documented from a threats and countermeasures perspective:

- Encrypt authentication data in storage and transit to mitigate risk of information disclosure and authentication protocol attacks.

- Encrypt passwords using nonreversible encryption such as a hashing algorithm and a salt to prevent dictionary attacks. *Salt* refers to inserting random bits into algorithms used for key generation to mitigate against dictionary attacks.

- Lock out accounts after reaching a login failure threshold and enforce password complexity to mitigate risk of brute-force password attacks.

- Display generic error messages upon validation of credentials to mitigate risk of account harvesting/enumeration.

- Mutually authenticate client and server to prevent nonrepudiation and man-in-the-middle (MITM) attacks.

Artifacts produced in the threat modeling process, such as threat trees and attack libraries, can then be used to derive negative test scenarios.

A threat tree will assume a root attack (e.g., attack might be able to read other users' messages) and identify different exploits of security controls (e.g., data validation fails because of a SQL injection vulnerability) and necessary countermeasures (e.g., implement data validation and parameterized queries) that could be tested for effectiveness in mitigating such attacks.

Typically, functional testing is used to test the functionality of implemented features or after the software feature is complete. However, code coverage is limited by the number of available use cases. If a test is not created for a specific use case, then a number of execution paths in the software will remain untested. Therefore, even if the functionality is validated for all available use cases, that is not a guarantee that the software is free of defects.

Logic testing is a type of functional testing that involves ensuring that business logic is predicated on the correct assumptions. Business logic is the code that satisfies the business purpose of cloud software and typically models and automates a "real-life" or "paper" business process such as e-commerce or inventory management. Business logic is composed of both business rules and workflows:

- Business rules that express business policy (such as channels, location, logistics, prices, and products)

- Workflows based on the ordered tasks of passing documents or data from one participant (a person or a software system) to another

Business logic flaws are typically specific to the cloud application being tested, and are difficult to detect. Automated tools do a poor job of discovering logic flaws because they do not understand the context of the decisions. Therefore, discovering logic flaws is typically a manual process performed by a human tester.

When looking for business logic flaws, the tester begins by considering the rules for the business function being provided by the cloud application. Next, the tester searches for any limits or restrictions on people's behavior. Then the application can be tested to validate that it enforces those rules. A classic example of a business logic flaw is the modification of prices that was sometimes allowed by e-commerce applications on the early Web-based Internet.

Setting the price of a product on an e-commerce site as a negative number could result in funds being credited to an attacker. A countermeasure to this vulnerability is to implement positive validation of the price so that the application allows only positive numbers in a specific numerical range. Of course, the application should never accept and process any data from the client that did not require user input in the first place.

Performance Testing

In an online report (`http://vote.nist.gov/vvsg-report.htm`), NIST states that "what distinguishes performance testing from functional testing is the form of the experimental result. A functional test yields a yes or no verdict, while a performance test yields a quantity." Performance testing measures how well the cloud software system executes according to its required response times, throughput, CPU, usage, and other quantifiable features in operation. The quantity resulting from a test may subsequently be reduced to a yes or no verdict by comparison with a benchmark.

Performance testing is also commonly known by other names and/or associated with other testing activities, such as stress testing, capacity testing, load testing, volume testing, and benchmark testing. These various performance testing activities all have approximately the same goal: "measuring the cloud software product under a real or simulated load."[19]

Typically, performance testing is conducted late in the software life cycle when the software is fully developed. In order to obtain accurate measurements, the cloud software is deployed and tested in an environment that simulates the operational environment. This can be achieved by creating a cloud "staging" environment, essentially a mirror copy of the production infrastructure, and simulating typical operating conditions.

A major benefit of performance testing is that it is typically designed specifically for pushing system limits over a long period of time. This form of testing has commonly been used to uncover unique failures not discovered during conformance or interoperability tests. In addition, benchmarking is typically used to provide competitive baseline performance comparisons. For instance, these tests are used to characterize performance prior to manufacturing as well as to compare performance characteristics of other software products prior to purchase.

Performance testing procedures provide steps for determining the ability of the cloud software to function properly, particularly when near or beyond the boundaries of its specified capabilities or requirements. These boundaries are usually stated in terms of the volume of information used. The specified metrics are usually stated in terms of time to complete an operation. Ideally, performance testing is conducted by running a software element against standard datasets or scenarios, known as *reference data*.

Performance measures and requirements are quantitative, which means they consist of numbers that can be measured and confirmed by rational experiments. A performance specification consists of a set of specified numbers that can be reduced to measured numbers, often in the form of a probability distribution. The numbers measured for the software product are either less than, more than, or equal to the specified values. If less than, the software product fails; if more than or equal to, the software product passes the tests. Every performance specification is a variation of these simple ideas. Common metrics used in performance testing include the following:

- **Throughput** — The rate at which the system processes transactions, commonly measured in bytes per second

- **Processing delay** — The time it takes to process those transactions, measured in seconds

- **Load** — The rate at which transactions are submitted to a software product, measured in arriving transactions per second

Stress testing is a kind of performance testing that involves increasing the load on a software system beyond normal operating capacity and observing the results. Stress testing can be used to ensure that the cloud software remains stable and reliable, and can continue to provide a specific quality of service, although the software is often tested to the point of failure. Extreme operating conditions, such as those associated with resource exhaustion — out of memory or hardware failures that might occur in a cloud environment — are simulated.

Stress testing can also be used to test the security properties of cloud software because it can induce anomalous behavior. For example, extreme operating conditions may cause an error that is poorly handled by the cloud application, causing it to fail insecurely. In a real-world scenario, a DoS attack targeted against a cloud application could slow down the execution of the application such that it exposes a race condition, which could subsequently be exploited as a security vulnerability.[20]

NOTE The Microsoft Web Application Stress Tool (www.microsoft.com) is a freely available tool that simulates multiple browsers requesting pages from a website. It can be used to gather performance and stability information about a Web application. It simulates a large number of requests with a relatively small number of client machines. The goal is to create an environment that is as close to production as possible so that problems can be discovered and eliminated in a Web application prior to deployment.

Security Testing

Security testing should assess the security properties and behaviors of cloud software as it interacts with external entities (human users, environment, other software) and as its own components interact with each other. Security testing should verify that software exhibits the following properties and behaviors, as summarized from the "Software Security Assurance State-of-the-Art Report (SOAR)":[21]

- Its behavior is predictable and secure.

- It exposes no vulnerabilities or weaknesses.

- Its error and exception handling routines enable it to maintain a secure state when confronted by attack patterns or intentional faults.

- It satisfies all of its specified and implicit nonfunctional security requirements.

- It does not violate any specified security constraints.

- As much of its runtime-interpretable source code and byte code as possible has been obscured or obfuscated to deter reverse engineering.

A security test plan should be included in the overall cloud software test plan and should define all testing activities, including the following:

- Security test cases or scenarios

- Test data, including attack patterns

- Test oracle (if one is to be used), which is used to determine if a software test has passed or failed

- Test tools (white box, black box, static, and dynamic)

- Analyses to be performed to interpret, correlate, and synthesize the results from the various tests and outputs from the various tools

Software security testing techniques can be categorized as white box, gray box, or black box:

- **White box** — Testing from an internal perspective, i.e., with full knowledge of the software internals; the source code, architecture and design documents, and configuration files are available for analysis.

- **Gray box** — Analyzing the source code for the purpose of designing the test cases, but using black box testing techniques; both the source code and the executable binary are available for analysis.

- **Black box** — Testing the software from an external perspective, i.e., with no prior knowledge of the software; only the binary executable or intermediate byte code is available for analysis.

An example of a white box testing technique is the static analysis of source code that should be performed iteratively as the software is being written. Table 3-3 lists other common security testing techniques and how they are typically categorized.

Table 3-3: Common Security Testing Techniques

TESTING TECHNIQUE	CATEGORY
Source code analysis	White box
Property-based	White box
Source code fault injection	White box, gray box
Dynamic code analysis	Gray box
Binary fault injection	Gray box, black box
Fuzz testing	Black box
Binary code analysis	Black box
Byte code analysis	Black box
Black box debugging	Black box
Vulnerability scanning	Black box
Penetration testing	Black box

Fault Injection

Fault injection is a technique used to improve code coverage by testing all code paths, especially error-handling code paths that may not be exercised during functional testing. In fault injection testing, errors are injected into the cloud software to simulate unintentional user errors and intentional attacks on the software through its environment, and attacks on the environment itself.

Source Code Fault Injection

In source code fault injection, the tester decides when environment faults should be triggered. The tester then "instruments" the source code by non-intrusively inserting changes into the program that reflect the changed environment data that would result from those faults.[22] The instrumented source code is then compiled and executed, and the tester observes how the executing software's state changes when the instrumented portions of code are executed. This enables the tester to observe the secure and nonsecure state changes in the software resulting from changes in its environment.

The tester can also analyze how the cloud software's state changes as a result of a fault propagating through the source code. This type of analysis is typically referred to as *fault propagation analysis,* and involves two techniques of source code fault injection: *extended propagation analysis* and *interface propagation analysis.*

To prepare for fault propagation analysis, the tester must generate a fault tree from the software's source code. To perform an extended propagation analysis, the tester injects faults into the fault tree, then traces how each injected fault propagates through the tree. This shows the impact a particular fault will have on the overall behavior of the software.

Interface propagation analysis focuses on how faults are propagated through the interfaces between the component/module and other cloud application-level and environment-level components. In interface propagation analysis, the tester injects a fault into the data inputs between components, views how the resulting faults propagate, and observes whether any new anomalies result. This type of analysis enables the tester to determine how the failure of one component can affect the failure of a neighboring component, particularly important if a neighboring cloud component is of high consequence.

Source code fault injection is particularly useful in detecting the following:

- Incorrect use of pointers and arrays
- Use of dangerous calls
- Race conditions

Source code fault injection should be performed iteratively as the software is being written. When new threats (attack types and intrusion techniques) are discovered, the source code can be re-instrumented with faults that are representative of those new threat types.

Binary Fault Injection

Binary fault injection is a runtime analysis technique whereby an executing cloud application is monitored as faults are injected. By monitoring system call traces, a tester can identify the names of system calls, the parameters to each call, and the call's return code. This enables the tester to discover the names and types of resources being accessed by the calling software, how the resources are being used, and the success or failure of each access attempt. In binary fault analysis, faults are injected into the environment resources that surround the cloud application. Environmental faults provide the tester with a number of benefits:

- They simulate real-world attack scenarios and can be easily automated.
- They simulate environment anomalies without requiring an understanding of how those anomalies actually occur in the real world. This enables fault injection by testers who do not have prior knowledge of the environment whose faults are being simulated.
- The tester can choose when to trigger a particular environmental fault. This avoids the problem of a full environment emulation in which the environment state when the application interacts with it may not be what is expected, or may not have the expected effect on the software's behavior.

It is difficult to predict the complex inputs the cloud software will actually receive in its target environment. Therefore, fault injection scenarios should be designed to give the tester the most complete understanding possible of the security of the behaviors, states, and properties of the software system under all possible operating conditions. Once the cloud application has been deployed to production, the tester can employ penetration testing and vulnerability scanning to provide an additional measure of the application's security posture.

Binary fault injection tools include binary fault injectors and brute-force testers. These tools should support the common functionality found in the application. For example, the commercial fault injection tool Holodeck (www.securityinnovation.com/holodeck/) is often used to simulate faults in Microsoft operating system applications. Holodeck injects faults for common functionality found in a typical Windows environment such as the following:

- **Network** — Cable disconnected, network not installed, wrong Winsock version, Winsock task limit reached, no ports available, network is down
- **Disk** — Insufficient disk space, cyclic redundancy check (CRC) errors, too many files open, disk is write-protected, no disk is in the drive
- **Memory** — Insufficient memory, failure to allocate, locked memory

Holodeck also supports monitoring an application to watch its interactions with the environment.

Dynamic Code Analysis

Dynamic code analysis examines the code as it executes in a running cloud application, with the tester tracing the external interfaces in the source code to the corresponding interactions in the executing code, so that any vulnerabilities or anomalies that arise in the executing interfaces are simultaneously located in the source code, where they can then be fixed.

Unlike static analysis, dynamic analysis enables the tester to exercise the software in ways that expose vulnerabilities introduced by interactions with users and changes in the configuration or behavior of environment components. Because the software isn't fully linked and deployed in its actual target environment, these interactions and their associated inputs and environment conditions are essentially simulated by the testing tool.

An example of a dynamic code analysis toolset is the open-source Valgrind (www.valgrind.org), which is useful in detecting memory management and thread bugs.

Property-Based Testing

Property-based testing is a formal analysis technique developed at the University of California at Davis.[23] Property-based testing validates that the software's implemented functionality satisfies its specifications. It does this by examining security-relevant properties revealed by the source code, such as the absence of insecure state changes. Then these security-relevant properties in the code are compared against the software's specification to determine whether the security assumptions have been met.

Like direct code analysis, property-based testing requires the full concentration of the tester and is a detail-oriented process. Because it requires the tester to dedicate a significant amount of time to the code, it is often used only to analyze code that implements high-consequence functions.

Black Box Debugging

Black box debugging[24] is a technique to monitor behaviors external to the binary component or system while it is executing, and thereby observe the data that passes between that component/system and external entities.

Additionally, by observing how data passes across the software's boundary, the analyst can also determine how externally sourced data might be manipulated to force the software down certain execution paths, or to cause the software to fail. This can reveal errors and failures that originate not in the cloud software itself, but are forced by the external entities with which it interacts, or by an incorrectly implemented API.

Interoperability Testing

Interoperability testing evaluates whether a cloud application can exchange data (interoperate) with other components or applications. Interoperability testing activities determine the capability of applications to exchange data via a common set of exchange formats, to read and write the same file formats, and to communicate using the same protocols. A major goal of interoperability testing is to detect interoperability problems between cloud software applications before these applications are put into operation. Interoperability testing requires the majority of the application to be completed before testing can occur.

Interoperability testing typically takes one of three approaches:

- **Testing all pairs** — This is often conducted by a third-party independent group of testers who are knowledgeable about the interoperability characteristics across software products and between software vendors.

- **Testing some of the combinations** — This approach involves testing only part of the combinations and assuming the untested combinations will also interoperate.

- **Testing against a reference implementation** — This approach establishes a reference implementation, e.g., using the accepted standard, and testing all products against the reference. In a paper on metrology in information technology, researchers in the NIST Information Technology Laboratory state that a typical procedure used to conduct interoperability testing includes "developing a representative set of test transactions in one software product for passage to another software product for processing verification."[25]

One challenge in cloud software component integration is how to build a secure composite system from components that may or may not be individually secure. In a paper by Verizon Communications and the University of Texas,[26] researchers describe a systematic approach for determining interoperability of components from a security perspective and unifying the security features, policies, and implementation mechanisms of components. This is a goal-oriented and model-driven approach to analyzing the security features of components to determine interoperability. Along with this approach, the researchers provide a guideline for integrating the components to fulfill the security goals of the composite system. Following the proposed analysis procedure could lead to discovery of some classes of security interoperability conflicts that help to determine whether or not the components should be used together.

Cloud Penetration Testing

A penetration test is a security testing methodology that gives the tester insight into the strength of the target's network security by simulating an attack from a malicious source. The process involves an active analysis of the cloud system for any potential vulnerabilities that may result from poor or improper system configuration, known and/or unknown hardware or software flaws, or operational weaknesses in process or technical countermeasures. This analysis is carried out from the position of a potential attacker, and can involve active exploitation of security vulnerabilities.

Any security issues that are found are presented to the system owner together with an assessment of their impact, and often with a proposal for mitigation or a technical solution. The intent of a penetration test is to proactively determine the feasibility of an attack or to retroactively determine the degree to which a successful exploit has affected the business. It is a component of a full security audit, which includes the following:

- **A Level I, high-level assessment** — A top-down look at the organization's policies, procedures, standards, and guidelines. A Level I assessment is not usually hands-on, in that the system's security is not actually tested.

- **A Level II, network evaluation** — More hands-on than a Level I assessment, a Level II assessment has some of the Level I activities plus more information gathering and scanning.

- **A Level III, penetration test** — A penetration test is not usually concerned with policies. It is more about taking the adversarial view of a hacker, by seeing what can be accomplished, and with what difficulty.

Several factors have converged in the cloud environment to make penetration testing a necessity. The evolution of information technology has focused on ease of use at the operational end, while exponentially increasing the complexity of the computing resources. Unfortunately, the administration and management requirements of cloud systems have increased for several reasons:

- The skill level required to execute a hacker exploit has steadily decreased.

- The size and complexity of the network environment has mushroomed.

- The number of network and cloud-based applications has increased.

- The detrimental impact of a security breach on corporate assets and good-will is greater than ever.

Penetration testing is most commonly carried out within a "black box," that is, with no prior knowledge of the infrastructure to be tested. At its simplest level, the penetration test involves three phases:

1. **Preparation** — A formal contract is executed containing nondisclosure of the client's data and legal protection for the tester. At a minimum, it also lists the IP addresses to be tested and the time to test.

2. **Execution** — In this phase the penetration test is executed, with the tester looking for potential vulnerabilities.

3. **Delivery** — The results of the evaluation are communicated to the tester's contact in the organization, and corrective action is advised.

Whether the penetration test is a full knowledge (white box) test, a partial knowledge (gray box) test, or a zero knowledge (black box) test, after the report and results are obtained, mitigation techniques have to be applied to reduce the risk of compromise to an acceptable or tolerable level. The test should address vulnerabilities and corresponding risks to such areas as applications, remote access systems, Voice over Internet Protocol (VoIP), wireless networks, and so on.

Legal and Ethical Implications

Because an ethical hacker conducting a penetration test works for an organization to assist in evaluating its network security, this individual must adhere to a high standard of conduct. In fact, there is a Certified Ethical Hacker (CEH) certification sponsored by the International Council of E-Commerce Consultants (EC-Council) at `www.eccouncil.org` that attests to the ethical hacker's knowledge and subscription to ethical principles. The EC-Council also provides the Licensed Penetration Tester (LPT) certification, which, to quote their website, provides the following benefits:

- Standardizes the knowledge base for penetration testing professionals by incorporating best practices followed by experienced experts in the field

- Ensures that each professional licensed by EC-Council follows a strict code of ethics

- Is exposed to the best practices in the domain of penetration testing

- Is aware of all the compliance requirements required by the industry

- Trains security professionals to analyze the security posture of a network exhaustively and recommend corrective measures

When an ethical hacker or licensed penetration tester agrees to conduct penetration tests for an organization, and to probe the weaknesses of their information systems, he or she can be open to dismissal and prosecution unless contract terms are included to protect the individuals conducting the test. It is vitally important that the organization and ethical hacking team have an identical understanding of what the team is authorized to do and what happens if the team inadvertently causes some damage.

Attacking a network from the outside carries ethical and legal risk to the tester, and remedies and protections must be spelled out in detail before the test begins. For example, the Cyber Security Enhancement Act of 2002 indicates life sentences for hackers who "recklessly" endanger the lives of others, and several other U.S. statutes address cyber crime. Statute 1030, "Fraud and Related Activity in Connection with Computers," specifically states that whoever intentionally accesses a protected computer without authorization, and as a result of such conduct, recklessly causes damage or impairs medical treatment, can receive a fine or imprisonment of five to twenty years. It is vital that the tester receive specific written permission to conduct the test from the most senior executive possible. A tester should be specifically indemnified against prosecution for the task of testing.

For his or her protection, the ethical hacking tester should keep the following items in mind:

- **Protect information uncovered during the penetration test** — In the course of gaining access to an organization's networks and computing resources, the ethical hacker will find that he or she has access to sensitive information that would be valuable to the organization's competitors or enemies. Therefore, this information should be protected to the highest degree possible and not divulged to anyone, either purposely or inadvertently.

- **Conduct business in an ethical manner** — Ethical is a relative term and is a function of a number of variables, including socio-economic background, religion, upbringing, and so on. However, the ethical hacker should conduct his or her activities in a trustworthy manner that reflects the best interests of the organization that commissioned the penetration testing. Similarly, the organization should treat the ethical hacker with the same respect and ethical conduct.

- **Limitation of liability** — As discussed earlier in this section, during a penetration test, the ethical hacking team will most likely have access to sensitive files and information. The ethical hacker is trained to not cause any harm, such as modifying files, deleting information, and so on, in the course of his or her activities; but because errors do occur, the organization and the ethical hacker should have terms in the contract between them that address the situation where harm is done inadvertently. There should be a limitation to the liability of the ethical hacker if this scenario occurs. Another commonly used option by consultants is to obtain an insurance policy that will cover the consultant's activities in his or her chosen profession.

- **Remain within the scope of the assignment** — The scope of the penetration testing should be delineated beforehand and agreed upon by all parties involved. With that accomplished, the testing team should conduct the testing strictly within those bounds. For example, the penetration testing should include only the networks and computing resources specified, as well as the methods and extent of trying to break in to the information system.

- **Develop a testing plan** — As with any endeavor, the ethical hacking team should develop a test plan in advance of the testing and have it approved by the hiring organization. The plan should include the scope of the test, resources to be tested, support provided by the hiring organization, times for the testing, location of the testing, the type of testing (white box, gray box, or black box), extent of the penetration, individuals to contact in the event of problems, and deliverables.

- **Comply with relevant laws and regulations** — Business organizations are required to comply with a variety of laws and regulations, including the Health Insurance Portability and Accountability Act (HIPAA), Sarbanes-Oxley, and the Gramm-Leach-Bliley Act (GLBA). These acts are one of the reasons why companies hire ethical hackers, and demonstrate that they are acting to protect their information resources.

The Open-Source Security Testing Methodology Manual, OSS OSSTMM 2.2, (`http://isecom.securenetltd.com/osstmm.en.2.2.pdf`), also provides rules of engagement for ethical practices in a number of areas, including penetration testing. The following list summarizes some of the pertinent rules from the OSSTMM 2.2:

- Testing of very insecure systems and installations is not to be performed until appropriate remediation measures have been taken.

- The auditor is required to ensure nondisclosure of client proprietary information.

- Contracts should limit the liability of the auditor.
- The engagement contract should provide permissions for the specific types of tests to be performed.
- The scope of the testing effort should be clearly defined.
- The auditor must operate legally.
- In reporting test results, the auditor must respect the privacy of all concerned.

The Three Pre-Test Phases

Penetration testing is usually initiated with *reconnaissance*, which comprises three pre-test phases: footprinting, scanning, and enumerating. These pre-test phases are very important and can make the difference between a successful penetration test that provides a complete picture of the target's network and an unsuccessful test that does not.

The reconnaissance process seeks to gather as much information about the target network as possible, using the following seven steps during the footprinting, scanning, and enumerating activities:

1. Gather initial information.
2. Determine the network range.
3. Identify active machines.
4. Discover open ports and access points (APs).
5. Fingerprint the operating system.
6. Uncover services on ports.
7. Map the network.

Footprinting

Footprinting is obtaining information concerning the security profile of an organization. It involves gathering data to create a blueprint of the organization's networks and systems. It is an important way for an attacker to gain information about an organization without the organization's knowledge.

Footprinting employs the first two steps of reconnaissance, gathering the initial target information and determining the network range of the target. It may also require manual research, such as studying the company's Web page for useful information such as the following:

- Company contact names, phone numbers, and e-mail addresses
- Company locations and branches

- Other companies with which the target company partners or deals
- News, such as mergers or acquisitions
- Links to other company-related sites
- Company privacy policies, which may help identify the types of security mechanisms in place

Other resources that may have information about the target company include the following:

- The U.S. Securities and Exchange Commission (SEC) EDGAR database, if the company is publicly traded
- Job boards, either internal to the company or external sites
- Disgruntled employee blogs
- The target organization's website and other related websites
- Business social networking websites such as LinkedIn
- Personal/business websites such as Facebook
- Trade press

Scanning

The next four steps of gathering information — identifying active machines, discovering open ports and access points, fingerprinting the operating system, and uncovering services on ports — are considered part of the scanning phase. The goal in this step is to discover open ports and applications by performing external or internal network scanning, pinging machines, determining network ranges, and scanning the ports of individual systems. (Scanning is discussed in more detail later in this chapter.)

Enumerating

The last step in reconnaissance, mapping the network, is the result of the scanning phase and leads to the enumerating phase. As the final pre-test phase, the goal of enumeration is to paint a fairly complete picture of the target.

To enumerate a target, a tester tries to identify valid user accounts or poorly protected resource elements by using directed queries and active connections to and from the target. The type of information sought by testers during the enumeration phase can be names of users and groups, network resources and shares, and applications.

The techniques used for enumerating include the following:

- Obtaining Active Directory information and identifying vulnerable user accounts
- Discovering the NetBIOS name with NBTscan

- Using the SNMPutil command-line utility for Simple Network Management Protocol (SNMP)
- Employing Windows DNS queries
- Establishing null sessions and connections

Penetration Testing Tools and Techniques

A variety of tools and techniques, including some used by malicious hackers, can be valuable in conducting penetration tests on cloud systems. Some tools, such as Whois and Nslookup, are public software that can help gather information about the target network. Whois is usually the first stop in reconnaissance. With it, you can find information such as the domain's registrant, its administrative and technical contacts, and a listing of their domain servers. Nslookup enables you to query Internet domain name servers. It displays information that can be used to diagnose Domain Name System (DNS) infrastructure and find additional IP addresses. It can also use the MX record to reveal the IP of the mail server.

Another information source is American Registry of Internet Numbers (ARIN). ARIN enables you to search the Whois database for a network's autonomous system numbers (ASNs), network-related handles, and other related point-of-contact information. ARIN's Whois function enables you to query the IP address to find information on the target's use of subnet addressing.

The common traceroute utility is also useful. Traceroute works by exploiting a feature of the Internet Protocol called *time-to-live (TTL)*. It reveals the path that IP packets travel between two systems by sending out consecutive User Datagram Protocol (UDP) packets with ever-increasing TTLs. As each router processes an IP packet, it decrements the TTL. When the TTL reaches zero, the router sends back a "TTL exceeded" Internet Control Message Protocol (ICMP) message to the origin. Thus, routers with DNS entries reveal their names, network affiliations, and geographic locations.

A utility called Visual Trace by McAfee displays the traceroute output visually in map view, node view, or IP view. Additional useful Windows-based tools for gathering information include the following:

- **VisualRoute** — VisualRoute by VisualWare includes integrated traceroute, ping tests, and reverse DNS and Whois lookups. It also displays the actual route of connections and IP address locations on a global map.
- **SmartWhois** — Like Whois, SmartWhois by TamoSoft obtains comprehensive info about the target: IP address; hostname or domain, including country, state or province; city; name of the network provider; administrator; and technical support contact information. Unlike Whois utilities, SmartWhois can find the information about a computer located in any part of the world, intelligently querying the right database and delivering all the related records within a few seconds.

- **Sam Spade** — This freeware tool, primarily used to track down spammers, can also be used to provide information about a target. It comes with a host of useful network tools, including ping, Nslookup, Whois, IP block Whois, dig, traceroute, finger, SMTP, VRFY, Web browser, keep-alive, DNS zone transfer, SMTP relay check, and more.

Port Scanners

Port scanning is one of the most common reconnaissance techniques used by testers to discover the vulnerabilities in the services listening to well-known ports. Once you've identified the IP address of a target through footprinting, you can begin the process of port scanning: looking for holes in the system through which you — or a malicious intruder — can gain access. A typical system has $2^{16}-1$ port numbers, each with its own Transmission Control Protocol (TCP) and UDP port that can be used to gain access, if unprotected.

NMap, the most popular port scanner for Linux, is also available for Windows. NMap can scan a system in a variety of stealth modes, depending upon how undetectable you want to be. NMap can determine a wealth of information about a target, including what hosts are available, what services are offered, and what OS is running.

Other port-scanning tools for Linux systems include SATAN, NSAT, VeteScan, SARA, PortScanner, Network Superscanner, CGI Port Scanner, and CGI Sonar.

Vulnerability Scanners

Nessus, a popular open-source tool, is an extremely powerful network scanner that can be configured to run a variety of scans. While a Windows graphical front end is available, the core Nessus product requires Linux to run.

Microsoft's Baseline Security Analyzer (MBSA) is a free Windows vulnerability scanner. MBSA can be used to detect security configuration errors on local computers or on computers across a network. It does have some issues with Windows Update, however, and can't always tell if a patch has been installed.

Popular commercial vulnerability scanners include Retina Network Security Scanner, which runs on Windows, and SAINT, which runs on several Unix/Linux variants, including Mac OS X.

Password Crackers

Password cracking doesn't have to involve fancy tools, but it is a fairly tedious process. If the target doesn't lock you out after a specific number of tries, you can spend an infinite amount of time trying every combination of alphanumeric characters. It's just a question of time and bandwidth before you break into the system.

The most common passwords found are password, root, administrator, admin, operator, demo, test, webmaster, backup, guest, trial, member, private, beta, [company_name], or [known_username].

Three basic types of password cracking methods can be automated with tools:

- **Dictionary** — A file of words is run against user accounts. If the password is a simple word, it can be found fairly quickly.

- **Hybrid** — A hybrid attack works like a dictionary attack, but adds simple numbers or symbols to the file of words. This attack exploits a weakness of many passwords: they are common words with numbers or symbols tacked on the end.

- **Brute force** — The most time-consuming but comprehensive way to crack a password. Every combination of character is tried until the password is broken.

Some common Web password-cracking tools are:

- **Brutus** — Brutus is a password-cracking tool that can perform both dictionary attacks and brute-force attacks whereby passwords are randomly generated from a given character. It can crack the multiple authentication types, HTTP (basic authentication, HTML form/CGI), POP3, FTP, SMB, and Telnet.

- **WebCracker** — WebCracker is a simple tool that takes text lists of usernames and passwords, and uses them as dictionaries to implement basic password guessing.

- **ObiWan** — ObiWan is a Web password-cracking tool that can work through a proxy. Using word lists, it alternates numeric or alphanumeric characters with roman characters to generate possible passwords.

- **Burp Intruder** — Burp Intruder is a Web application security tool that can be used to configure and automate attacks. It can be used to test for Web application vulnerabilities to such attacks as buffer overflow, SQL injection, path traversal, and cross-site scripting.

- **Burp Repeater** — Burp Repeater is a manual tool that can be used to attack Web applications. It operates by supporting the reissuing of HTTP requests from the same window. It also provides a graphical environment to support the manual Web application testing procedures, and complements other tools such as Burp Intruder.

Trojan Horses

A *Trojan horse* is a program that performs unknown and unwanted functions. It can take one or more of the following forms:

- An unauthorized program contained within a legitimate program

- A legitimate program that has been altered by the placement of unauthorized code within it

- Any program that appears to perform a desirable and necessary function but does something unintended

Trojan horses can be transmitted to the computer in several ways — through e-mail attachments, freeware, physical installation, ICQ/IRC chat, phony programs, or infected websites. When the user signs on and goes online, the Trojan horse is activated and the attacker gains access to the system.

Unlike a worm, a Trojan horse doesn't typically self-replicate. The exact type of attack depends on the type of Trojan horse, which can be any of the following:

- Remote access Trojan horses
- Keystroke loggers or password-sending Trojan horses
- Software detection killers
- Purely destructive or denial-of-service Trojan horses

The list of Trojan horses in the wild is expanding quickly, but a few of the earliest have remained relevant since the beginning, and many of these serve as platforms for the development of more lethal variations.

Back Orifice 2000, known as BO2K, is the grandfather of Trojan horses and has spawned a considerable number of imitators. Once installed on a target PC or server machine, BO2K gives the attacker complete control of the victim.

BO2K has stealth capabilities, will not show up on the task list, and runs completely in hidden mode. Back Orifice and its variants have been credited with the highest number of infestations of Windows systems.

Another Trojan horse that has been around for a considerable time is SubSeven, although it is becoming less and less of a problem. SubSeven is a back-door program that enables others to gain full access to Windows systems through the network.

Other common Trojans and spyware currently in the wild include Rovbin, Canary, Remacc.RCPro, Jgidol, IRC.mimic, and NetBus. The SANS Internet Storm Center (http://isc.sans.org/) is a good source of information on the latest malware exploits and attack activity.

Buffer Overflows

A *buffer overflow* (or overrun) occurs when a program allocates a specific block length of memory for something, but then attempts to store more data than the block was intended to hold. This overflowing data can overwrite memory areas and interfere with information crucial to the normal execution of the program. While buffer overflows may be a side effect of poorly written code, they can also be triggered intentionally to create an attack.

A buffer overflow can allow an intruder to load a remote shell or execute a command, enabling the attacker to gain unauthorized access or escalate user privileges. To generate the overflow, the attacker must create a specific data feed to induce the error, as random data will rarely produce the desired effect.

For a buffer overflow attack to work, the target system must fail to test the data or stack boundaries and must also be able to execute code that resides in the data or stack segment. Once the stack is smashed, the attacker can deploy his or her payload and take control of the attacked system.

Three common ways to test for a buffer overflow vulnerability are as follows:

- Look for strings declared as local variables in functions or methods, and verify the presence of boundary checks in the source code.

- Check for improper use of input/output or string functions.

- Feed the application large amounts of data and check for abnormal behavior.

Products like Immunix's StackGuard and ProPolice employ stack-smashing protection to detect buffer overflows on stack-allocated variables. Also, vulnerability scanners like Proventia can help protect against buffer overflow.

Buffer overflow vulnerabilities can be detected by manual auditing of the code as well as by boundary testing. Other countermeasures include updating C and C++ software compilers and C libraries to more secure versions, and disabling stack execution in the program.

SQL Injection Attack

SQL injection is an example of a class of injection exploits that occur when one scripting language is embedded inside another scripting language.

The injection targets the data residing in a database through the firewall in order to alter the SQL statements and retrieve data from the database or execute commands. It accomplishes this by modifying the parameters of a Web-based application.

Preventing SQL injection vulnerability involves enforcing better coding practices and database administration procedures. Here are some specific steps to take:

- Disable verbose error messages that give information to the attacker.

- Protect the system account `sa`. It's very common for the `sa` password to be `blank`.

- Enforce the concept of *least privilege* at the database connection.

- Secure the application by auditing the source code to restrict length of input.

Cross-Site Scripting (XSS)

Web application attacks are often successful because the attack is not noticed immediately. One such attack exploits the cross-site scripting (XSS) vulnerability. An XSS vulnerability is created by the failure of a Web-based application to validate user-supplied input before returning it to the client system.

Attackers can exploit XSS by crafting malicious URLs and tricking users into clicking on them. These links enable the attacker's client-side scripting language, such as JavaScript or VBScript, to execute on the victim's browser.

If the application accepts only expected input, then the XSS vulnerability can be significantly reduced. Many Web application vulnerabilities can be minimized by adhering to proper design specifications and coding practices, and implementing security early in the application's development life cycle.

Another piece of advice: Don't rely on client-side data for critical processes during the application development process; and use an encrypted session, such as SSL, without hidden fields.

Social Engineering

Social engineering describes the acquisition of sensitive information or inappropriate access privileges by an outsider, by manipulating people. It exploits the human side of computing, tricking people into providing valuable information or allowing access to that information.

Social engineering is the hardest form of attack to defend against because it cannot be prevented with hardware or software alone. A company may have rock-solid authentication processes, VPNs, and firewalls, but still be vulnerable to attacks that exploit the human element.

Social engineering can be divided into two types: human-based, person-to-person interaction, and computer-based interaction using software that automates the attempt to engineer information.

Common techniques used by an intruder to gain either physical access or system access are as follows:

- Asserting authority or pulling rank
- Professing to have the authority, perhaps supported with altered identification, to enter a facility or system
- Attempting to intimidate an individual into providing information
- Praising, flattering, or sympathizing
- Using positive reinforcement to coerce a subject into providing access or information for system access

Some examples of successful social engineering attacks include the following:

- E-mails to employees from a tester requesting their passwords to validate the organizational database after a network intrusion has occurred
- E-mails to employees from a tester requesting their passwords because work has to be done over the weekend on the system

- An e-mail or phone call from a tester impersonating an official who is conducting an investigation for the organization and requires passwords for the investigation

- An improper release of medical information to individuals posing as medical personnel and requesting data from patients' records

- A computer repair technician who convinces a user that the hard disk on his or her PC is damaged and irreparable, and installs a new hard disk, taking the old hard disk, extracting the information, and selling it to a competitor or foreign government

The only real defense against social engineering attacks is an information security policy that addresses such attacks and educates users about these types of attacks.

Regression Testing

As software evolves, new features are added and existing features are modified. Sometimes these new features and modifications "break" existing functionality — that is, cause accidental damage to existing software components. According to the IEEE Software Engineering Body of Knowledge (IEEE610.12-90), regression testing is the "selective retesting of a system or component to verify that modifications have not caused unintended effects." Regression testing can indicate that software which previously passed the tests no longer does. The problem code can then be identified and fixed to restore the lost functionality. However, as software evolves, a fault that was previously fixed sometimes "reemerges." This kind of reemergence of faults is common and occurs for a number of reasons, including the following:

- **Poor revision control practices** — The fix was not documented properly or the change was accidentally reversed.

- **Software brittleness** — The fix for the initial fault was too narrow in scope. As the software ages and the code base grows larger (becoming "legacy" software), new problems emerge relating to the initial fault but are more difficult to fix without negatively affecting other areas of the software.

- **Repetition of mistakes** — Problematic code is sometimes copied from one area of the software to another; or when a feature is redesigned, the same mistakes are made in the redesign that were made in the original implementation of the feature.

Increasing the code execution coverage of regression testing can help prevent the reemergence of software faults. For example, regression tests could be varied — such as by introducing new sample data or combining tests — to catch problems that were missed with the existing tests. In this way, regression testing would not only verify that previous tests still work, but also mitigate the risk of unintended side effects caused by changes.

For greater assurance, regression testing should also be more extensive for code surrounding vulnerability fixes, code that may contain the same class of vulnerability, and other high-consequence areas of the software. A regression security test plan should be developed containing misuse/abuse cases and attack scenarios (based in part on relevant attack patterns). Earlier test cases can be augmented by any new abuse/misuse cases and attack scenarios suggested by real-world attacks that have emerged since the software was last tested.

Regression testing is often performed by different stakeholders in the software life cycle. During the coding phase, programmers run unit tests to verify that individual units of source code are working properly. The unit is the smallest testable part of the software, often a function or method and its encapsulated data. Unit testing as part of a software development methodology, such as extreme programming, typically relies upon an automated unit testing framework, such as JUnit (www.junit.org). The automated unit testing framework integrates with an IDE and enables the developer to generate a stub for a unit test that can then be completed with sample data and additional business logic. In test-driven development, unit code should be created for every software unit. When a programmer follows this discipline, it can result in more confident coding, and enable a programmer to verify that a fault has been fixed earlier in the life cycle (reducing overall development costs).

At the system level, regression testing is a form of functional testing that the software quality assurance team performs by using an automated testing suite. Typically, if a software fault is discovered in the process of testing, it is submitted to the bug-tracking system and assigned to a programmer for remediation. Once the bug is fixed, the software needs to be run through all the regression test cases once again. Consequently, fixing a bug at the quality assurance stage is more expensive than during coding.

According to the IEEE Computer Society, testing is defined as "an activity performed for evaluating product quality, and for improving it, by identifying defects and problems. Software testing consists of the dynamic verification of the behavior of a program on a finite set of test cases, suitably selected from the usually infinite executions domain, against the expected behavior."[27]

Secure software testing involves testing for quality assurance through functional, white box and black box, environment, and defect testing. Penetration tests, fuzzing, and simulation tests complemented by conducting cloud system scans provide additional secure software test tools.

Cloud Computing and Business Continuity Planning/Disaster Recovery

Business continuity planning (BCP) and disaster recovery planning (DRP) involve the preparation, testing, and updating of the actions required to protect critical business processes from the effects of major system and network failures. From the cloud perspective, these important business processes are heavily dependent on cloud-based applications and software robustness and security. BCP comprises scoping and initiating the planning, conducting a business impact assessment (BIA), and developing the plan. DRP includes developing the DRP processes, testing the plan, and implementing the disaster recovery procedures.

Designing, developing, and implementing a quality and effective BCP and DRP is a major undertaking, involving many person-hours and, in many instances, high hardware or software costs. These efforts and costs are worthwhile and necessary, but they impact a large number of organizational resources. Cloud computing offers an attractive alternative to total, in-house BCP/DRP implementations. Before exploring cloud computing solutions to BCP/DRP, it is important to establish baseline definitions of key related terms.

Definitions

A *disaster* is a rapidly occurring or unstoppable event that can cause suffering, loss of life, or damage. In many instances, the aftermath of a disaster can impact social or natural conditions for a long period of time.

A DRP is a comprehensive statement of consistent actions to be taken before, during, and after a disruptive event that causes a significant loss of information systems resources. The number one priority of DRP is personnel safety and evacuation, followed by the recovery of data center operations and business operations and processes.

Specific areas that can be addressed by cloud providers include the following:

- Protecting an organization from a major computer services failure
- Providing extended backup operations during an interruption
- Providing the capability to implement critical processes at an alternate site
- Guaranteeing the reliability of standby systems through testing and simulations
- Returning to the primary site and normal processing within a time frame that minimizes business loss by executing rapid recovery procedures.
- Minimizing the decision-making required by personnel during a disaster

- Proving an organized way to make decisions if a disruptive event occurs
- Minimizing the risk to the organization from delays in providing service

A business continuity plan addresses the means for a business to recover from disruptions and continue support for critical business functions. It is designed to protect key business processes from natural or man-made failures or disasters and the resultant loss of capital due to the unavailability of normal business processes. A BCP includes a business impact assessment (BIA), which, in turn, contains a vulnerability assessment.

A BIA is a process used to help business units understand the impact of a disruptive event. A vulnerability assessment is similar to a risk assessment in that it contains both a quantitative (financial) section and a qualitative (operational) section. It differs in that it is smaller than a full risk assessment and is focused on providing information that is used solely for the business continuity plan or disaster recovery plan.

General Principles and Practices

Several major steps are required to produce an effective DRP and BCP. In this section, the principles and practices behind DRB and BCP are reviewed in the context of their ability to be provided through cloud services.

Disaster Recovery Planning

As mentioned in the preceding section, the primary objective of a disaster recovery plan is to provide the capability to implement critical processes at an alternate site and return to the primary site and normal processing within a time frame that minimizes loss to the organization by executing rapid recovery procedures. In many scenarios, the cloud platforms already in use by a customer are extant alternate sites. Disasters primarily affect availability, which impacts the ability of staff to access the data and systems, but it can also affect the other two tenets, confidentiality and integrity. In the recovery plan, a classification scheme such as the one shown in Table 3-4 can be used to classify the recovery time-frame needs of each business function.

The DRP should address all information processing areas of the company:

- Cloud resources being utilized
- LANs, WANs, and servers
- Telecommunications and data communication links
- Workstations and workspaces
- Applications, software, and data

- Media and records storage

- Staff duties and production processes

Table 3-4: Recovery Time Frame Requirements Classification

RATING CLASS	RECOVERY TIME FRAME REQUIREMENTS
AAA	Immediate recovery needed; no downtime allowed
AA	Full functional recovery required within four hours
A	Same-day business recovery required
B	Up to 24 hours downtime acceptable
C	24 to 72 hours downtime acceptable
D	Greater than 72 hours downtime acceptable

The means of obtaining backup services are important elements in the disaster recovery plan. The typically used alternative services are as follows:

- **Mutual aid agreements** — An arrangement with another company that might have similar computing needs. The other company may have similar hardware or software configurations or may require the same network data communications or Internet access.

- **Subscription services** — Third-party commercial services that provide alternate backup and processing facilities. An organization can move its IT processing to the alternate site in the event of a disaster.

- **Multiple centers** — Processing is spread over several operations centers, creating a distributed approach to redundancy and sharing of available resources. These multiple centers could be owned and managed by the same organization (in-house sites) or used in conjunction with a reciprocal agreement.

- **Service bureaus** — Setting up a contract with a service bureau to fully provide all alternate backup-processing services. The disadvantages of this arrangement are primarily the expense and resource contention during a large emergency.

Recovery plan maintenance techniques must be employed from the outset to ensure that the plan remains fresh and usable. It's important to build maintenance procedures into the organization by using job descriptions that centralize responsibility for updates. In addition, create audit procedures that can report regularly on the state of the plan. It is important to ensure that multiple versions of the plan don't exist because that could create confusion during an emergency.

The Foreign Corrupt Practices Act of 1977 imposes civil and criminal penalties if publicly held organizations fail to maintain adequate controls over their information systems. Organizations must take reasonable steps to ensure not only the integrity of their data, but also the system controls the organization put in place.

Disaster Recovery Plan Testing

The major reasons to test a disaster recovery plan are summarized as follows:

- To inform management of the recovery capabilities of the enterprise
- To verify the accuracy of the recovery procedures and identify deficiencies
- To prepare and train personnel to execute their emergency duties
- To verify the processing capability of the alternate backup site or cloud provider

Certain fundamental concepts apply to the testing procedure. Primarily, the testing must not disrupt normal business functions, and the test should begin with the least complex case and gradually work up to major simulations.

Management Roles

The plan should also detail the roles of senior management during and following a disaster:

- Remaining visible to employees and stakeholders
- Directing, managing, and monitoring the recovery
- Rationally amending business plans and projections
- Clearly communicating new roles and responsibilities
- Monitoring employee morale
- Providing employees and family with counseling and support
- Reestablishing accounting processes, such as payroll, benefits, and accounts payable
- Reestablishing transaction controls and approval limits

WHEN A DISASTER CAN BE DECLARED TO BE OVER

A disaster is not over until all operations have been returned to their normal location and function. A very large window of vulnerability exists when transaction processing returns from the alternate backup site to the original production site. If cloud computing resources provide a large portion of the backup for the organization, any possible vulnerabilities will be mitigated. The disaster can be officially declared over only when all areas of the enterprise are back to normal in their original home, and all data has been certified as accurate.

Business Continuity Planning

A BCP is designed to keep a business running, reduce the risk of financial loss, and enhance a company's capability to recover promptly following a disruptive event. The four principle components of a BCP are as follows:

- **Scope and plan initiation** — Creating the scope and other elements needed to define the plan's parameters

- **Business impact assessment (BIA)** — Assisting the business units in understanding the impact of a disruptive event. This phase includes the execution of a vulnerability assessment.

- **Business continuity plan development** — Using information collected in the BIA to develop the actual business continuity plan. This process includes the areas of plan implementation, plan testing, and ongoing plan maintenance.

- **Plan approval and implementation** — Obtaining the final senior management sign-off, creating enterprise wide awareness of the plan, and implementing a maintenance procedure for updating the plan as needed.

The BIA

A key element of the BCP process is conducting a BIA. The purpose of a BIA is to create a document that outlines what impact a disruptive event would have on the business. The impact might be financial (quantitative) or operational (qualitative), such as the inability to respond to customer complaints. A vulnerability assessment is often part of the BIA process. A BIA has three primary goals:

- **Criticality prioritization** — Every critical business unit process must be identified and prioritized, and the impact of a disruptive event must be evaluated.

- **Downtime estimation** — The BIA is used to help estimate the maximum tolerable downtime (MTD) that the business can withstand and still remain viable; that is, what is the longest period of time a critical process can remain interrupted before the company can never recover? The BIA process often determines that this time period is much shorter than expected.

- **Resource requirements** — The resource requirements for the critical processes are also identified at this time, with the most time-sensitive processes receiving the most resource allocation.

A BIA generally involves four steps:

1. Gathering the needed assessment materials
2. Performing the vulnerability assessment

3. Analyzing the information compiled

4. Documenting the results and presenting recommendations

The Vulnerability Assessment

The vulnerability assessment is often part of a BIA. It is similar to a risk assessment but it is smaller than a full risk assessment and is focused on providing information that is used solely for the business continuity plan or disaster recovery plan.

The function of a vulnerability assessment is to conduct a loss impact analysis. Because there are two parts to the assessment, a financial assessment and an operational assessment, it is necessary to define loss criteria both quantitatively and qualitatively.

Quantitative loss criteria can be defined as follows:

- Incurring financial losses from loss of revenue, capital expenditure, or personal liability resolution
- Incurring additional operational expenses due to the disruptive event
- Incurring financial loss resulting from the resolution of violating contract agreements
- Incurring financial loss resulting from the resolution of violating regulatory or compliance requirements

Qualitative loss criteria can consist of the following:

- The loss of competitive advantage or market share
- The loss of public confidence or credibility, or incurring public embarrassment

During the vulnerability assessment, critical support areas must be defined in order to assess the impact of a disruptive event. A critical support area is defined as a business unit or function that must be present to sustain continuity of the business processes, protect life, provide safety, or avoid public relations embarrassment.

Critical support areas could include the following:

- Telecommunications, data communications, or information technology areas
- Physical infrastructure or plant facilities, transportation services
- Accounting, payroll, transaction processing, customer service, purchasing

Typical steps in performing a vulnerability assessment are as follows:

1. List potential disruptive events (i.e., natural, technological, and man-made).

2. Estimate the likelihood of occurrence of a disruptive event.

3. Assess the potential impact of the disruptive event on the organization (i.e., human impact, property impact, and business impact).

4. Assess external and internal resources required to deal with the disruptive event.

Enterprise wide awareness of the plan is important because an organization's ability to recover from an event will most likely depend on the efforts of many individuals. Employee awareness of the plan also emphasizes the organization's commitment to its employees. Specific training may be required for certain personnel to carry out their tasks; and quality training is perceived as a benefit, which increases the interest and commitment of personnel in the BCP process.

Using the Cloud for BCP/DRP

Adopting a cloud strategy for BCP/DRP offers significant benefits without large amounts of capital and human resource investments. Effective cloud-based BCP/DRP requires planning, preparation, and selecting the cloud provider that best meets an organization's needs. A critical issue is the stability and viability of the vendor. The vendor should have the financial, technical, and organizational resources to ensure it will be around for both the short term and the long term. In addition, in order for cloud BCP/DRP to reach its full potential, standardization across a variety of architectures has to evolve.

Proper design of a cloud-based IT system that meets the requirements of a BCP and DRP should include the following:

- Secure access from remote locations
- A distributed architecture with no single point of failure
- Integral redundancy of applications and information
- Geographical dispersion

Redundancy Provided by the Cloud

Cloud-based BCP and DRP eliminate the need for expensive alternative sites and the associated hardware and software to provide redundancy. This approach also provides for low cost and widely available, dynamically scalable, and virtualized resources.

With a cloud computing paradigm, the backup infrastructure is always in place. Thus, data access and running business applications are available on cloud servers. Another option is to implement a hybrid cloud with collocation of resources and services. Cloud service providers also offer organizations the option to control the backup process thorough the use of storage area networks (SANs). Examples of elements that require backup are application data, media files, files that have changed, recent documents, the operating system, and archival files.

Secure Remote Access

In order for cloud-based BCP/DRP to be effective, the cloud applications and data must be securely accessible from all parts of the globe. One solution is for the cloud vendor to establish a global traffic management system that provides the following customer services:

- Meets service-level agreements for availability and performance
- Regulates and controls traffic among virtual machines located at multiple data centers
- Maximizes speed and performance by directing traffic to the closest and most logical cloud data center

These services have to be implemented and conducted in a secure environment to protect both the cloud consumer and cloud provider from compromises and attacks.

Integration into Normal Business Processes

Services provided by a cloud vendor at a remote location are, in almost all cases, isolated geographically from the customer's facilities. The cloud enterprise is strongly protected both physically and technically. At the consumer's site, if cloud processing and data storage are integrated into the daily routine of the business, recovery from a disruptive event at the user organization can be more rapid and involve less time and personnel. In many instances, the cloud resources will be used in normal operations and will be available during a disruptive event at the organization's location without large amounts of transfer activity.

Summary

Security of cloud-based applications and data is one of the principal concerns of cloud customers. Secure software and secure software life cycle management are intrinsic to the protection of cloud services. The information security of cloud systems depends on the classical principles of confidentiality, availability, and integrity, but applied to distributed, virtualized, and dynamic architectures. Important secure software design and application principles include least privilege, separation of duties, defense in depth, fail-safe, and open design.

Secure cloud software also depends on applying software requirements engineering, design principles, code practices, security policy implementation and decomposition, and secure software testing. Valuable testing types are penetration testing, functional testing, performance testing, and vulnerability testing.

The availability of an organization's applications and data residing on cloud servers is a prime consideration of acquiring cloud services. Business continuity planning and disaster recovery planning are important activities for any organization. Cloud computing can offer a low entry cost into providing redundant, resilient, backup capabilities for an organization, and minimize interference in business processes during and following a disruptive event.

Notes

1. Cloud Security Alliance Guidance Version 2.1, 2009, (http://www.cloud-securityalliance.org/guidance/csaguide.pdf).

2. Information Assurance Technology Analysis Center (IATAC), Data and Analysis Center for Software (DACS), Software Security Assurance, State-of-the-Art Report (SOAR), July 31, 2007.

3. Komaroff, M., and Baldwin, K., DoD Software Assurance Initiative, September 13, 2005 (https://acc.dau.mil/CommunityBrowser.aspx?id=25749).

4. Goertzel, K., Winograd, T., et al., "Enhancing the Development Life Cycle to Produce Secure Software," Draft Version 2.0. Rome, New York: United States Department of Defense Data and Analysis Center for Software, July 2008.

5. Saltzer, J. H., and Schroeder, M. D., "The Protection of Information in Computer Systems," Fourth ACM Symposium on Operating Systems Principles, October 1974.

6. National Security Agency, "Information Assurance Technical Framework (IATF)," Release 3.1, September 2002.

7. Goertzel, K., Winograd, T., et al., "Enhancing the Development Life Cycle to Produce Secure Software.

8. van Lamsweerde A., Brohez, S., De Landtsheer, R., and Janssens, D., "From System Goals to Intruder Anti-Goals: Attack Generation and Resolution for Security Requirements Engineering," in *Proceedings of the Requirements for High Assurance Workshop*, Monterey Bay, CA, September 8, 2003, pp. 49–56.

9. Chung, L., "Representing and Using Nonfunctional Requirements," Ph.D. Thesis, Dept. of Computer Science, University of Toronto, 1993.

10. Goertzel, Winograd, T., et al., "Enhancing the Development Life Cycle to Produce Secure Software."

11. van Lamsweerde, Brohez, De Landtsheer, and Janssens, "From System Goals to Intruder Anti-Goals: Attack Generation and Resolution for Security Requirements Engineering."

12. Goertzel, Winograd, et al., "Enhancing the Development Life Cycle to Produce Secure Software."

13. NIST FIPS Publication 200, "Minimum Security Requirements for Federal Information and Information Systems," March 2006.

14. Goertzel, Winograd, et al., "Enhancing the Development Life Cycle to Produce Secure Software."

15. American Institute of Certified Public Accountants (AICPA), "Accounting for the Costs of Computer Software Developed or Obtained for Internal Use," AICPA Statement of Position (SOP) No. 98-1, March 1998, www.aicpa.org.

16. ISACA, "IS Auditing Guideline on Due Professional Care," Information Systems Audit and Control Association, March 1, 2008, www.isaca.org.

17. Tassey, G., "The Economic Impacts of Inadequate Infrastructure for Software Testing," National Institute of Standards and Technology, Technical Report, 2002.

18. Sun, X., Feng, C., Shen, Y., and Lombardi, F., *Protocol Conformance Testing Using Unique Input/Output Sequences* (Hackensack, NJ: World Scientific Publishing Co., 1997).

19. Tassey, G., "The Economic Impacts of Inadequate Infrastructure for Software Testing."

20. Du, W., and Mathur, A. P., "Testing for Software Vulnerability Using Environment Perturbation," *Proceedings of the International Conference on Dependable Systems and Networks (DSN 2000)*, Workshop on Dependability versus Malicious Faults, New York, NY, June 25–28, 2000 (Los Alamitos, CA: IEEE Computer Society Press, 2000), pp. 603–12.

21. Information Assurance Technology Analysis Center (IATAC)/Data and Analysis Center for Software (DACS), "Software Security Assurance State-of-the-Art Report (SOAR)," July 31, 2007.

22. Goertzel, K. M., Winograd, T., et al., "Enhancing the Development Life Cycle to Produce Secure Software."

23. Fink, G., and Bishop, M., "Property-Based Testing: A New Approach to Testing for Assurance," *SIGSOFT Software Engineering Notes* 22, 4 (July 1997): 74–80.

24. Whittaker, J. A., and Thompson, H. H., "Black Box Debugging," *Queue 1*, 9 (December/January 2003–2004).

25. National Institute of Standards and Technology (NIST), 1997, "Metrology for Information Technology (IT)," www.nist.gov/itl/lab/nistirs/ir6025 .htm.

26. Oladimeji, E. A., and Chung, L., "Analyzing Security Interoperability during Component Integration," in *Proceedings of the 5th IEEE/ACIS International Conference on Computer and Information Science and 1st IEEE/ACIS International Workshop on Component-Based Software Engineering, Software Architecture and Reuse* (July 10–12, 2006). ICIS-COMSAR, IEEE Computer Society, Washington, DC, pp. 121–29.

27. Abran, A., Moore J., (executive editors), Bourque, P., Dupuis, R., and Tripp, L. (editors), "Guide to the Software Engineering Body of Knowledge," IEEE Computer Society, 2004.

Cloud Computing Risk Issues

Institutions will try to preserve the problem to which they are the solution.
—Clay Shirky

In addition to the risks and threats inherent in traditional IT computing, cloud computing presents an organization with its own set of security issues.

This chapter examines cloud computing risk to privacy assurance and compliance regulations, how cloud computing presents a unique risk to "traditional" concepts of data, identity, and access management traversing infrastructure, and how those risks and threats may be unique to cloud service providers (CSP).

The CIA Triad

The three fundamental tenets of information security — confidentiality, integrity, and availability (CIA) — define an organization's security posture. All of the information security controls and safeguards, and all of the threats, vulnerabilities, and security processes are subject to the CIA yardstick.

Confidentiality

Confidentiality is the prevention of the intentional or unintentional unauthorized disclosure of contents. Loss of confidentiality can occur in many ways. For example, loss of confidentiality can occur through the intentional release of private company information or through a misapplication of network rights.

Some of the elements of telecommunications used to ensure confidentiality are as follows:

- Network security protocols
- Network authentication services
- Data encryption services

Integrity

Integrity is the guarantee that the message sent is the message received and that the message is not intentionally or unintentionally altered. Loss of integrity can occur through an intentional attack to change information (for example, a website defacement) or, more commonly, unintentionally (data is accidentally altered by an operator). Integrity also contains the concept of nonrepudiation of a message source, which we will describe later.

Some of the elements used to ensure integrity include the following:

- Firewall services
- Communications security management
- Intrusion detection services

Availability

This concept refers to the elements that create reliability and stability in networks and systems. It ensures that connectivity is accessible when needed, allowing authorized users to access the network or systems.

Also included in that assurance is the guarantee that security services for the security practitioner are usable when they are needed. The concept of availability also tends to include areas in an information system (IS) that are traditionally not thought of as pure security (such as guarantee of service, performance, and up time), yet are obviously affected by breaches such as a denial-of-service (DoS) attack.

Some of the elements that are used to ensure availability are as follows:

- Fault tolerance for data availability, such as backups and redundant disk systems
- Acceptable logins and operating process performance
- Reliable and interoperable security processes and network security mechanisms

Other Important Concepts

There are also several other important concepts and terms that apply equally well to traditional IT computing and cloud computing:

- **Identification** — The means by which users claim their identities to a system. Most commonly used for access control, identification is necessary for authentication and authorization.

- **Authentication** — The testing or reconciliation of evidence of a user's identity. It establishes the user's identity and ensures that the users are who they say they are.

- **Accountability** — A system's capability to determine the actions and behaviors of a single individual within a system and to identify that particular individual. Audit trails and logs support accountability.

- **Authorization** — The rights and permissions granted to an individual or process that enable access to a computer resource. Once a user's identity and authentication are established, authorization levels determine the extent of a user's system rights.

- **Privacy** — The level of confidentiality and privacy protection given to a user in a system. This is often an important component of security controls. Privacy not only guarantees the fundamental tenet of confidentiality of company data, but also guarantees the data's level of privacy, which is being used by the operator. We examine privacy risks in more detail in the following section.

Privacy and Compliance Risks

One area that is greatly affected by cloud computing is privacy. It's important to remember that although the control of cloud computing privacy has many threats and vulnerabilities in common with noncloud processes and infrastructure, it also has unique security issues.

For example, a successful identity theft exploit can result in a privacy loss that has a huge impact on an enterprise. The organization can suffer short-term losses due to remediation, investigation, and restitution costs. It can also incur longer term problems for the organization due to loss of credibility, confidence, and negative publicity.

Another mistake organizations often make is in assigning responsibility for privacy controls to the IT dept, rather than a business unit that owns the data. Information systems security frameworks have defined, standardized processes that apply to cloud computing — and its potential privacy breaches. This section examines the legal and standard processes that affect privacy control in the cloud.

An individual's right to privacy is embodied in the fundamental principles of privacy:

- **Notice** — Regarding the collection, use, and disclosure of personally identifiable information (PII)
- **Choice** — To opt out or opt in regarding disclosure of PII to third parties
- **Access** — By consumers to their PII to permit review and correction of information
- **Security** — To protect PII from unauthorized disclosure
- **Enforcement** — Of applicable privacy policies and obligations

Privacy definitions vary widely, especially when we start to wander out of the United States. The definition of personally identifiable information (PII) as described by the Office of Management and Budget (OMB) is as follows:

Information which can be used to distinguish or trace an individual's identity, such as their name, social security number, biometric records, etc. alone, or when combined with other personal or identifying information which is linked or linkable to a specific individual, such as date and place of birth, mother's maiden name, etc.[1]

Variations of this definition are used by compliance regulations such as HIPAA and EU directive 95/46/EC:

. . . "personal data" shall mean any information relating to an identified or identifiable natural person ("data subject"); an identifiable person is one who can be identified, directly or indirectly, in particular by reference to an identification number or to one or more factors specific to his physical, physiological, mental, economic, cultural or social identity. . .[2]

The Payment Card Industry Data Security Standard (PCI DSS)

PCI compliance refers to a 12-step security certification standard called the Payment Card Industry Data Security Standard (PCI DSS), which is required in order to help minimize privacy loss and reduce identity theft vulnerabilities in the credit card industry. Any organization that stores, processes, or transmits card data is covered by PCI, regardless of the number of transactions per year. How the organization must verify this compliance varies according to its volume of annual card transactions.

The consequences of noncompliance depend on the rules of the specific enforcement program. If the audit finds some gaps in meeting the requirements, usually the organization is expected to develop a plan for addressing the gaps, setting specific target dates. However, if there are gaping holes in their security, if they suffer a breach, or if they haven't had an audit or even started a compliance program, then it would likely be a different story. Noncompliance can result in fines for merchants and service providers — that is, whether cardholder data is processed and stored by the company or by a third party.

Proving compliance depends on the number of transactions that they process. Merchants and service providers with higher levels of transactions have to pass an on-site audit every year. Those with lower levels of transactions must submit documentation stating that they meet the requirements, called a self-assessment questionnaire.

The PCI DSS contains the following set of 12 high-level requirements that are supported by a series of more detailed requirements:[3]

- Install and maintain a firewall configuration to protect cardholder data.
- Do not use vendor-supplied defaults for system passwords and other security parameters.
- Protect stored cardholder data.
- Encrypt transmission of cardholder data across open, public networks.
- Use and regularly update antivirus software.
- Develop and maintain secure systems and applications.
- Restrict access to cardholder data based on the business's need to know.
- Assign a unique ID to each person with computer access.
- Restrict physical access to cardholder data.
- Track and monitor all access to network resources and cardholder data.
- Regularly test security systems and processes.
- Maintain a policy that addresses information security.

As of the writing of this book, there is much discussion within the PCI QSA (Qualified Security Assessor) community regarding the proper process to audit and certify a cloud computing environment that requires PCI DSS compliance.

There is no reason why the 12 PCI requirements can't be applied to cloud computing and virtualization. However, it is questionable whether a company that has all of its infrastructure and processes in the cloud can actually be PCI compliant, or whether all compliance-related activities can only be properly executed by the CSP.

THE PCI DSS AND VIRTUALIZATION

The most current revision of the PCI DSS (v1.2) still doesn't have any reference to cloud computing. The PCI SSC Virtualization Special Interest Group (SIG) is developing an Information Supplement to the PCI Data Security Standard (DSS) to provide guidance on the use of virtualization technology, with its final release targeted for the calendar year 2010.

The PCI DSS states that an assessor must clearly state which third party components should be included within a PCI assessment. The third party must have a PCI assessment conducted; however, this assessment can be conducted at the time of the assessment of the original company. This means that cooperation from cloud computing service providers may be required to gain PCI-compliance for components within the cloud.

Some points regarding PCI and cloud computing can be addressed right now (thanks to Nick Coblentz, senior consultant within AT&T Consulting Services' Application Security Practice, for this list):

■ Segmentation needs to be evaluated as it applies to virtual infrastructure, such as Amazon's physical infrastructure.

■ Companies will need to establish compliance with at least some of the cloud provider's components *and* companies will likely need cooperation from cloud providers in obtaining PCI compliance.

■ Companies may need to plan ahead and/or get cooperation from cloud providers regarding logging and forensics. Specialized virtual images can be created to assist with forensics or incident investigation.

■ Companies should verify and document the cloud provider's use of anti-virus software on host operating systems, cloud storage, and other components.

FOR MORE INFORMATION

For more information on the privacy implications of cloud computing, see the May 2008 report by Ann Cavoukian, "Privacy in the Clouds: A White Paper on Privacy and Digital Identity: Implications for the Internet" (Information and Privacy Commissioner of Ontario), www.ipc.on.ca/images/Resources/privacyintheclouds.pdf.

Information Privacy and Privacy Laws

There are many types of legal systems in the world, and they differ in how they treat evidence, the rights of the accused, and the role of the judiciary. These laws have a significant privacy impact on cloud computing environments, yet vary widely.

Examples of these different legal systems are common law, Islamic and other religious law, and civil law. The common law system is employed in the United States, United Kingdom, Australia, and Canada. Civil law systems are used in France, Germany, and Quebec, to name a few.

Organizations develop and publish privacy policies that describe their approach to handling PII. The websites of organizations usually have their privacy policies available to read online, and these policies usually cover the following areas:

- Statement of the organization's commitment to privacy
- The type of information collected, such as names, addresses, credit card numbers, phone numbers, and so on
- Retaining and using e-mail correspondence
- Information gathered through cookies and Web server logs and how that information is used
- How information is shared with affiliates and strategic partners
- Mechanisms to secure information transmissions, such as encryption and digital signatures
- Mechanisms to protect PII stored by the organization
- Procedures for review of the organization's compliance with the privacy policy
- Evaluation of information protection practices
- Means for the user to access and correct PII held by the organization
- Rules for disclosing PII to outside parties
- Providing PII that is legally required

Privacy laws attempt to provide protection to an individual from unauthorized disclosure of the individual's personally identifiable information (PII). For example, the Health Insurance Portability & Accountability Act (HIPAA) lists the following 16 items as a person's individual identifiers:

- Names
- Postal address information, other than town or city, state, and zip code
- Telephone numbers
- Fax numbers
- Electronic mail addresses
- Social security numbers
- Medical record numbers

- Health plan beneficiary numbers
- Account numbers
- Certificate/license numbers
- Vehicle identifiers and serial numbers, including license plate numbers
- Device identifiers and serial numbers
- Web Universal Resource Locators (URLs)
- Internet Protocol (IP) address numbers
- Biometric identifiers, including fingerprints and voiceprints
- Full face photographic images and any comparable images

Privacy Legislation

The following list summarizes some important legislation and recommended guidelines for privacy:

- *The Cable Communications Policy Act* provides for discretionary use of PII by cable operators internally but imposes restrictions on disclosures to third parties.
- *The Children's Online Privacy Protection Act* (COPPA) is aimed at providing protection to children under the age of 13.
- *Customer Proprietary Network Information Rules* apply to telephone companies and restrict their use of customer information both internally and to third parties.
- *The Financial Services Modernization Act* (*Gramm-Leach-Bliley*) requires financial institutions to provide customers with clear descriptions of the institution's policies and procedures for protecting the PII of customers.
- *The Telephone Consumer Protection Act* restricts communications between companies and consumers, such as telemarketing.
- *The 1973 U.S. Code of Fair Information Practices* states that:

  1. There must not be personal data record-keeping systems whose very existence is secret.
  2. There must be a way for a person to find out what information about them is in a record and how it is used.
  3. There must be a way for a person to prevent information about them, which was obtained for one purpose, from being used or made available for another purpose without their consent.

4. Any organization creating, maintaining, using, or disseminating records of identifiable personal data must ensure the reliability of the data for their intended use and must take precautions to prevent misuses of that data.

Health Insurance Portability and Accountability Act (HIPAA)

An excellent example of the requirements and application of individual privacy principles is in the area of health care. The protection from disclosure and misuse of a private individual's medical information is a prime example of a privacy law. Some of the common health care security issues are as follows:

- Access controls of most health care information systems do not provide sufficient granularity to implement the principle of least privilege among users.

- Most off-the-shelf applications do not incorporate adequate information security controls.

- Systems must be accessible to outside partners, members, and some vendors.

- Providing users with the necessary access to the Internet creates the potential for enabling violations of the privacy and integrity of information.

- Criminal and civil penalties can be imposed for the improper disclosure of medical information.

- A large organization's misuse of medical information can cause the public to change its perception of the organization.

- Health care organizations should adhere to the following information privacy principles (based on European Union principles):

  - An individual should have the means to monitor the database of stored information about themselves and should have the ability to change or correct that information.

  - Information obtained for one purpose should not be used for another purpose.

  - Organizations collecting information about individuals should ensure that the information is provided only for its intended use and should provide safeguards against the misuse of this information.

  - The existence of databases containing personal information should not be kept secret.

HIPAA addresses the issues of health care privacy and plan portability in the United States. With respect to privacy, this Act states, "Not later than the date that is 12 months after the date of the enactment of this Act, the Secretary of Health and Human Services shall submit . . . detailed recommendations on standards with respect to the privacy of individually identifiable health information." This Act further states "the recommendations . . . shall address at least the following:

- The rights that an individual who is a subject of individually identifiable health information should have
- The procedures that should be established for the exercise of such rights
- The uses and disclosures of such information that should be authorized or required"

The Final Privacy Rule refers to security issues as illustrated in the following statements:

"1. Standard: safeguards. A covered entity must have in place appropriate administrative, technical, and physical safeguards to protect the privacy of protected health information.

2. Implementation specification: safeguards. A covered entity must reasonably safeguard protected health information from any intentional or unintentional use or disclosure that is in violation of the standards, implementation specifications or other requirements of this subpart."

HITECH Act

The security and privacy rules of HIPAA (Health Insurance Portability and Accountability Act) took effect in 2003, but the healthcare industry did not take any of it seriously, as there was a lack of any real enforcement. The passing of the Health Information Technology for Economic and Clinical Health (HITECH) Act in 2009 is expected to change all of that. The HITECH Act not only strengthens HIPAA requirements, but also adds additional incentives for companies to switch over to electronic records while ensuring security.

One immediate impact of the HITECH Act is the significant expansion in the number of entities covered under HIPAA and increased accountability and liability to business associates. It expands the HIPAA Privacy Rule and security standards, adds provisions for breach notification, and changes the rules for business associates.

Platform for Privacy Preferences (P3P)

The Platform for Privacy Preferences (P3P) was developed by the World Wide Web Consortium (W3C) to implement privacy practices on websites. The W3C P3P Specification states that "P3P enables Web sites to express their privacy practices in a standard format that can be retrieved automatically and interpreted easily by user agents. P3P user agents will allow users to be informed of site practices (in both machine- and human-readable formats) and to automate decision-making based on these practices when appropriate. Thus users need not read the privacy policies at every site they visit."

- The W3C P3P document can be found at www.w3.org/TR. With P3P, an organization can post its privacy policy in machine-readable form (XML) on its website. This policy statement should include the following:

    - Who has access to collected information

    - The type of information collected

    - How the information is used

    - The legal entity making the privacy statement

The P3P specification contains the following items:

- A standard vocabulary for describing a website's data practices

- A set of data elements that websites can refer to in their P3P privacy policies

- A standard schema for data a website may wish to collect, known as the *P3P base data schema*

- A standard set of uses, recipients, data categories, and other privacy disclosures

- An XML format for expressing a privacy policy

- A means of associating privacy policies with Web pages or sites and cookies

- A mechanism for transporting P3P policies over HTTP

A useful consequence of implementing P3P on a website is that website owners are required to answer multiple-choice questions about their privacy practices. This forces the organization sponsoring the website to think about and evaluate its privacy policy and practices if it hasn't already done so. After answering the necessary P3P privacy questions, an organization can then proceed to develop its policy. A number of sources provide free policy editors and assistance in writing privacy policies.[4]

P3P also supports user agents that allow a user to configure a P3P-enabled Web browser with the user's privacy preferences. Then, when the user attempts to access a website, the user agent compares the user's stated preferences with the privacy policy in machine-readable form at the website. Access will be granted if the preferences match the policy. Otherwise, either access to the website will be blocked or a pop-up window will appear notifying the user that he or she must change the privacy preferences. Microsoft's Internet Explorer 6 (IE6) and above Web browser supports P3P and can be used to generate and display a report describing a particular website's P3P-implemented privacy policy.

Another P3P implementation is provided by AT&T's Privacy Bird software, a browser add-on that inserts an icon of a bird in the top-right corner of a user's Web browser. The AT&T software reads the XML privacy policy statements from a website, causing the bird to chirp and change color if the user's listed privacy preference settings are satisfied by the website's P3P policy statements. Clicking on the bird provides more detailed information concerning mismatches between the website's policy practices and the user's provided preferences.

PATRIOT Act

The 2001 USA Provide Appropriate Tools Required to Intercept and Obstruct Terrorism (PATRIOT) Act permits the following:

- Subpoena of electronic records
- Monitoring of Internet communications
- Search and seizure of information on live systems (including routers and servers), backups, and archives

This act gives the U.S. government powers to subpoena electronic records and monitor Internet traffic. In monitoring information, the government can require the assistance of ISPs and network operators. This monitoring can extend even into individual organizations. In the PATRIOT Act, Congress permits investigators to gather information about e-mail without having to show probable cause that the person to be monitored has committed a crime or was intending to commit a crime. Routers, servers, backups, and so on now fall under existing search and seizure laws.

A new twist to the PATRIOT Act is delayed notification of a search warrant. Under the PATRIOT Act, if it is suspected that notification of a search warrant would cause a suspect to flee, a search can be conducted before notification of a search warrant is given.

Federal Information Security Management Act (FISMA)

In order to increase the security of federal information systems, the Federal Information Security Management Act (FISMA), which is Title III of the E-Government Act of December, 2002 (Public Law 107-347), was passed. FISMA was enacted to:

1. Provide a comprehensive framework for ensuring the effectiveness of information security controls over information resources that support Federal operations and assets.

2. Recognize the highly networked nature of the current Federal computing environment and provide effective government-wide management and oversight of the related information security risks, including coordination of information security efforts throughout the civilian, national security, and law enforcement communities.

3. Provide for development and maintenance of minimum controls required to protect Federal information and information systems.

4. Provide a mechanism for improved oversight of Federal agency information security programs.

FISMA, the Paperwork Reduction Act (PRA) of 1980, as amended by the Paperwork Reduction Act of 1995 (44 U.S.C. Chapter 35), and the Clinger-Cohen Act (also known as the Information Technology Management Reform Act of 1996) (Pub. L. 104-106, Division E) promote a risk-based policy for cost effective security. The Clinger-Cohen Act supplements the information resources management policies contained in the PRA by establishing a comprehensive approach for executive agencies to improve the acquisition and management of their information resources. FISMA also specifies that national security classified information should be handled in accordance with the appropriate national security directives as provided by the DoD and the NSA.

FISMA charges the Director of the Office of Management and Budget (OMB) with the responsibility of overseeing the security policies and practices of all agencies of the executive branch of the federal government, including "coordinating the development of standards and guidelines between NIST and the NSA and other agencies with responsibility for national security systems." Agencies of the executive branch of the U.S. government are defined as:

- An Executive Department specified in 5 U.S.C., Section 101
- Within the Executive Office of the President, only OMB and the Office of Administration
- A Military Department specified in 5 U.S.C., Section 102
- An independent establishment as defined in 5 U.S.C., Section 104(1)
- A wholly owned government corporation fully subject to the provisions of 31 U.S.C., Chapter 91

OMB Circular A-130, Appendix III, "Security of Federal Automated Information Resources," specifies that federal government agencies perform the following functions:

- Plan for security.
- Ensure that appropriate officials are assigned security responsibility.
- Review the security controls in their information systems.
- Authorize system processing prior to operations and periodically thereafter.

OMB Circular A-130, Appendix III, also requires that each agency perform security accreditation, which is considered "a form of quality control and challenges managers and technical staffs at all levels to implement the most effective security controls possible in an information system, given mission requirements, technical constraints, operational constraints, and cost/schedule constraints. By accrediting an information system, an agency official accepts responsibility for the security of the system and is fully accountable for any adverse impacts to the agency if a breach of security occurs."

The actions that FISMA requires each government agency to perform in developing and implementing an agency-wide information security program are specified in NIST Special Publication 800-37, "Guide for the Security Certification and Accreditation of Federal Information Systems," Second Public Draft, June 2003. FISMA specifies that the program must include:

1. Periodic assessments of risk, including the magnitude of harm that could result from the unauthorized access, use, disclosure, disruption, modification, or destruction of information and information systems that support the operations and assets of the agency

2. Policies and procedures that are based on risk assessments, cost-effectively reduce information security risks to an acceptable level, and ensure that information security is addressed throughout the life cycle of each agency information system

3. Subordinate plans for providing adequate information security for networks, facilities, information systems, or groups of information systems, as appropriate

4. Security awareness training to inform personnel (including contractors and other users of information systems that support the operations and assets of the agency) of the information security risks associated with their activities and their responsibilities in complying with agency policies and procedures designed to reduce these risks

5. Periodic testing and evaluation of the effectiveness of information security policies, procedures, practices, and security controls to be performed with a frequency depending on risk, but no less than annually

6. A process for planning, implementing, evaluating, and documenting remedial action to address any deficiencies in the information security policies, procedures, and practices, of the agency

7. Procedures for detecting, reporting, and responding to security incidents

8. Plans and procedures to ensure continuity of operations for information systems that support the operations and assets of the agency

Other Privacy-Related Acts

In addition to the privacy acts we've just described, it's important to know a little about a few other privacy-related acts that have a bearing on cloud privacy.

1974 U.S. Federal Privacy Act (amended in 1980) — Applies to federal agencies; provides for the protection of information about private individuals that is held in federal databases, and grants access by the individual to these databases.

The law imposes civil and criminal penalties for violations of the provisions of the act. The act assigns the U.S. Treasury Department the responsibilities of implementing physical security practices, information management practices, and computer and network controls.

1978 Foreign Intelligence Surveillance Act (FISA) — FISA can be used to conduct electronic surveillance and physical searches under a court order and without a warrant in cases of international terrorism, spying, or sabotage activities that are conducted by a foreign power or its agent. FISA is not intended for use in prosecuting U.S. citizens.

1984 U.S. Medical Computer Crime Act — Addresses illegal access or alteration of computerized medical records through phone or data networks

1986 U.S. Electronic Communications Privacy Act — Prohibits eavesdropping or the interception of message contents without distinguishing between private or public systems. This law updated the federal privacy clause in the Omnibus Crime Control and Safe Streets Act of 1968 to include digitized voice, data, or video, whether transmitted over wire, microwave, or fiber optics. Court warrants are required to intercept wire or oral communications, except for phone companies, the FCC, and police officers who are party to a call with the consent of one of the parties.

1987 U.S. Computer Security Act — Places requirements on federal government agencies to conduct security-related training, to identify sensitive systems, and to develop a security plan for those sensitive systems. A category of sensitive information called *Sensitive But Unclassified (SBU)* has to be considered. This category, formerly called Sensitive Unclassified Information (SUI), pertains to information below the government's classified level that is important enough to protect, such as medical information, financial information, and research and development knowledge. This act also partitioned the government's responsibility for security between the National Institute of Standards and Technology (NIST) and the National Security Agency (NSA). NIST was given responsibility for information security in general, primarily for the commercial and SBU arenas, and NSA retained the responsibility for cryptography for classified government and military applications.

The Computer Security Act established the *National Computer System Security and Privacy Advisory Board (CSSPAB)*, which is a 12-member advisory group of experts in computer and telecommunications systems security.

1994 U.S. Computer Abuse Amendments Act — This act accomplished the following:

1. Changed the federal interest computer to a computer used in interstate commerce or communications

2. Covers viruses and worms

3. Included intentional damage as well as damage done with "reckless disregard of substantial and unjustifiable risk"

4. Limited imprisonment for the unintentional damage to one year

5. Provides for civil action to obtain compensatory damages or other relief

1995 Council Directive (Law) on Data Protection for the European Union (EU) — Declares that each EU nation is to enact protections similar to those of the OECD Guidelines.

1996 U.S. Economic and Protection of Proprietary Information Act — Addresses industrial and corporate espionage and extends the definition of property to include proprietary economic information in order to cover the theft of this information

1996 U.S. National Information Infrastructure Protection Act — Enacted in October 1996 as part of Public Law 104-294, it amended the Computer Fraud and Abuse Act, which is codified as 18 U.S.C. § 1030. The amended Computer Fraud and Abuse Act is patterned after the OECD Guidelines for the Security of Information Systems and addresses the protection of the confidentiality, integrity, and availability of data and systems. This path is intended to encourage other countries to adopt a similar framework, thus creating a more uniform approach to addressing computer crime in the existing global information infrastructure.

1996, Title I, Economic Espionage Act — The Economic Espionage Act address the numerous acts concerned with economic espionage and the national security aspects of the crime. The theft of trade secrets is also defined in the act as a federal crime.

European Union (EU) Principles

The protection of information about private individuals from intentional or unintentional disclosure or misuse is the goal of information privacy laws. The intent and scope of these laws widely varies from country to country. The European Union (EU) has defined privacy principles that in general are more protective of individual privacy than those applied in the United States. Therefore, the transfer of personal information from the EU to the United States, when equivalent personal protections are not in place in the United States, is prohibited. The EU principles include the following:

- Data should be collected in accordance with the law.
- Information collected about an individual cannot be disclosed to other organizations or individuals unless authorized by law or by consent of the individual.
- Records kept on an individual should be accurate and up to date.
- Individuals have the right to correct errors contained in their personal data.
- Data should be used only for the purposes for which it was collected, and it should be used only for a reasonable period of time.

- Individuals are entitled to receive a report on the information that is held about them.

- Transmission of personal information to locations where equivalent personal data protection cannot be assured is prohibited.

Threats to Infrastructure, Data, and Access Control

To properly understand the threats that cloud computing presents to the computing infrastructure, it's important to understand communications security techniques to prevent, detect, and correct errors so that integrity, availability, and the confidentiality of transactions over networks may be maintained.

This includes the following:

- Communications and network security as it relates to voice, data, multimedia, and facsimile transmissions in terms of local area, wide area, and remote access networks

- Internet/intranet/extranet in terms of firewalls, routers, gateways, and various protocols

---

THE IRONY OF SCALE

There is an ironic element to infrastructure security when addressing the cloud: smaller companies with minimal IT departments often see a bigger security return by using cloud infrastructure offered by a public cloud service provider (CSP) than larger, better-funded organizations with complex infrastructure. Large, established companies have a bigger investment in traditional IT and its accompanying security architecture, whereas a newer company can more readily employ the security features offered by a CSP.

Common Threats and Vulnerabilities

A threat is simply any event that, if realized, can cause damage to a system and create a loss of confidentiality, availability, or integrity. Threats can be malicious, such as the intentional modification of sensitive information, or they can be accidental — such as an error in a transaction calculation or the accidental deletion of a file.

A *vulnerability* is a weakness in a system that can be exploited by a threat. Reducing the vulnerable aspects of a system can reduce the risk and impact of threats on the system. For example, a password-generation tool, which helps users choose robust passwords, reduces the chance that users will select poor passwords (the vulnerability) and makes the password more difficult to crack (the threat of external attack).

Common threats to both cloud and traditional infrastructure include the following:

- **Eavesdropping** — Data scavenging, traffic or trend analysis, social engineering, economic or political espionage, sniffing, dumpster diving, keystroke monitoring, and shoulder surfing are all types of eavesdropping to gain information or to create a foundation for a later attack. Eavesdropping is a primary cause of the failure of confidentiality.

- **Fraud** — Examples of fraud include collusion, falsified transactions, data manipulation, and other altering of data integrity for gain.

- **Theft** — Examples of theft include the theft of information or trade secrets for profit or unauthorized disclosure, and physical theft of hardware or software.

- **Sabotage** — Sabotage includes denial-of-service (DoS) attacks, production delays, and data integrity sabotage.

- **External attack** — Examples of external attacks include malicious cracking, scanning, and probing to gain infrastructure information, demon dialing to locate an unsecured modem line, and the insertion of a malicious code or virus.

PRIVATE CLOUDS VS. PUBLIC CLOUDS

Cloud computing infrastructure security is greatly affected by whether the cloud employed is a private cloud or a public cloud. Private cloud infrastructure security almost exactly duplicates traditional IT security architecture, such that they are nearly indistinguishable from one another. The security tools and processes in place for the traditional infrastructure will apply pretty well for the private cloud, and are similar to a private extranet implementation.

The public cloud infrastructure, however, requires that an organization rethink security architecture and processes and address how its network fits with the CSP's network. In either case, a secure cloud implementation must reduce risk to confidentiality, integrity, and availability, as well as protect data storage and ensure proper access control (authentication, authorization, and auditing.)

Many network attacks and abuses share a commonality with traditional infrastructure and cloud infrastructure. Attacks against computers, networks, and cryptographic systems have a variety of motivations. Some attacks are aimed at disrupting service, others focus on illegally acquiring sensitive information, and others attempt to deceive or defraud. In general, such attacks target the CIA components of information security.

This section explores the most common types of attacks. Although these attacks are constantly evolving, most networked systems attacks can be grouped into several general areas.

Logon Abuse

Logon abuse can refer to legitimate users accessing services of a higher security level that would normally be restricted to them. Unlike network intrusion, this type of abuse focuses primarily on those users who might be legitimate users of a different system or users who have a lower security classification.

Masquerading is the term used when one user pretends to be another user, such as an attacker socially engineering passwords from an Internet Service Provider (ISP).

Inappropriate System Use

This style of network abuse refers to the nonbusiness or personal use of a network by otherwise authorized users, such as Internet surfing to inappropriate content sites (travel, pornography, sports, and so forth). As per the International Information Systems Security Certification Consortium (ISC) Code of Ethics and the Internet Advisory Board (IAB) recommendations, the use of networked services for other than business purposes can be considered abuse of the system. While most employers do not enforce extremely strict Web surfing rules, occasional harassment litigation may result from employees accessing pornography sites and employees operating private Web businesses using the company's infrastructure.

Eavesdropping

This type of network attack consists of the unauthorized interception of network traffic. Certain network transmission methods, such as satellite, wireless, mobile, PDA, and so on, are vulnerable to eavesdropping attacks. *Tapping* refers to the physical interception of a transmission medium (like the splicing of a cable or the creation of an induction loop to pick up electromagnetic emanations from copper). Eavesdropping can take one of two forms:

- **Passive eavesdropping** — Covertly monitoring or listening to transmissions that are unauthorized by either the sender or receiver

- **Active eavesdropping** — Tampering with a transmission to create a covert signaling channel, or actively probing the network for infrastructure information

Eavesdropping and probing are often the preliminary steps to session hijacking and other network intrusions. Covert channel eavesdropping refers to using a hidden, unauthorized network connection to communicate unauthorized information. A covert channel is a connection intentionally created to transmit unauthorized information from inside a trusted network to a partner at an outside, untrusted node.

War walking (or war driving) refers to scanning for 802.11-based wireless network information by either driving or walking with a laptop, a wireless adapter in promiscuous mode, some type of scanning software such as NetStumbler or AiroPeek, and a Global Positioning System (GPS).

Network Intrusion

This type of attack refers to the use of unauthorized access to break into a network primarily from an external source. Unlike a logon abuse attack, the intruders are not considered to be known to the company. Most common hacks belong to this category. Also known as a *penetration attack*, it exploits known security vulnerabilities in the security perimeter.

Back doors are very hard to trace, as an intruder will often create several avenues into a network to be exploited later. The only real way to ensure that these avenues are closed after an attack is to restore the operating system from the original media, apply the patches, and restore all data and applications.

Piggy-backing, in the network domain, refers to an attacker gaining unauthorized access to a system by using a legitimate user's connection. A user leaves a session open or incorrectly logs off, enabling an unauthorized user to resume the session.

Denial-of-Service (DoS) Attacks

The DoS attack might use some of the following techniques to overwhelm a target's resources:

- Filling up a target's hard drive storage space by using huge e-mail attachments or file transfers
- Sending a message that resets a target host's subnet mask, causing a disruption of the target's subnet routing
- Using up all of a target's resources to accept network connections, resulting in additional network connections being denied

Session Hijacking Attacks

Unauthorized access to a system can be achieved by session hijacking. In this type of attack, an attacker hijacks a session between a trusted client and network server. The attacking computer substitutes its IP address for that of the trusted client and the server continues the dialog, believing it is communicating with the trusted client.

Highjacking attacks include IP spoofing attacks, TCP sequence number attacks, and DNS poisoning.

Fragmentation Attacks

IP fragmentation attacks use varied IP datagram fragmentation to disguise their TCP packets from a target's IP filtering devices. The following are two examples of these types of attacks:

- A *tiny fragment attack* occurs when the intruder sends a very small fragment that forces some of the TCP header field into a second fragment. If the target's filtering device does not enforce minimum fragment size, this illegal packet can then be passed on through the target's network.

- An *overlapping fragment attack* is another variation on a datagram's zero-offset modification. Subsequent packets overwrite the initial packet's destination address information, and then the second packet is passed by the target's filtering device. This can happen if the target's filtering device does not enforce a minimum fragment offset for fragments with non-zero offsets.

DIALING ATTACKS

War dialing is a method used to hack into computers by using a software program to automatically call a large pool of telephone numbers to search for those that have a modem attached.

Cloud Access Control Issues

The cost of access control in the cloud must be commensurate with the value of the information being protected. The value of this information is determined through qualitative and quantitative methods. These methods incorporate factors such as the cost to develop or acquire the information, the importance of the information to an organization and its competitors, and the effect on the organization's reputation if the information is compromised.

Proper access controls enable full availability. Availability ensures that a system's authorized users have timely and uninterrupted access to the information in the system. The additional access control objectives are reliability and utility.

Access control must offer protection from an unauthorized, unanticipated, or unintentional modification of information. This protection should preserve the data's internal and external consistency. The confidentiality of the information must also be similarly maintained, and the information should be available on a timely basis. These factors cover the integrity, confidentiality, and availability components of information system security.

Accountability is another facet of access control. Individuals on a system are responsible for their actions. This accountability property enables system activities to be traced to the proper individuals. Accountability is supported by audit trails that record events on both the system and the network. Audit trails can be used for intrusion detection and for the reconstruction of past events. Monitoring individual activities, such as keystroke monitoring, should be accomplished in accordance with the company policy and appropriate laws. Banners at logon time should notify the user of any monitoring being conducted.

The following measures compensate for both internal and external access violations:

- Backups
- RAID (Redundant Array of Independent Disks) technology
- Fault tolerance
- Business continuity planning
- Insurance

Database Integrity Issues

Database integrity requires the following three goals:

- Prevention of the modification of information by unauthorized users
- Prevention of the unauthorized or unintentional modification of information by authorized users
- Preservation of both internal and external consistency:

  - *Internal consistency* — Ensures that internal data is consistent. For example, assume that an internal database holds the number of units of a particular item in each department of an organization. The sum of the number of units in each department should equal the total number of units that the database has recorded internally for the whole organization.

  - *External consistency* — Ensures that the data stored in the database is consistent with the real world. Using the preceding example, external consistency means that the number of items recorded in the database for each department is equal to the number of items that physically exist in that department.

Cloud Service Provider Risks

Using virtualized systems introduces many new risks, while maintaining many if not most of the risks inherent in using traditional systems. The publication by the Burton Group, "Attacking and Defending Virtual Environments,"[5] groups these risk as follows:

- All existing attacks still work.
- As a separate system that must be protected, the hypervisor is risk additive.
- Aggregating separate systems into VMs increases risk.
- An untrusted hypervisor with a trusted VM has a higher risk than a trusted hypervisor with an untrusted VM.

Based on these parameters, we can identify several areas of risk to virtualized systems, including the following:

- **Complexity of configuration** — Virtual systems add more layers of complexity to networks and systems, greatly increasing the possibility of improper configuration or the induction of heretofore unseen vulnerabilities.

- **Privilege escalation** — A hacker may be able to escalate his or her privileges on a system by leveraging a virtual machine using a lower level of access rights, then attack a VM with a higher level of security controls through the hypervisor.

- **Inactive virtual machines** — Virtual machines that are not active (i.e., are dormant), could store data that is sensitive. Monitoring access to that data in a dormant VM is virtually impossible, but provides a security risk through the loss of or access to the VM. Also, monitoring tools for VM systems are not as mature as traditional tools, but are expected to improve quickly.

- **Segregation of duties** — A virtualized system poses risk to organizations through the improper definition of user access roles. Because the VM provides access to many type of components from many directions, proper segregation of duties may be difficult to maintain.

- **Poor access controls** — The virtual machine's hypervisor facilitates hardware virtualization and mediates all hardware access for the running virtual machines. This creates a new attack vector into the VM, due to its single point of access. Therefore, the hypervisor can expose the trusted network through poorly designed access control systems, deficient patching, and lack of monitoring. This vulnerability also applies to virtualized databases.

It is important for the information security professional to understand and identify other types of attacks. These attacks are summarized in the following sections.

Back-Door

A back-door attack takes place using dial-up modems or asynchronous external connections. The strategy is to gain access to a network through bypassing of control mechanisms, getting in through a "back door" such as a modem.

Spoofing

Intruders use IP spoofing to convince a system that it is communicating with a known, trusted entity in order to provide the intruder with access to the system. IP spoofing involves alteration of a packet at the TCP level, which is used to attack Internet-connected systems that provide various TCP/IP services. The attacker sends a packet with an IP source address of a known, trusted host instead of its own IP source address to a target host. The target host may accept the packet and act upon it.

Man-in-the-Middle

The man-in-the-middle attack involves an attacker, A, substituting his or her public key for that of another person, P. Then, anyone desiring to send an encrypted message to P using P's public key is unknowingly using A's public key. Therefore, A can read the message intended for P. A can then send the message on to P, encrypted in P's real public key, and P will never be the wiser. Obviously, A could modify the message before resending it to P.

Replay

The replay attack occurs when an attacker intercepts and saves old messages and then tries to send them later, impersonating one of the participants. One method of making this attack more difficult to accomplish is through the use of a random number or string called a *nonce*. For example, if Bob wants to communicate with Alice, he sends a nonce along with the first message to Alice. When Alice replies, she sends the nonce back to Bob, who verifies that it is the one he sent with the first message. Anyone trying to use these same messages later will not be using the newer nonce. Another approach to countering the replay attack is for Bob to add a timestamp to his message. This timestamp indicates the time that the message was sent. Thus, if the message is used later, the timestamp will show that an old message is being used.

TCP Hijacking

In this type of attack, an attacker steals, or hijacks, a session between a trusted client and network server. The attacking computer substitutes its IP address for that of the trusted client, and the server continues the dialog believing it is communicating with the trusted client.

Social Engineering

This attack uses social skills to obtain information such as passwords or PIN numbers to be used against information systems. For example, an attacker may impersonate someone in an organization and make phone calls to employees of that organization requesting passwords for use in maintenance operations. The following are additional examples of social engineering attacks:

- E-mails to employees from a cracker requesting their passwords to validate the organizational database after a network intrusion has occurred

- E-mails to employees from a cracker requesting their passwords because work has to be done over the weekend on the system

- E-mails or phone calls from a cracker impersonating an official who is conducting an investigation for the organization and requires passwords for the investigation

- Improper release of medical information to individuals posing as doctors and requesting data from patients' records

- A computer repair technician convinces a user that the hard disk on his or her PC is damaged and irreparable and installs a new hard disk. The technician then takes the hard disk, extracts the information, and sells the information to a competitor or foreign government.

Dumpster Diving

Dumpster diving involves the acquisition of information that is discarded by an individual or organization. In many cases, information found in trash can be very valuable to a cracker. Discarded information may include technical manuals, password lists, telephone numbers, credit card numbers, and organization charts. Note that in order for information to be treated as a trade secret, it must be adequately protected and not revealed to any unauthorized individuals. If a document containing an organization's trade secret information is inadvertently discarded and found in the trash by another person, the other person can use that information, as it was not adequately protected by the organization.

Password Guessing

Because passwords are the most commonly used mechanism to authenticate users to an information system, obtaining passwords is a common and effective attack approach. Gaining access to a person's password can be obtained by physically looking around their desk for notes with the password, "sniffing" the connection to the network to acquire unencrypted passwords, social engineering, gaining access to a password database, or outright guessing. The last approach can be done in a random or systematic manner.

An effective means to prevent password guessing is to place a limit on the number of user attempts to enter a password. For example, a limit could be set such that a user is "locked out" of a system for a period of time after three unsuccessful tries at entering the password. This approach must be used carefully, however. For example, consider the consequences of employing this type of control in a critical application such as a Supervisory Control and Data Acquisition (SCADA) System. SCADA systems are used to run real-time processes such as oil refineries, nuclear power stations, and chemical plants. Consider the consequences of a panicked operator trying to respond to an emergency in the plant, improperly typing in his or her password a number of times, and then being locked out of the system. Clearly, the lock-out approach should be carefully evaluated before being applied to systems requiring rapid operator responses.

Trojan Horses and Malware

Trojan horses hide malicious code inside a host program that seems to do something useful. Once these programs are executed, the virus, worm, or other type of malicious code hidden in the Trojan horse program is released to attack the workstation, server, or network, or to allow unauthorized access to those devices. Trojans are common tools used to create back doors into the network for later exploitation by crackers. Trojan horses can be carried via Internet traffic such as FTP downloads or downloadable applets from websites, or distributed through e-mail.

Some Trojans are programmed to open specific ports to allow access for exploitation. If a Trojan is installed on a system it often opens a high-numbered port. Then the open Trojan port could be scanned and located, enabling an attacker to compromise the system.

A *logic bomb* is an instantiation of a Trojan horse that is activated upon the occurrence of a particular event. For example, the malicious code might be set to run when a specific piece of code is executed or at a certain time and date. Similarly, *a time bomb* is set to activate after a designated period of time has elapsed.

Summary

While the benefits of cloud computing are varied, the related risk issues are also just as varied. We started by examining the basic tenets of information systems security, confidentiality, integrity, and availability, and looked at how those three tenets affect other security concepts, such as data protection, identity protection, and access management.

We also took a look at how cloud computing can create risk to privacy assurance and compliance regulations, and examined in more detail those privacy regulations that can adversely be affected by the adoption of virtualization. And we finished by looking at some risks and threats that may be unique to cloud service providers (CSP).

In Chapter 5, we'll cover cloud computing security opportunities in the areas of security policy implementation, computer intrusion detection and response, and virtualization security management.

Notes

1. M-07-16 Subject: Safeguarding Against and Responding to the Breach of Personally Identifiable Information. From: Clay Johnson III, Deputy Director for Management (2007/05/22).

2. `www.oecd.org/document/18/0,3343,en_2649_34255_1815186_1_1_1_1,00` `.html`.

3. Payment Card Industry (PCI) Data Security Standard Requirements and Security Assessment Procedures, Version 1.2, October 2008.

4. Some of these resources can be found at `www.w3.org/P3P/` and `http://` `p3ptoolbox.org/`.

5. "Attacking and Defending Virtual Environments," The Burton Group, `www.burtongroup.com/Guest/Srms/AttackingDefendingVirtual.aspx`.

CHAPTER 5

Cloud Computing Security Challenges

In these days, a man who says a thing cannot be done is quite apt to be interrupted by some idiot doing it.
—Elbert Green Hubbard (1865–1915) U. S. author, editor, printer

The introduction of cloud services presents many challenges to an organization. When an organization migrates to consuming cloud services, and especially public cloud services, much of the computing system infrastructure will now be under the control of a third-party Cloud Services Provider (CSP).

Many of these challenges can and should be addressed through management initiatives. These management initiatives will require clearly delineating the ownership and responsibility roles of both the CSP (which may or may not be the organization itself) and the organization functioning in the role as customer.

Security managers must be able to determine what detective and preventative controls exist to clearly define the security posture of the organization. Although proper security controls must be implemented based on asset, threat, and vulnerability risk assessment matrices, and are contingent upon the level of data protection needed, some general management processes will be required regardless of the nature of the organization's business. These include the following:

- Security policy implementation
- Computer intrusion detection and response
- Virtualization security management

Let's look at each of these management initiatives.

Security Policy Implementation

Security policies are the foundation of a sound security implementation. Often organizations will implement technical security solutions without first creating this foundation of policies, standards, guidelines, and procedures, unintentionally creating unfocused and ineffective security controls.

A *policy* is one of those terms that can mean several things. For example, there are security policies on firewalls, which refer to the access control and routing list information. Standards, procedures, and guidelines are also referred to as policies in the larger sense of a global information security policy.

A good, well-written policy is more than an exercise created on white paper — it is an essential and fundamental element of sound security practice. A policy, for example, can literally be a lifesaver during a disaster, or it might be a requirement of a governmental or regulatory function. A policy can also provide protection from liability due to an employee's actions, or it can control access to trade secrets.

Figure 5-1 shows how the policies relate to each other hierarchically.

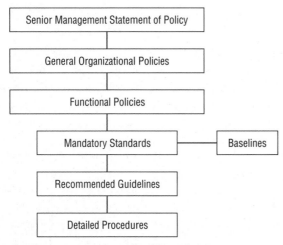

Figure 5-1: Security policy hierarchy

Policy Types

In the corporate world, when we refer to specific polices, rather than a group policy, we generally mean those policies that are distinct from the standards, procedures, and guidelines. Policies are considered the first and highest level of documentation, from which the lower-level elements of standards, procedures, and guidelines flow.

This is not to say, however, that higher-level policies are more important than the lower elements. These higher-level policies, which reflect the more general policies and statements, should be created first in the process, for strategic reasons, and then the more tactical elements can follow.

Management should ensure the high visibility of a formal security policy. This is because nearly all employees at all levels will in some way be affected, major organizational resources will be addressed, and many new terms, procedures, and activities will be introduced.

Including security as a regular topic at staff meetings at all levels of the organization can be helpful. In addition, providing visibility through such avenues as management presentations, panel discussions, guest speakers, question/answer forums, and newsletters can be beneficial.

Senior Management Statement of Policy

The first policy of any policy creation process is the *senior management statement of policy*. This is a general, high-level policy that acknowledges the importance of the computing resources to the business model; states support for information security throughout the enterprise; and commits to authorizing and managing the definition of the lower-level standards, procedures, and guidelines.

Regulatory Policies

Regulatory policies are security policies that an organization must implement due to compliance, regulation, or other legal requirements. These companies might be financial institutions, public utilities, or some other type of organization that operates in the public interest. Such policies are usually very detailed and specific to the industry in which the organization operates.

Advisory Policies

Advisory policies are security policies that are not mandated but strongly suggested, perhaps with serious consequences defined for failure to follow them (such as termination, a job action warning, and so forth). A company with such policies wants most employees to consider these policies mandatory. Most policies fall under this broad category.

Informative Policies

Informative policies are policies that exist simply to inform the reader. There are not implied or specified requirements, and the audience for this information could be certain internal (within the organization) or external parties. This does not mean that the policies are authorized for public consumption but that they are general enough to be distributed to external parties (vendors accessing an extranet, for example) without a loss of confidentiality.

Computer Security Incident Response Team (CSIRT)

As you read in Chapter 7, as part of a structured incident-handling program of intrusion detection and response, a Computer Emergency Response Team (CERT) or computer security incident response team (CSIRT) is commonly created. The main tasks of a CSIRT are as follows:

- Analysis of an event notification
- Response to an incident if the analysis warrants it
- Escalation path procedures
- Resolution, post-incident follow-up, and reporting to the appropriate parties

The prime directive of every CIRT is incident response management, which reflects a company's response to events that pose a risk to its computing environment. This management often consists of the following:

- Coordinating the notification and distribution of information pertaining to the incident to the appropriate parties (those with a need to know) through a predefined escalation path
- Mitigating risk to the enterprise by minimizing the disruptions to normal business activities and the costs associated with remediating the incident (including public relations)
- Assembling teams of technical personnel to investigate the potential vulnerabilities and resolve specific intrusions

Additional examples of CIRT activities are:

- Management of the network logs, including collection, retention, review, and analysis of data
- Management of an incident's resolution, management of a vulnerability's remediation, and post-event reporting to the appropriate parties

Response includes notifying the appropriate parties to take action in order to determine the extent of an incident's severity and to remediate the incident's effects. According to NIST, an organization should address computer security incidents by developing an incident-handling capability. The incident-handling capability should be used to do the following:

- Provide the ability to respond quickly and effectively
- Contain and repair the damage from incidents. When left unchecked, malicious software can significantly harm an organization's computing

resources, depending on the technology and its connectivity. Containing the incident should include an assessment of whether the incident is part of a targeted attack on the organization or an isolated incident.

- Prevent future damage. An incident-handling capability should assist an organization in preventing (or at least minimizing) damage from future incidents. Incidents can be studied internally to gain a better understanding of the organization's threats and vulnerabilities.

Virtualization Security Management

Although the global adoption of virtualization is a relatively recent event, threats to the virtualized infrastructure are evolving just as quickly. Historically, the development and implementation of new technology has preceded the full understanding of its inherent security risks, and virtualized systems are no different. The following sections examine the threats and vulnerabilities inherent in virtualized systems and look at some common management solutions to those threats.

VIRTUALIZATION TYPES

The Virtual Machine (VM), Virtual Memory Manager (VMM), and hypervisor or host OS are the minimum set of components needed in a virtual environment. They comprise virtual environments in a few distinct ways:

- Type 1 virtual environments are considered "full virtualization" environments and have VMs running on a hypervisor that interacts with the hardware (see Figure 5-2).

- Type 2 virtual environments are also considered "full virtualization" but work with a host OS instead of a hypervisor (see Figure 5-3).

- Para-virtualized environments offer performance gains by eliminating some of the emulation that occurs in full virtualization environments.

- Other type designations include hybrid virtual machines (HVMs) and hardware-assisted techniques.

These classifications are somewhat ambiguous in the IT community at large. The most important thing to remember from a security perspective is that there is a more significant impact when a host OS with user applications and interfaces is running outside of a VM at a level lower than the other VMs (i.e., a Type 2 architecture). Because of its architecture, the Type 2 environment increases the potential risk of attacks against the host OS. For example, a laptop running VMware with a Linux VM on a Windows XP system inherits the attack surface of both OSs, plus the virtualization code (VMM).[1]

VIRTUALIZATION MANAGEMENT ROLES

Typically, the VMware Infrastructure is managed by several users performing different roles. The roles assumed by administrators are the Virtualization Server Administrator, Virtual Machine Administrator, and Guest Administrator. VMware Infrastructure users may have different roles and responsibilities, but some functional overlap may occur. The roles assumed by administrators are configured in VMS and are defined to provide role responsibilities:

- **Virtual Server Administrator** — This role is responsible for installing and configuring the ESX Server hardware, storage, physical and virtual networks, service console, and management applications.

- **Virtual Machine Administrator** — This role is responsible for creating and configuring virtual machines, virtual networks, virtual machine resources, and security policies. The Virtual Machine Administrator creates, maintains, and provisions virtual machines.

- **Guest Administrator** — This role is responsible for managing a guest virtual machine or machines. Tasks typically performed by Guest Administrators include connecting virtual devices, adding system updates, and managing applications that may reside on the operating system.

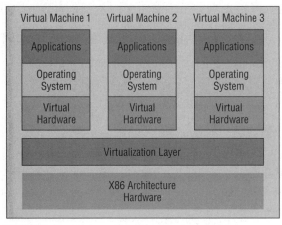

Figure 5-2: Type 1 virtualized environment

Virtual Threats

Some threats to virtualized systems are general in nature, as they are inherent threats to all computerized systems (such as denial-of-service, or DoS, attacks). Other threats and vulnerabilities, however, are unique to virtual machines. Many VM vulnerabilities stem from the fact that a vulnerability in one VM system can be exploited to attack other VM systems or the host systems, as multiple virtual machines share the same physical hardware, as shown in Figure 5-4.

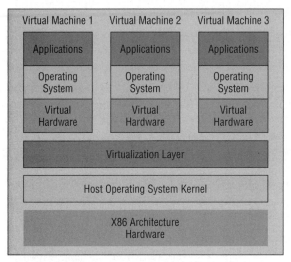

Figure 5-3: Type 2 virtualized environment

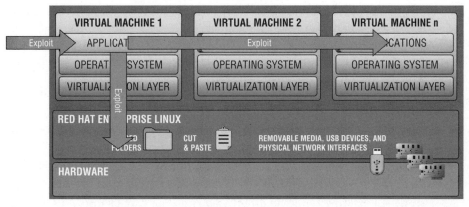

Figure 5-4: Basic VM system vulnerability

Various organizations are currently conducting security analysis and proof-of-concept (PoC) attacks against virtualized systems, and recently published research regarding security in virtual environments highlights some of the vulnerabilities exposed to any malicious-minded individuals:

- **Shared clipboard** — Shared clipboard technology allows data to be transferred between VMs and the host, providing a means of moving data between malicious programs in VMs of different security realms.

■ **Keystroke logging** — Some VM technologies enable the logging of keystrokes and screen updates to be passed across virtual terminals in the virtual machine, writing to host files and permitting the monitoring of encrypted terminal connections inside the VM.

■ **VM monitoring from the host** — Because all network packets coming from or going to a VM pass through the host, the host may be able to affect the VM by the following:

■ Starting, stopping, pausing, and restart VMs

■ Monitoring and configuring resources available to the VMs, including CPU, memory, disk, and network usage of VMs

■ Adjusting the number of CPUs, amount of memory, amount and number of virtual disks, and number of virtual network interfaces available to a VM

■ Monitoring the applications running inside the VM

■ Viewing, copying, and modifying data stored on the VM's virtual disks

■ **Virtual machine monitoring from another VM** — Usually, VMs should not be able to directly access one another's virtual disks on the host. However, if the VM platform uses a virtual hub or switch to connect the VMs to the host, then intruders may be able to use a hacker technique known as "ARP poisoning" to redirect packets going to or from the other VM for sniffing.

■ **Virtual machine backdoors** — A backdoor, covert communications channel between the guest and host could allow intruders to perform potentially dangerous operations.[2]

Table 5-1 shows how VMware's ESX server vulnerabilities can be categorized, as interpreted by the DoD (see also Figure 5-5).

According to the Burton Group five immutable laws of virtualization security must be understood and used to drive security decisions:

Law 1: All existing OS-level attacks work in the exact same way.

Law 2: The hypervisor attack surface is additive to a system's risk profile.

Law 3: Separating functionality and/or content into VMs will reduce risk.

Law 4: Aggregating functions and resources onto a physical platform will increase risk.

Law 5: A system containing a "trusted" VM on an "untrusted" host has a higher risk level than a system containing a "trusted" host with an "untrusted" VM.[3]

The current major virtualization vendors are VMware, Microsoft Hyper-V, and Citrix Systems XenServer (based on the Xen open-source hypervisor).

Table 5-1: ESX Server Application Vulnerability Severity Code Definitions

CATEGORY	ESX SERVER APPLICATION
Category I — Vulnerabilities that allow an attacker immediate access into a machine, allow super-user access, or bypass a firewall	Vulnerabilities that may result in malicious attacks on virtual infrastructure resources or services. Attacks may include, but are not limited to, malware at the VMM, virtual machine–based rootkit (SubVirt), Trojan, DOS, and executing potentially malicious actions.
Category II — Vulnerabilities that provide information that have a high potential of giving access to an intruder	Vulnerabilities that may result in unauthorized users accessing and modifying virtual infrastructure resources or services.
Category III — Vulnerabilities that provide information that potentially could lead to compromise	Vulnerabilities that may result in unauthorized users viewing or possibly accessing virtual infrastructure resources or services.

Source: ESX Server V1R1 DISA Field Security Operations, 28 April 2008, Developed by DISA for the DoD.

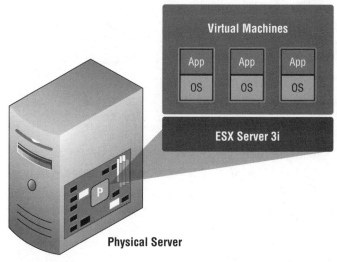

Figure 5-5: VMware ESX Server 3i

Figure 5-6 shows VMware's approach to virtualized infrastructure, and Figure 5-7 shows a little more detail into VMware's ESX server architecture.

VM THREAT LEVELS

When categorizing the threat posed to virtualized environments, often the vulnerability/threat matrix is classified into three levels of compromise:

■ **Abnormally terminated** — Availability to the virtual machine is compromised, as the VM is placed into an infinite loop that prevents the VM administrator from accessing the VM's monitor.

(continued)

VM THREAT LEVELS *(continued)*

■ **Partially compromised** — The virtual machine allows a hostile process to interfere with the virtualization manager, contaminating stet checkpoints or over-allocating resources.

■ **Totally compromised** — The virtual machine is completely overtaken and directed to execute unauthorized commands on its host with elevated privileges.[4]

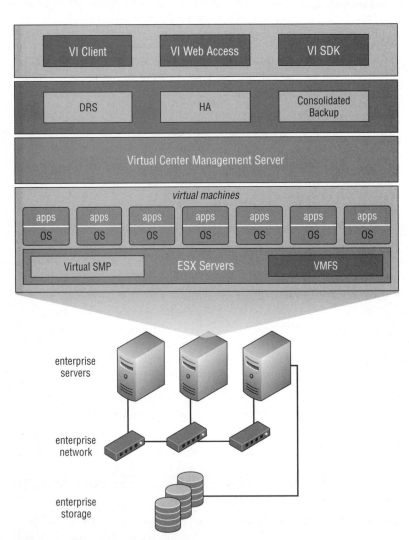

Figure 5-6: VMwARE Infrastructure

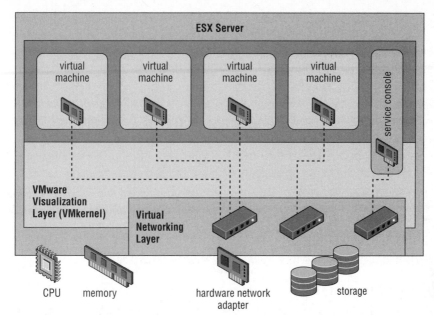

Figure 5-7: ESX server architecture

Hypervisor Risks

The *hypervisor* is the part of a virtual machine that allows host resource sharing and enables VM/host isolation. Therefore, the ability of the hypervisor to provide the necessary isolation during intentional attack greatly determines how well the virtual machine can survive risk.

One reason why the hypervisor is susceptible to risk is because it's a software program; risk increases as the volume and complexity of application code increases. Ideally, software code operating within a defined VM would not be able to communicate or affect code running either on the physical host itself or within a different VM; but several issues, such as bugs in the software, or limitations to the virtualization implementation, may put this isolation at risk. Major vulnerabilities inherent in the hypervisor consist of rogue hypervisor rootkits, external modification to the hypervisor, and VM escape.

Rogue Hypervisors

As you've seen in previous chapters, in a normal virtualization scenario, the guest operating system (the operating system that is booted inside of a virtualized environment) runs like a traditional OS managing I/O to hardware and network traffic, even though it's controlled by the hypervisor. The hypervisor, therefore, has a great level of control over the system, not only in the VM but also on the host machine.

Rootkits that target virtualization, and in particular the hypervisor, have been gaining traction in the hacker community. VM-based rootkits can hide from normal malware detection systems by initiating a "rogue" hypervisor and creating a cover channel to dump unauthorized code into the system.

Proof-of-concept (PoC) exploits have demonstrated that a hypervisor rootkit can insert itself into RAM, downgrade the host OS to a VM, and make itself invisible. A properly designed rootkit could then stay "undetectable" to the host OS, resisting attempts by malware detectors to discover and remove it.[5]

This creates a serious vulnerability in all virtualized systems. Detectability of malware code lies at the heart of intrusion detection and correction, as security researchers analyze code samples by running the code and viewing the result.

In addition, some malware tries to avoid detection by anti-virus processes by attempting to identify whether the system it has infected is traditional or virtual. If found to be a VM, it remains inactivated and hidden until it can penetrate the physical host and execute its payload through a traditional attack vector.

External Modification of the Hypervisor

In additional to the execution of the rootkit payload, a poorly protected or designed hypervisor can also create an attack vector. Therefore, a self-protected virtual machine may allow direct modification of its hypervisor by an external intruder. This can occur in virtualized systems that don't validate the hypervisor as a regular process.

VM Escape

Due to the host machine's fundamentally privileged position in relationship to the VM, an improperly configured VM could allow code to completely bypass the virtual environment, and obtain full root or kernel access to the physical host. This would result in a complete failure of the security mechanisms of the system, and is called *VM escape*.

Virtual machine escape refers to the attacker's ability to execute arbitrary code on the VM's physical host, by "escaping" the hypervisor. Sometimes called the "Holy Grail" of virtualization security research, VM escape has been the subject of a series of PoCs conducted by security researchers such as Tavis Ormandy of Google, and Tom Liston and Ed Skoudis at Intelguardians Network Intelligence.

Liston and Ormandy showed that VM escapes could occur through virtual machine shared resources called VMchat, VMftp, VMcat, and VMdrag-n-sploit.[6]

Increased Denial of Service Risk

The threat of denial-of-service (DoS) attacks against a virtualized system is as prevalent as it is against nonvirtualized systems; but because the virtual machines share the host's resources, such as memory, processor, disk, I/O devices, and so on, a denial-of-service attack risk against another VM, the host, or an external service is actually greatly increased.

Because the VM has more complex layers of resource allocation than a traditional system, DoS prevention techniques can become equally more complex. Like IT protections traditionally implemented against denial-of-service attacks, limiting the consumption of host resources through resource allocation may help lessen the exposure to DoS attacks.

VM Security Recommendations

As we've just described a host of security issues inherent in virtualized computing, let's examine some ways to protect the virtual machine. First we'll look at standard best practice security techniques that apply to traditional computer systems, and then we'll examine security techniques that are unique to virtualized systems.

Best Practice Security Techniques

The following security implementation techniques are required for most computer systems, and are still best practices for virtualized systems. These areas include physical security, patching, and remote management techniques.

Hardening the Host Operating System

Vulnerabilities inherent in the operating system of the host computer can flow upward into the virtual machine operating system. While a compromise on the VM OS would hopefully only compromise the guest domain, a compromise of the underlying host OS would give an intruder access to all services on all virtual machines hosted by the machine.

Therefore, best practice hardening techniques must be implemented to maintain the security posture of the underlying technology. Some of these techniques include the following:

- Use strong passwords, such as lengthy, hard to guess passwords with letters, numbers, and symbol combinations, and change them often.

- Disable unneeded services or programs, especially networked services.

- Require full authentication for access control.

- The host should be individually firewalled.

- Patch and update the host regularly, after testing on a nonproduction unit.

Use vendor-supplied best practice configuration guides for both the guest and host domains, and refer to some of the published standards in this area, such as the following:

- NIST Computer Resource Center (`http://csrc.nist.gov`)
- Defense Information Systems Agency (DISA) Security Technical Implementation Guides (STIGS) (`http://iase.disa.mil/stigs/index.html`)
- Center for Internet Security (`http://cisecurity.org`)
- SANS Institute (`http://www.sans.org`)
- National Security Agency (NSA) (`http://www.nsa.gov`)

We'll describe some of these techniques in detail.

Limiting Physical Access to the Host

Basic physical host security is required to prevent intruders from attacking the hardware of the virtual machine. When attackers can access a host they can do the following:

- Use OS-specific keystrokes to kill processes, monitor resource usage, or shut down the machine, commonly without needing a valid login account and password
- Reboot the machine, booting to external media with a known root password
- Steal files using external media (floppy, CD/DVD-RW, USB/flash drives, etc.)
- Capture traffic coming into or out of the network interfaces
- Remove one or more disks, mounting them in a machine with a known administrator or root password, potentially providing access to the entire contents of the host and guest VMs
- Simply remove the entire machine

Standard physical controls must also be implemented on the server room itself:

- Require card or guard access to the room with the machines.
- Use locks to anchor the machines to the building, and/or lock the cases to prevent removal of the hard drives.
- Remove floppy and CD drives after initial setup.
- In the BIOS, disable booting from any device except the primary hard drive. Also, password protect the BIOS so the boot choice cannot be changed.
- Control all external ports through host and guest system configuration or third-party applications.[7]

Using Encrypted Communications

Encryption technologies, such as Secure HTTP (HTTPS), encrypted Virtual Private Networks (VPNs), Transport Layer Security (TLS), Secure Shell (SSH), and so on should be used to provide secure communications links between the host domain and the guest domain, or from hosts to management systems. Encryption will help prevent such exploits as man-in-the-middle (MITM), spoofed attacks, and session hijacking.

In addition, standard traditional authentication techniques, such as failed login timeouts, strong passwords, BIOS passwords, warning banners, and password masking should be implemented.

Disabling Background Tasks

Most traditional server operating systems have multiple low-priority processes that are scheduled to run after primary business hours, when the server is expected to be less busy. Disabling, limiting, or off-loading these processes to other servers may be advisable if the host is beginning to suffer from resource contention.

The primary problem with background task detection on a virtual machine is that the virtual idle process is not fully aware of the state of the other virtual machines, and may not be able to make an accurate determination as to whether the host processor is really idle or not. This may lead to a situation where the background task demands more processor cycles than was initially intended.

In addition, several hacker exploits are designed to piggyback off of these processes, in an attempt to be less detectable to malware detection. Some of these processes may include file indexing tools, logging tools, and defragmenters.

Updating and Patching

Most standards organizations enforce the concept of timely patching and updating of systems. Unfortunately, the proliferation of VMs in an organization adds complexity to the patch control process. This means that not only must you patch and update the host OS promptly, but each of the virtual machines requires the same patching schedule. This is one reason standardization of an operating system throughout an enterprise is very important, if at all possible.

The patch schedule also requires management of the shutdown process, as most patches require rebooting after the patch is applied, and the administrator may have a very narrow maintenance window in which to apply the patch. Now you're shutting down not only the host, but every system that's on that host, and updating every VM on the host, as well as the host itself.

It's also imperative that the patch be tested on a nonproduction system representative of the system to be updated. While it's important that both the host and guest VMs receive the latest security patch, a research and testing control process must be implemented to demonstrate what effect an update may have on your specific configuration. A large part of integration resource is expended when an update has unforeseen consequences, and must be rolled back or results in required patching of other system components.

Keep up to date via mailing lists and news groups for information about the latest patches for your systems, and to research update implementation issues, especially for organizations that have systems comparable to yours. Also, some patches must be specifically modified by the virtualization vendor prior to implementation, so keep in close contact with your virtualization vendor through the patching and updating process.

Enabling Perimeter Defense on the VM

Perimeter defense devices are some of the oldest and most established ways of enforcing the security policy, by regulating data traffic ingress and egress. In fact, a common error of IT management is allocating too many resources (time and money) to purely perimeter defense, in the form of firewalls and hardened DMZ routers, while neglecting hardening the internal, trusted network. This often creates what's referred to as an *M&M* network security posture: crunchy on the outside but soft on the inside. The network is difficult to get into, but it lacks adequate controls once an intruder succeeds in penetrating the perimeter.

One advantage of enabling firewalls or intrusion detection systems through virtual machines on the host OS is that successful compromise of the guest domain may not compromise the host domain if the VM has been configured properly. Because the host domain controls the actual network traffic and makes final routing determinations after the VM has communicated, network-based intrusion detection or firewall products can very successfully be implemented at this choke point, and further helps the organization to implement a "defense-in-depth" strategy.

Implementing File Integrity Checks

One of the tenets of information systems security is the preservation of file integrity — that is, the guarantee that the contents of a file haven't been subjected to unauthorized alterations, either intentionally or unintentionally. File integrity checking is the process of verifying that the files retain the proper consistency, and serves as a check for intrusion into the system.

While the security classification level of the data to be hosted in the VM will determine the intensity and focus of the checking, it's recommended that file integrity checking be implemented at the host operating system level.

One way of implementing file integrity checking is by storing hash values of core OS files offline, as these files should not change often. Tripwire (www .tripwire.com), is one of the most established vendors of file integrity checking, and has recently begun focusing on virtualized environments in addition to traditional physical environments.

Maintaining Backups

We shouldn't even have to tell you this, but unfortunately we do. Perform image backups frequently for all production VMs. This will aid recovery of both individual files or the complete server image.

Protection of the physical backup is also a part of best practices. This includes protection of the data stream of the backup, which should be encrypted to prevent the interception of a server image by capturing the packets in the backup, as well as physical control of the backup media transport and storage.

THE ATTACK SURFACE

Attack surface **is a term that refers to the all of a host's running services that expose it to attack. The security profession tries to shrink the attack surface to as small a footprint as possible, while still maintaining business functionality. Shrinking reduces the vulnerability exposure the attack surface provides an attacker, and has the added benefit of lowering the complexity and resources needed to secure a system.**

AUDITING VM

It's very important that system auditors and assessors understand the inherent risks of any virtualized system that engages a connection to public networks (such as the Internet). Many standards and guidelines are being built to guide auditors in assessing the security posture of a virtualized environment, including guidelines from the U.S. Department of Defense (DoD) Defense Information Systems Agency (DISA),[8] the Center for Internet Security (CIS),[9] and various consulting organizations, such as the Burton Group.[10] These guidelines also provide recommendations for implementing the controls necessary to secure virtual machines and their hypervisors.

VM-Specific Security Techniques

A fundamental requirement for a successful virtualization security process is recognizing the dynamic nature of virtual machines. Therefore, many of the following security techniques are fairly unique to virtualized systems, and should be implemented in addition to the traditional best practice techniques just described.

Hardening the Virtual Machine

Virtual machines need to be configured securely, according to vendor-provided or industry best practices. Because this hardening may vary according to the vendor's implementation of virtualization, follow the vendor recommendations for best practice in this area.

This hardening can include many steps, such as the following:

- Putting limits on virtual machine resource consumption

- Configuring the virtual network interface and storage appropriately

- Disabling or removing unnecessary devices and services

- Ensuring that components that might be shared across virtual network devices are adequately isolated and secured

- Keeping granular and detailed audit logging trails for the virtualized infrastructure

It's important to use vendor supplied best practice configuration guides for both the guest and host domains, and refer to some of the published standards in this area, such as:

- NIST Computer Resource Center (http://csrc.nist.gov/)

- Defense Information Systems Agency (DISA) Security Technical Implementation Guides (STIGS) (http://iase.disa.mil/stigs/index.html)

- Center for Internet Security (http://cisecurity.org)

- SANS Institute (http://www.sans.org/)

- National Security Agency (NSA) (http://www.nsa.gov/)

Let's look at some important VM hardening techniques.

Harden the Hypervisor

It is critical to focus on the hypervisor as an attack vector, and strive to ensure that the hypervisor is deployed securely. Even before this stage, when you are evaluating various vendors' virtualization technology, place a premium on a vendor's track record of identifying vulnerabilities to its technology and the frequency of patch distribution.

Employ change and configuration controls to manage the virtual system patches and configuration changes to the hypervisor, and implement a testing process to test for publish vulnerabilities. Engaging a third-party testing service is standard best practice also.

Root Secure the Monitor

Because most operating systems can be compromised through privilege escalation, the VM monitor should be "root secure." This means that no level of privilege within the virtualized guest environment permits interference with the host system.

Implement Only One Primary Function per VM

While contemporary servers and virtual machines are adept at multi-tasking many functions, it's a lot easier to maintain secure control if the virtual machine is configured with process separation. It greatly complicates the hacker's ability to compromise multiple system components if the VM is implemented with one primary function per virtual server or device.

Firewall Any Additional VM Ports

The virtual machine may open multiple ports linked to the host's external IP address, besides the usual ports opened by the host. These ports are used to connect remotely to the virtual machine layer to view or configure virtual machines, share drives, or perform other tasks.

   Therefore, the host system should be independently firewalled with a minimum of access allowed. Remote management of the host and VM will likely be required, but this communication should only take place on a separate NIC for administrative access only.

Harden the Host Domain

The Center for Internet Security (CIS) recently published a Xen benchmark study[11] that incorporates a lot of valuable security advice for hardening the host domain: "Before any virtual machines can be secure, the Host Domain of the host Linux operating system must be secure. A compromise of the Host Domain makes compromising the Guest Domains a simple task. Thus steps should be taken to reduce the attack surface of the Host Domain. These include but are not limited to:

- Remove unnecessary accounts and groups.
- Disable unnecessary services.
- Remove unnecessary binaries, libraries, and files.
- Firewall network access to the host.
- Install monitoring or Host Intrusion Detection Systems.
- Ensure that the Host Domain is not accessible from the Guest Domains.
- Ensure that monitoring or remote console interfaces for the Host Domain are not accessible via the Guest Domains.
- Ensure that the Guest Domains cannot directly affect any network storage or other resources that the Host Domain relies on for boot, configuration, or authentication.

   The Host Domain host should only be used as a resource for virtualizing other operating environments. The Host Domain system should not host any other services or resources itself, including web, email and file servers. If such services are required, migrate the services to another system or consider creating a virtual machine to host them inside of a Guest Domain."

Use Unique NICs for Sensitive VMs

If possible, VMs that contain confidential databases and encrypted or sensitive information should have their network interface address bound to distinct and separate physical network interfaces (NICs). This external NIC would be the primary attack vector for intrusion, and isolation can help protect the VM.

Disconnect Unused Devices

It's advisable to disconnect the unneeded default virtual machine device connections when configuring the VM. Because the VM can control physical devices on the host, it's possible to insert media with undesired code into the device, enabling the code to execute when the VM mounts. Enable host access to devices only when explicitly required by the VM.

Additional VM Recommendations

Tavis Ormandy[12] also has additional recommendations for hardening virtualized systems:

- Treat Virtual Machines like services that can be compromised; use chroot, systrace, acls, least privileged users, etc.

- Disable emulated hardware you don't need, and external services you don't use (DHCP daemons, etc.) to reduce the attack surface exposed to hostile users.

- Xen is worth watching in future; separating domains should limit the impact of a compromise.

- Maintain the integrity of guest operating systems, protect the kernel using standard procedures of disabling modules: `/dev/mem`, `/dev/port`, etc.

- Keep guest software up-to-date with published vulnerabilities. If an attacker cannot elevate their privileges within the guest, the likelihood of compromising the VMM is significantly reduced.

- Keep Virtual Machine software updated to ensure all known vulnerabilities have been corrected.

- Avoid guests that do not operate in protected mode, and make use of any security features offered, avoid running untrusted code with root-equivalent privileges within the guest.

Securing VM Remote Access

Many virtual machine systems are rack-mounted, and may be located in a server farm physically distinct from the administration location. This usually requires the system administrator to access the virtualized system remotely for management tasks. This requires secure remote communications techniques.

Although each vendor's implementation of virtualization technology may differ, some general standard best practices exist when using remote services to access a system for administration. Most systems utilize a dedicated management NIC, and running service processes that are used to create a secure connection with the remote administrator.

Standard practices for remote administration include the following:

- Strong authentication practices should be employed:
  - Two-factor authentication
  - Strong passwords
  - One-time passwords
  - Private/public PKI key pairs

- Use encrypted communications only, such as a SSH or VPNs.
- MAC address or IP address filtering should be employed.
- Telnet access to the unit should be denied, as it does not encrypt the communications channel.

THE VALUE OF SSH

SSH (Secure Shell) is a terminal connection emulator that resembles Telnet but is a more secure tool for running management tasks remotely. SSH is cross-platform and can run both purely text-based sessions as well as X-Windows graphical applications. SSH is flexible enough to enable administrators to run the same set of management tools used in the nonvirtual, traditional environment, and it includes a wealth of various add-on tools built upon the SSH technology, such as SFTP (secure FTP) and PuTTY (see http://www.chiark .greenend.org.uk/~sgtatham/putty/download.html**).**

It is best practice in SSH implementation to disable the less secure version 1 of the SSH protocol (SSH-1) and use only SSH-2. In addition, employ role-based access control (RBAC), or another access control mechanism, that forces users to use defined login accounts, to enforce accountability.

Summary

With the adoption of cloud technology comes many challenges to an organization, especially in the area of secure computing. Managing the security of the organization's private cloud as well as supervising the actions of the Cloud Services Provider can well become a monumental task.

To help lessen the size of the task, clearly defined management initiatives must be instituted which delineate clear ownership and responsibility of the data security. Therefore in this chapter we examined detective, preventative, and best practice controls to ensure that virtualization doesn't break the security posture of the company.

To this end we looked at the need and function of security policies, and gave some examples of what types of polices are usually developed. We also touched upon computer intrusion detection and response and the creation of a Computer Security Incident Response Team (CSIRT).

We spent the rest of the chapter examining various virtualization security management best practices. We looked first at some specific threats to the virtual environment, then examined a few general security best practices, and then ended with details of hardening techniques that are unique to virtualized systems.

Notes

1. "Attacking and Defending Virtual Environments," the Burton Group, `http://www.burtongroup.com/Guest/Srms/AttackingDefendingVirtual.aspx`

2. Virtual Machine Security Guidelines Version 1.0, September 2007, the Center for Internet Security

3. "Attacking and Defending Virtual Environments," the Burton Group, `http://www.burtongroup.com/Guest/Srms/AttackingDefendingVirtual.aspx`

4. "An Empirical Study into the Security Exposure to Hosts of Hostile Virtualized Environments," Tavis Ormandy, Google, Inc.

5. `http://theinvisiblethings.blogspot.com/2006/06/introducing-blue-pill.html`

6. "Attacking and Defending Virtual Environments," the Burton Group, `http://www.burtongroup.com/Guest/Srms/AttackingDefendingVirtual.aspx`

7. Virtual Machine Security Guidelines, Version 1.0, the Center for Internet Security

8. "Virtual Machine Security Technical Implementation Guide," U.S. Department of Defense Information Systems Agency, `http://iase.disa.mil/stigs/stig/vm_stig_v2r2.pdf`

9. "CIS Level 1 Benchmark for Virtual Machines," Center for Internet Security, `http://www.cisecurity.org/bench_vm.htm`

10. "Attacking and Defending Virtual Environments," the Burton Group, `http://www.burtongroup.com/Guest/Srms/AttackingDefendingVirtual.aspx`

11. Benchmark for Xen 3.2 Version 1.0, May 2008, the Center for Internet Security (CIS)

12. "An Empirical Study into the Security Exposure to Hosts of Hostile Virtualized Environments, " Tavis Ormandy, Google, Inc.

Cloud Computing Security Architecture

It is much more secure to be feared than to be loved.
—Niccolo Machiavelli

With all the advantages of the cloud paradigm and its potential for decreasing costs and reducing the time required to start new initiatives, cloud security will always be a major concern. Virtualized resources, geographically dispersed servers, and co-location of processing and storage pose challenges and opportunities for cloud providers and users.

The security posture of a cloud system is based on its security architecture. While there is no standard definition for security architecture, the Open Security Alliance (OSA) defines *security architecture* as "the design artifacts that describe how the security controls (= security countermeasures) are positioned, and how they relate to the overall IT Architecture. These controls serve the purpose to maintain the system's quality attributes, among them confidentiality, integrity, availability, accountability and assurance" (`http://www.opensecurityarchitecture.org/cms/definitions`).

A second definition developed by the Information Security Society Switzerland (ISSS) describes a *security architecture* as "a cohesive security design, which addresses the requirements (e.g., authentication, authorization, etc.) and in particular the risks of a particular environment/scenario, and specifies what security controls are to be applied where. The design process should be reproducible" (`http://www.isss.ch/fileadmin/publ/agsa/Security_Architecture.pdf`).

In this chapter, the general security architecture issues involved, the architectural components of trusted cloud computing, core security architectural functions, and the potential of autonomic systems to implement secure architectures will be presented.

Architectural Considerations

A variety of factors affect the implementation and performance of cloud security architecture. There are general issues involving regulatory requirements, adherence to standards, security management, information classification, and security awareness. Then there are more specific architecturally related areas, including trusted hardware and software, providing for a secure execution environment, establishing secure communications, and hardware augmentation through microarchitectures. These important concepts are addressed in this section.

General Issues

A variety of topics influence and directly affect the cloud security architecture. They include such factors as compliance, security management, administrative issues, controls, and security awareness.

Compliance with legal regulations should be supported by the cloud security architecture. As a corollary, the cloud security policy should address classification of information, what entities can potentially access information, under what conditions the access has to be provided, the geographical jurisdiction of the stored data, and whether or not the access is appropriate. Proper controls should be determined and verified with assurance methods, and appropriate personnel awareness education should be put in place.

Compliance

In a public cloud environment, the provider does not normally inform the clients of the storage location of their data. In fact, the distribution of processing and data storage is one of the cloud's fundamental characteristics. However, the cloud provider should cooperate to consider the client's data location requirements. In addition, the cloud vendor should provide transparency to the client by supplying information about storage used, processing characteristics, and other relevant account information. Another compliance issue is the accessibility of a client's data by the provider's system engineers and certain other employees. This factor is a necessary part of providing and maintaining cloud services, but the act of acquiring sensitive information should be monitored, controlled, and protected by safeguards such as separation of duties. In situations where information is stored in a foreign jurisdiction, the ability of local law enforcement agencies to access a client's sensitive data is a concern. For example, this scenario might occur when a government entity conducts a computer forensics investigation of a cloud provider under suspicion of illegal activity.

The cloud provider's claims for data protection and compliance must be backed up by relevant certifications, logging, and auditing. In particular, at a minimum, a cloud provider should undergo a Statement on Auditing Standard # 70 (SAS 70) "Service Organizations" Type II Audit (www.SaS70.com). This audit evaluates a service organization's internal controls to determine whether accepted best practices are being applied to protect client information. Cloud vendors are required to undergo subsequent audits to retain their SAS 70 Type II Audit certification.

Another source of direction for the cloud provider is given in Domain 4 of the "Cloud Security Alliance Security Guidance for Critical Areas of Focus in Cloud Computing" (http://www.cloudsecurityalliance.org/). Domain 4 stresses the roles of cloud customers, cloud providers, and auditors with respect to compliance responsibilities, the requirements of compliance evidence, and the need to acquaint assessors with the unique characteristics of cloud computation.

A related issue is the management policy associated with data stored in the cloud. When a client's engagement with the cloud provider is terminated, compliance and privacy requirements have to be considered. In some cases, information has to be preserved according to regulatory requirements and in other instances the provider should not hold a client's data in primary or backup storage if the client believes it has been destroyed. If stored in a foreign jurisdiction, the data might be subject to that country's privacy laws and not the laws applicable in the client's geographic location.

The evolution and application of appropriate cloud standards focused on legal requirements will also serve to meet the cloud's compliance requirements and provide the necessary protections. A number of standards organizations have joined forces under the title of the Cloud Standards Coordination Working Group to develop a cloud computing standardization approach. The Working Group includes the Object Management Group, the Distributed Management Task Force, the TeleManagement (TM) Forum, the Organization for the Advancement of Structured Information Standards, the Open Grid Forum, the Cloud Security Alliance, the Open Cloud Consortium, the Storage and Network Industry Association, and the Cloud Computing Interoperability Forum. Standards efforts are discussed in more detail in Chapter 7.

Security Management

Security architecture involves effective security management to realize the benefits of cloud computation. Proper cloud security management and administration should identify management issues in critical areas such as access control, vulnerability analysis, change control, incident response, fault tolerance, and disaster recovery and business continuity planning. These areas are enhanced and supported by the proper application and verification of cloud security controls.

Controls

The objective of cloud security controls is to reduce vulnerabilities to a tolerable level and minimize the effects of an attack. To achieve this, an organization must determine what impact an attack might have, and the likelihood of loss. Examples of loss are compromise of sensitive information, financial embezzlement, loss of reputation, and physical destruction of resources. The process of analyzing various threat scenarios and producing a representative value for the estimated potential loss is known as a *risk analysis (RA)*. Controls function as countermeasures for vulnerabilities. There are many kinds of controls, but they are generally categorized into one of the following four types:[1]

- **Deterrent controls** — Reduce the likelihood of a deliberate attack.
- **Preventative controls** — Protect vulnerabilities and make an attack unsuccessful or reduce its impact. Preventative controls inhibit attempts to violate security policy.
- **Corrective controls** — Reduce the effect of an attack.
- **Detective controls** — Discover attacks and trigger preventative or corrective controls. Detective controls warn of violations or attempted violations of security policy and include such controls as intrusion detection systems, organizational policies, video cameras, and motion detectors.

OMB CIRCULAR A-130

The U.S. Office of Management and Budget Circular A-130, revised November 30, 2000, requires that a review of the security controls for each major U.S. government application be performed at least every three years. For general support systems, OMB Circular A-130 requires that the security controls are either reviewed by an independent audit or self-reviewed. Audits can be self-administered or independent (either internal or external). The essential difference between a self-audit and an independent audit is objectivity; however, some systems may require a fully independent review.

Complementary Actions

Additional activities involved in cloud security management include the following:

- Management and monitoring of service levels and service-level agreements
- Acquisition of adequate data to identify and analyze problem situations through instrumentation and dashboards

- Reduction of the loss of critical information caused by lack of controls.

- Proper management of data on an organization's distributed computing resources. Data centralized on the cloud reduces the potential for data loss in organizations with large numbers of laptop computers and other personal computing devices.

- Monitoring of centrally stored cloud information, as opposed to having to examine data distributed throughout an organization on a variety of computing and storage devices.

- Provisioning for rapid recovery from problem situations.

Cloud security management should also foster improved capabilities to conduct forensic analysis on cloud-based information using a network forensic model. This model will provide for more rapid acquisition and verification of evidence, such as taking advantage of automatic hashing that is applied when storing data on a cloud.

Cloud security management can also be enhanced by the selective use of automation and by the application of emerging cloud management standards to areas such as interoperable security mechanisms, quality of service, accounting, provisioning, and API specifications. APIs provide for control of cloud resources through program interfaces, and remote APIs should be managed to ensure that they are documented and consistent.

Cloud security management should address applications with the goal of enterprise cost containment through scalability, pay as you go models, on-demand implementation and provisioning, and reallocation of information management operational activities to the cloud.

Information Classification

Another major area that relates to compliance and can affect the cloud security architecture is information classification. The information classification process also supports disaster recovery planning and business continuity planning.

Information Classification Objectives

There are several good reasons to classify information. Not all data has the same value to an organization. For example, some data is more valuable to upper management, because it aids them in making strategic long-range or short-range business direction decisions. Some data, such as trade secrets, formulas, and new product information, is so valuable that its loss could create a significant problem for the enterprise in the marketplace — either by creating public embarrassment or by causing a lack of credibility.

For these reasons, it is obvious that information classification has a higher, enterprise-level benefit. Information stored in a cloud environment can have an impact on a business globally, not just on the business unit or line operation levels. Its primary purpose is to enhance confidentiality, integrity, and availability (the CIA triad described in Chapter 3), and minimize risks to the information. In addition, by focusing the protection mechanisms and controls on the information areas that most need it, you achieve a more efficient cost-to-benefit ratio.

Information classification has the longest history in the government sector. Its value has long been established, and it is a required component when securing trusted systems. In this sector, information classification is used primarily to prevent the unauthorized disclosure of information and the resultant failure of confidentiality.

Information classification supports privacy requirements and enables regulatory compliance. A company might wish to employ classification to maintain a competitive edge in a tough marketplace. There might also be sound legal reasons for an organization to employ information classification on the cloud, such as to minimize liability or to protect valuable business information.

Information Classification Benefits

In addition to the aforementioned reasons, employing information classification has several clear benefits to an organization engaged in cloud computing. Some of these benefits are as follows:

- It demonstrates an organization's commitment to security protections.
- It helps identify which information is the most sensitive or vital to an organization.
- It supports the tenets of confidentiality, integrity, and availability as it pertains to data.
- It helps identify which protections apply to which information.
- It might be required for regulatory, compliance, or legal reasons.

Information Classification Concepts

The information that an organization processes must be classified according to the organization's sensitivity to its loss or disclosure. The information system owner is responsible for defining the sensitivity level of the data. Classification according to a defined classification scheme enables security controls to be properly implemented.

The following classification terms are typical of those used in the private sector and are applicable to cloud data:

- **Public data** — Information that is similar to unclassified information; all of a company's information that does not fit into any of the next categories can be considered public. While its unauthorized disclosure may be against policy, it is not expected to impact seriously or adversely the organization, its employees, and/or its customers.

- **Sensitive data** — Information that requires a higher level of classification than normal data. This information is protected from a loss of confidentiality as well as from a loss of integrity due to an unauthorized alteration. This classification applies to information that requires special precautions to ensure its integrity by protecting it from unauthorized modification or deletion. It is information that requires a higher-than-normal assurance of accuracy and completeness.

- **Private data** — This classification applies to personal information that is intended for use within the organization. Its unauthorized disclosure could seriously and adversely impact the organization and/or its employees. For example, salary levels and medical information are considered private.

- **Confidential data** — This classification applies to the most sensitive business information that is intended strictly for use within the organization. Its unauthorized disclosure could seriously and adversely impact the organization, its stockholders, its business partners, and/or its customers. This information is exempt from disclosure under the provisions of the Freedom of Information Act or other applicable federal laws or regulations. For example, information about new product development, trade secrets, and merger negotiations is considered confidential.

An organization may use a high, medium, or low classification scheme based upon its CIA needs and whether it requires high, medium, or low protective controls. For example, a system and its information may require a high degree of integrity and availability, yet have no need for confidentiality.

The designated owners of information are responsible for determining data classification levels, subject to executive management review. Table 6-1 shows a simple High/Medium/Low (H/M/L) data classification schema for sensitive information.

Table 6-1: High/Medium/Low Classifications

CLASSIFICATION	IMPACT
High	Could cause loss of life, imprisonment, major financial loss, or require legal remediation if the information is compromised
Medium	Could cause noticeable financial loss if the information is compromised
Low	Would cause only minor financial loss or require minor administrative action for correction if the information is compromised

From NIST SP 800-26, "Security Self-Assessment Guide for Information Technology Systems."

Classification Criteria

Several criteria may be used to determine the classification of an information object:

- **Value** — Value is the number one commonly used criteria for classifying data in the private sector. If the information is valuable to an organization or its competitors, then it needs to be classified.

- **Age** — The classification of information might be lowered if the information's value decreases over time. In the U.S. Department of Defense, some classified documents are automatically declassified after a predetermined time period has passed.

- **Useful life** — If the information has been made obsolete due to new information, substantial changes in the company, or other reasons, the information can often be declassified.

- **Personal association** — If information is personally associated with specific individuals or is addressed by a privacy law, it might need to be classified. For example, investigative information that reveals informant names might need to remain classified.

Information Classification Procedures

There are several steps in establishing a classification system. These are the steps in priority order:

1. Identify the appropriate administrator and data custodian. The data custodian is responsible for protecting the information, running backups, and performing data restoration.

2. Specify the criteria for classifying and labeling the information.

3. Classify the data by its owner, who is subject to review by a supervisor.

4. Specify and document any exceptions to the classification policy.

5. Specify the controls that will be applied to each classification level.

6. Specify the termination procedures for declassifying the information or for transferring custody of the information to another entity.

7. Create an enterprise awareness program about the classification controls.

Distribution of Classified Information

External distribution of sensitive or classified information stored on a cloud is often necessary, and the inherent security vulnerabilities need to be addressed. Some of the instances when this distribution is required are as follows:

■ **Court order** — Classified or sensitive information might need to be disclosed to comply with a court order.

■ **Government contracts** — Government contractors might need to disclose classified or sensitive information in accordance with (IAW) the procurement agreements related to a government project.

■ **Senior-level approval** — A senior-level executive might authorize the release of classified or sensitive information to external entities or organizations. This release might require the signing of a confidentiality agreement by the external party.

Employee Termination

It is important to understand the impact of employee terminations on the integrity of information stored in a cloud environment. This issue applies to employees of the cloud client as well as the cloud provider. Typically, there are two types of terminations, friendly and unfriendly, and both require specific actions.

Friendly terminations should be accomplished by implementing a standard set of procedures for outgoing or transferring employees. This activity normally includes the following:[2]

■ The removal of access privileges, computer accounts, authentication tokens.

■ The briefing on the continuing responsibilities of the terminated employee for confidentiality and privacy.

■ The return of company computing property, such as laptops.

■ Continued availability of data. In both the manual and the electronic worlds, this may involve documenting procedures or filing schemes, such as how documents are stored on the hard disk and how they are backed up. Employees should be instructed whether or not to "clean up" their PC before leaving.

■ If cryptography is used to protect data, the availability of cryptographic keys to management personnel must be ensured.

Given the potential for adverse consequences during an unfriendly termination, organizations should do the following:

■ System access should be terminated as quickly as possible when an employee is leaving a position under less-than-friendly terms. If employees are to be fired, system access should be removed at the same time (or just before) the employees are notified of their dismissal.

- When an employee resigns and it can be reasonably assumed that it is on unfriendly terms, system access should be immediately terminated, or as soon as feasible.

- During the *notice of termination* period, it may be necessary to restrict the individual to a given area and function. This may be particularly true for employees capable of changing programs or modifying the system or applications.

- In some cases, physical removal from the offices may be necessary.

In either scenario, network access and system rights must be strictly controlled.

Security Awareness, Training, and Education

Security awareness is often overlooked as an element affecting cloud security architecture because most of a security practitioner's time is spent on controls, intrusion detection, risk assessment, and proactively or reactively administering security. Employees must understand how their actions, even seemingly insignificant actions, can greatly impact the overall security position of an organization.

Employees of both the cloud client and the cloud provider must be aware of the need to secure information and protect the information assets of an enterprise. Operators need ongoing training in the skills that are required to fulfill their job functions securely, and security practitioners need training to implement and maintain the necessary security controls, particularly when using or providing cloud services.

All employees need education in the basic concepts of security and its benefits to an organization. The benefits of the three pillars of security awareness training — awareness, training, and education — will manifest themselves through an improvement in the behavior and attitudes of personnel and through a significant improvement in an enterprise's security.

The purpose of computer security awareness, training, and education is to enhance security by doing the following:

- Improving awareness of the need to protect system resources

- Developing skills and knowledge so computer users can perform their jobs more securely

- Building in-depth knowledge, as needed, to design, implement, or operate security programs for organizations and systems

An effective computer security awareness and training program requires proper planning, implementation, maintenance, and periodic evaluation. In general, a computer security awareness and training program should encompass the following seven steps:[3]

1. Identify program scope, goals, and objectives.

2. Identify training staff.

3. Identify target audiences.

4. Motivate management and employees.

5. Administer the program.

6. Maintain the program.

7. Evaluate the program.

Making cloud system users and providers aware of their security responsibilities and teaching them correct practices helps change their behavior. It also supports individual accountability because without knowledge of the necessary security measures and to how to use them, personnel cannot be truly accountable for their actions.

Security Awareness

As opposed to training, the security awareness of an organization refers to the degree to which its personnel are collectively aware of the importance of security and security controls. In addition to the benefits and objectives previously mentioned, security awareness programs also have the following benefits:

- They can reduce the unauthorized actions attempted by personnel.
- They can significantly increase the effectiveness of the protection controls.
- They help to prevent the fraud, waste, and abuse of computing resources.

Personnel are considered "security aware" when they clearly understand the need for security, how security affects viability and the bottom line, and the daily risks to cloud computing resources.

It is important to have periodic awareness sessions to orient new employees and refresh senior employees. The material should always be direct, simple, and clear. It should be fairly motivational and should not contain a lot of techno-jargon, and you should convey it in a style that the audience easily understands. These sessions are most effective when they demonstrate how the security interests of the organization parallel the interests of the audience.

The following activities can be used to improve security within an organization without incurring large costs or draining resources:

- **Live/interactive presentations** — Lectures, videos, and computer-based training (CBT)
- **Publishing/distribution** — Posters, company newsletters, bulletins, and the intranet
- **Incentives** — Awards and recognition for security-related achievements

■ **Reminders** — Log-in banner messages and marketing paraphernalia such as mugs, pens, sticky notes, and mouse pads

Training and Education

Training is different from awareness in that it provides security information in a more formalized manner, such as classes, workshops, or individualized instruction. The following types of training are related to cloud security:

■ Security-related job training for operators and specific users

■ Awareness training for specific departments or personnel groups with security-sensitive positions

■ Technical security training for IT support personnel and system administrators

■ Advanced training for security practitioners and information systems auditors

■ Security training for senior managers, functional managers, and business unit managers

In-depth training and education for systems personnel, auditors, and security professionals is critical, and typically necessary for career development. In addition, specific product training for cloud security software and hardware is vital to the protection of the enterprise.

Motivating the personnel is always the prime directive of any training, and their understanding of the value of security's impact to the bottom line is also vital. A common training technique is to create hypothetical cloud security vulnerability scenarios and then solicit input on possible solutions or outcomes.

Trusted Cloud Computing

Trusted cloud computing can be viewed as a computer security architecture that is designed to protect cloud systems from malicious intrusions and attacks, and ensure that computing resources will act in a specific, predictable manner as intended. A trusted cloud computing system will protect data in use by hypervisors and applications, protect against unauthorized access to information, provide for strong authentication, apply encryption to protect sensitive data that resides on stolen or lost devices, and support compliance through hardware and software mechanisms.

Trusted Computing Characteristics

In a cloud computational system, multiple processes might be running concurrently. Each process has the capability to access certain memory locations and to execute a subset of the computer's instruction set. The execution and memory space assigned to each process is called a *protection domain*. This domain can be extended to virtual memory, which increases the apparent size of real memory by using disk storage. The purpose of establishing a protection domain is to protect programs from all unauthorized modification or executional interference.

A *trusted computing base (TCB)* is the total combination of protection mechanisms within a computer system, which includes the hardware, software, and firmware that are trusted to enforce a security policy. Because the TCB components are responsible for enforcing the security policy of a computing system, these components must be protected from malicious and untrusted processes. The TCB must also provide for memory protection and ensure that the processes from one domain do not access memory locations of another domain. The *security perimeter* is the boundary that separates the TCB from the remainder of the system. A *trusted path* must also exist so that users can access the TCB without being compromised by other processes or users. Therefore, a *trusted computer system* is one that employs the necessary hardware and software assurance measures to enable its use in processing multiple levels of classified or sensitive information. This system meets the specified requirements for reliability and security.

Another element associated with trusted computing is the *trusted platform module (TPM)*. The TPM stores cryptographic keys that can be used to attest to the operating state of a computing platform and to verify that the hardware and software configuration has not been modified. However, the standard TPM cannot be used in cloud computing because it does not operate in the virtualized cloud environment. To permit a TPM version to perform in the cloud, specifications have been generated for a virtual TPM (VTM)[4] that provides software instances of TPMs for each virtual machine operating on a trusted server.

Trusted computing also provides the capability to ensure that software that processes information complies with specified usage policies and is running unmodified and isolated from other software on the system. In addition, a trusted computing system must be capable of enforcing mandatory access control (MAC) rules. MAC rules are discussed in more detail later in this chapter.

Numerous trust-related issues should be raised with, and satisfied by, a cloud provider. They range from concerns about security, performance, cost, control, availability, resiliency, and vendor lock in. Following are some of the critical questions that should be asked to address these concerns:

- Do I have any control or choice over where my information will be stored? Where will my data reside and what are the security and privacy laws in effect in those locations?
- Are your cloud operations available for physical inspection?
- Can you provide an estimate of historical downtimes at your operation?

■ Are there any exit charges or penalties for migrating from your cloud to another vendor's cloud operation? Do you delete all my data from your systems if I move to another vendor?

■ Can you provide documentation of your disaster recovery policies and procedures and how they are implemented?

These questions related to basic trust issues associated with cloud computing arise from the characteristics and architecture of cloud resources. The cloud handles multi-party, co-located applications, and this capability brings with it corresponding security issues and requirements to minimize risk. The cloud provider must conduct quality risk assessments at regular, known intervals to meet the trust expectations of clients and auditors, and demonstrate that risk is being managed effectively. Additional factors that inspire trust include the following:

■ Use of industry-accepted standards.

■ Provision for interoperability and transparency.

■ Robust authentication and authorization mechanisms in access control.

■ Management of changing personnel and relationships in both the cloud client and provider organizations.

■ Establishment of accountability with respect to security and privacy requirements in a multi-party, flexible service delivery setting.

■ Use of information system security assurance techniques and metrics to establish the effectiveness of hardware and software protection mechanisms.

■ Establishment of effective policies and procedures to address multiple legal jurisdictions associated with cloud international services and compliance requirements.

■ Application of Information Rights Management (IRM) cryptographic techniques to protect sensitive cloud-based documents and provide an audit trail of accesses and policy changes. IRM prevents protected documents from screen capture, being printed, faxed, or forwarded, and can prohibit messages and attachments from being accessed after a specified period of time.

Also, because of the high volume of data that is being moved around in various locations, authorization privileges and rights management constraints must be attached to the data itself to restrict access only to authorized users.

Because of legal and forensic requirements, a trusted cloud provider should also have a Security Information and Event Management (SIEM) capability that can manage records and logs in a manner that meets legal constraints. An SEIM is a software mechanism that provides for centralized acquisition, storage, and analysis of recorded events and logs generated by other tools on an enterprise network.

Information stored in a SEIM can be used for data mining to discover significant trends and occurrences, and to provide for reliable and legally acceptable storage of information. It can also be used by report generators, and provide for backup of log data that might be lost at the source of the data.

Secure Execution Environments and Communications

In a cloud environment, applications are run on different servers in a distributed mode. These applications interact with the outside world and other applications and may contain sensitive information whose inappropriate access would be harmful to a client. In addition, cloud computing is increasingly being used to manage and store huge amounts of data in database applications that are also co-located with other users' information. Thus, it is extremely important for the cloud supplier to provide a secure execution environment and secure communications for client applications and storage.

Secure Execution Environment

Configuring computing platforms for secure execution is a complex task; and in many instances it is not performed properly because of the large number of parameters that are involved. This provides opportunities for malware to exploit vulnerabilities, such as downloading code embedded in data and having the code executed at a high privilege level.

In cloud computing, the major burden of establishing a secure execution environment is transferred from the client to the cloud provider. However, protected data transfers must be established through strong authentication mechanisms, and the client must have practices in place to address the privacy and confidentiality of information that is exchanged with the cloud. In fact, the client's port to the cloud might provide an attack path if not properly provisioned with security measures. Therefore, the client needs assurance that computations and data exchanges are conducted in a secure environment. This assurance is affected by trust enabled by cryptographic methods. Also, research into areas such as compiler-based virtual machines promises a more secure execution environment for operating systems.

Another major concern in secure execution of code is the widespread use of "unsafe" programming languages such as C and C++ instead of more secure languages such as object-oriented Java and structured, object-oriented C#.

Secure Communications

As opposed to having managed, secure communications among the computing resources internal to an organization, movement of applications to the cloud requires a reevaluation of communications security. These communications apply to both data in motion and data at rest.

Secure cloud communications involves the structures, transmission methods, transport formats, and security measures that provide confidentiality, integrity, availability, and authentication for transmissions over private and public communications networks. Secure cloud computing communications should ensure the following:

- **Confidentiality** — Ensures that only those who are supposed to access data can retrieve it. Loss of confidentiality can occur through the intentional release of private company information or through a misapplication of network rights. Some of the elements of telecommunications used to ensure confidentiality are as follows:

  - Network security protocols
  - Network authentication services
  - Data encryption services

- **Integrity** — Ensures that data has not been changed due to an accident or malice. Integrity is the guarantee that the message sent is the message received and that the message is not intentionally or unintentionally altered. Integrity also contains the concept of nonrepudiation of a message source. Some of the constituents of integrity are as follows:

  - Firewall services
  - Communications Security Management
  - Intrusion detection services

- **Availability** — Ensures that data is accessible when and where it is needed, and that connectivity is accessible when needed, allowing authorized users to access the network or systems. Also included in that assurance is the guarantee that security services for the security practitioner are usable when they are needed. Some of the elements that are used to ensure availability are as follows:

  - Fault tolerance for data availability, such as backups and redundant disk systems
  - Acceptable logins and operating process performances
  - Reliable and interoperable security processes and network security mechanisms

APIs

Common vulnerabilities such as weak antivirus software, unattended computing platforms, poor passwords, weak authentication mechanisms, and inadequate intrusion detection that can impact communications must be more stringently analyzed, and proper APIs must be used.

For example, in using IaaS, a cloud client typically communicates with cloud server instances through Representational State Transfer (REST) client/server model or Simple Object Access Protocol (SOAP) APIs. REST is a software architecture such as used in the World Wide Web and was developed with the HTTP/1.1 protocol. With SOAP, applications running on different operating systems and using different programming languages can communicate with each other.

Virtual Private Networks

Another important method to secure cloud communications is through a virtual private network (VPN). A VPN is created by building a secure communications link between two nodes by emulating the properties of a point-to-point private link. A VPN can be used to facilitate secure remote access into the cloud, securely connect two networks together, or create a secure data tunnel within a network.

The portion of the link in which the private data is encapsulated is known as the *tunnel*. It may be referred to as a secure, encrypted tunnel, although it's more accurately defined as an encapsulated tunnel, as encryption may or may not be used. To emulate a point-to-point link, data is encapsulated, or wrapped, with a header that provides routing information. Most often the data is encrypted for confidentiality. This encrypted part of the link is considered the actual virtual private network connection. Figure 6-1 shows a common VPN configuration with example IP addresses for remote access into an organization's intranet through the Internet. Address 192.168.123.2 designates the organization's router.

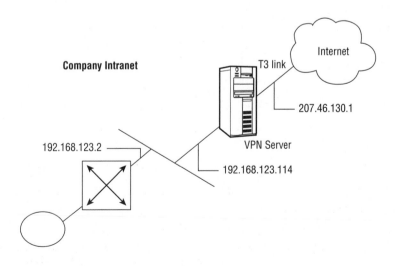

Figure 6-1: VPN configuration

The two general types of VPNs relevant to cloud computing are remote access and network-to-network. These VPN types are described in the following sections.

Remote Access VPNs

A VPN can be configured to provide remote access to corporate resources over the public Internet to maintain confidentiality and integrity. This configuration enables the remote user to utilize whatever local ISP is available to access the Internet without forcing the user to make a long-distance or 800 call to a third-party access provider. Using the connection to the local ISP, the VPN software creates a virtual private network between the dial-up user and the corporate VPN server across the Internet. Figure 6-2 shows a remote user VPN connection.

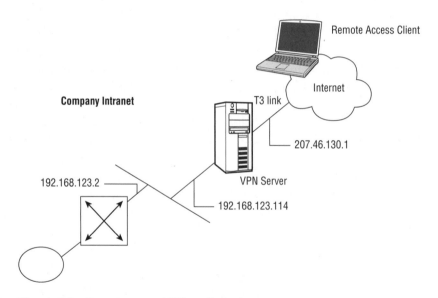

Figure 6-2: Remote access VPN configuration

Network-to-Network VPNs

A VPN is commonly used to connect two networks, perhaps the main corporate LAN and a remote branch office LAN, through the Internet. This connection can use either dedicated lines to the Internet or dial-up connections to the Internet. However, the corporate hub router that acts as a VPN server must be connected to a local ISP with a dedicated line if the VPN server needs to be available 24/7. The VPN software uses the connection to the local ISP to create a VPN tunnel between the branch office router and the corporate hub router across the Internet. Figure 6-3 shows a remote branch office connected to the corporate main office using a VPN tunnel through the Internet.

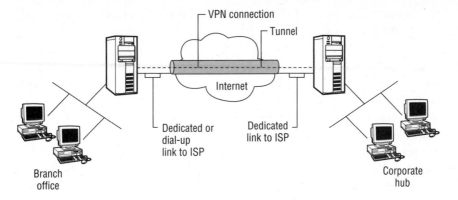

Figure 6-3: A network-to-network VPN configuration

VPN Tunneling

Tunneling is a method of transferring data from one network to another network by encapsulating the packets in an additional header. The additional header provides routing information so that the encapsulated payload can traverse the intermediate networks, as shown in Figure 6-4.

For a tunnel to be established, both the tunnel client and the tunnel server must be using the same tunneling protocol. Tunneling technology can be based on either a Layer 2 or a Layer 3 tunneling protocol. These layers correspond to the Open Systems Interconnection (OSI) Reference Model.

Tunneling, and the use of a VPN, is not intended as a substitute for encryption/decryption. In cases where a high level of security is necessary, the strongest possible encryption should be used within the VPN itself, and tunneling should serve only as a convenience.

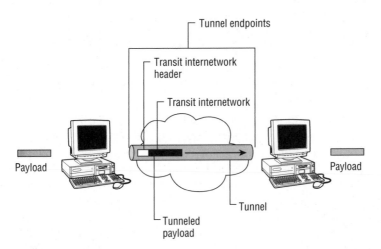

Figure 6-4: A VPN tunnel and payload

A popular tunneling protocol for network-to-network connectivity is IPSec, which encapsulates IP packets in an additional IP header. IPSec operates at the Network Layer of the OSI Reference Model and allows multiple simultaneous tunnels. IPSec contains the functionality to encrypt and authenticate IP data. It is built into the new IPv6 standard and is used as an add-on to the current IPv4. IPSec tunnel mode allows IP packets to be encrypted and then encapsulated in an IP header to be sent across a corporate IP Intranetwork or a public IP Internetwork, such as the Internet.

IPSec uses an authentication header (AH) to provide source authentication and integrity without encryption, and it uses the Encapsulating Security Payload (ESP) to provide authentication and integrity along with encryption. With IPSec, only the sender and recipient know the key. If the authentication data is valid, then the recipient knows that the communication came from the sender and was not changed in transit.

Public Key Infrastructure and Encryption Key Management

To secure communications, data that is being exchanged with a cloud should be encrypted, calls to remote servers should be examined for imbedded malware, and digital certificates should be employed and managed. A certification process can be used to bind individuals to their public keys as used in public key cryptography. A *certificate authority (CA)* acts as notary by verifying a person's identity and issuing a certificate that vouches for a public key of the named individual. This certification agent signs the certificate with its own private key. Therefore, the individual is verified as the sender if that person's public key opens the data.

The certificate contains the subject's name, the subject's public key, the name of the certificate authority, and the period in which the certificate is valid. To verify the CA's signature, its public key must be cross-certified with another CA. (The X.509 standard defines the format for public key certificates.) This certificate is then sent to a repository, which holds the certificates and *certificate revocation lists (CRLs)* that denote the revoked certificates. Figure 6-5 illustrates the use of digital certificates in a transaction between a subscribing entity and a transacting party. Digital certificates are discussed in more detail in the following sections.

The integration of digital signatures and certificates and the other services required for e-commerce is called the *public key infrastructure (PKI)*. These services provide integrity, access control, confidentiality, authentication, and nonrepudiation for electronic transactions. The PKI includes the following elements:

- Digital certificates
- Certificate authority (CA)
- Registration authorities

- Policies and procedures
- Certificate revocation
- Nonrepudiation support
- Timestamping
- Lightweight Directory Access Protocol (LDAP)
- Security-enabled applications

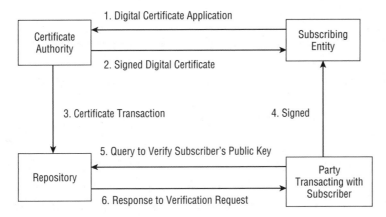

Figure 6-5: A transaction with digital certificates

Digital Certificates

The digital certificate and management of the certificate are major components of PKI. Remember: The purpose of a digital certificate is to verify to all that an individual's public key — posted on a public "key ring" — is actually his or hers. A trusted, third-party CA can verify that the public key is that of the named individual and then issue a certificate attesting to that fact. The CA accomplishes the certification by digitally signing the individual's public key and associated information.

Certificates and CRLs can be held in a repository, with responsibilities defined between the repository and the CA. The repository access protocol determines how these responsibilities are assigned. In one protocol, the repository interacts with other repositories, CAs, and users. The CA deposits its certificates and CRLs into the repository. The users can then access the repository for this information.

Directories and X.500

In PKI, a repository is usually referred to as a *directory*. The directory contains entries associated with an object class. An object class can refer to individuals or other computer-related entities. The class defines the attributes of the object. Attributes for PKI are defined in RFC 2587, "Internet X.509 Public Key Infrastructure LDAP v2 Schema," by Boeyen, Howes, and Richard, published in April 1999. Additional information on attributes can be found in RFC 2079, "Definition of an X.500 Attribute Type and an Object Class to Hold Uniform Resource Identifiers (URLs)," by M. Smith, published in January 1997.

The X.509 certificate standard defines the authentication bases for the X.500 directory. The X.500 directory stores information about individuals and objects in a distributed database residing on network servers. Some of the principal definitions associated with X.500 include the following:

- Directory user agents (DUAs) — Clients
- Directory server agents (DSAs) — Servers
- Directory Service Protocol (DSP) — Enables information exchanges between DSAs
- Directory Access Protocol (DAP) — Enables information exchanges from a DUA to a DSA
- Directory Information Shadowing Protocol (DISP) — Used by a DSA to duplicate or "shadow" some or all of its contents

DSAs accept requests from anonymous sources as well as authenticated requests. They share information through a *chaining* mechanism.

The Lightweight Directory Access Protocol

The Lightweight Directory Access Protocol (LDAP) was developed as a more efficient version of the DAP and has evolved into a second version (see RFC 1777, "Lightweight Directory Access Protocol," by Yeong, Y., T. Howes, and S. Killie, 1995). LDAP servers communicate through referrals — that is, a directory receiving a request for information it does not have will query the tables of remote directories. If it finds a directory with the required entry, it sends a referral to the requesting directory.

LDAP provides a standard format to access the certificate directories. These directories are stored on network LDAP servers and provide public keys and corresponding X.509 certificates for the enterprise. A directory contains information such as individuals' names, addresses, phone numbers, and public key certificates. The standards under X.500 define the protocols and information models for computer directory services that are independent of the platforms and other related entities. LDAP servers are subject to attacks that affect availability and integrity. For example, denial-of-service attacks on an LDAP server could prevent access to the CRLs and thus permit the use of a revoked certificate.

The DAP protocol in X.500 was unwieldy and led to most client implementations using LDAP. LDAP version 3 provides extensions that offer shadowing and chaining capabilities.

X.509 Certificates

The original X.509 certificate (CCITT, *The Directory-Authentication Framework*, Recommendation X.509, 1988) was developed to provide the authentication foundation for the X.500 directory. Since then, a version 2 and a version 3 have been developed. Version 2 of the X.509 certificate addresses the reuse of names, and version 3 provides for certificate extensions to the core certificate fields. These extensions can be used as needed by different users and different applications. A version of X.509 that takes into account the requirements of the Internet was published by the IETF (see RFC 2459, "Internet X.509 Public Key Infrastructure Certificate and CRL Profile," by Housley, R., W. Ford, W. Polk, and D. Solo, 1999).

The Consultation Committee, International Telephone and Telegraph, International Telecommunications Union (CCITT-ITU)/International Organization for Standardization (ISO) has defined the basic format of an X.509 certificate. This structure is outlined in Figure 6-6.

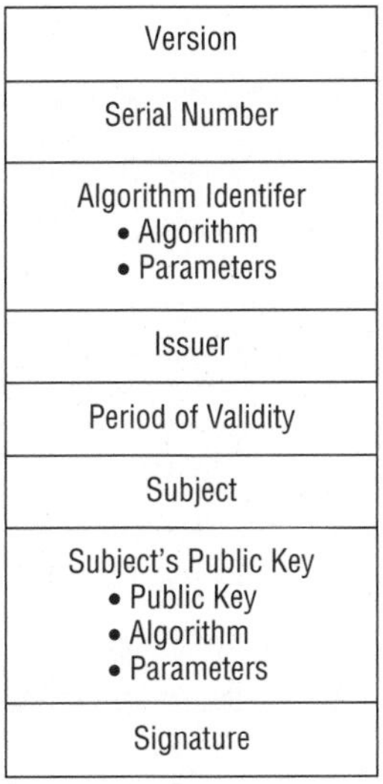

Version
Serial Number
Algorithm Identifer • Algorithm • Parameters
Issuer
Period of Validity
Subject
Subject's Public Key • Public Key • Algorithm • Parameters
Signature

Figure 6-6: The CCITT-ITU/ ISO X.509 certificate format

If version 3 certificates are used, the optional extensions field can be used. It comes before the signature field components in the certificate. Some typical extensions are the entity's name and supporting identity information, the attributes of the key, certificate policy information, and the type of the subject. The digital signature serves as a tamper-evident envelope.

Some of the different types of certificates that are issued include the following:

- **CA certificates** — Issued to CAs, these certificates contain the public keys used to verify digital signatures on CRLs and certificates.

- **End entity certificates** — Issued to entities that are not CAs, these certificates contain the public keys that are needed by the certificate's user in order to perform key management or verify a digital signature.

- **Self-issued certificates** — These certificates are issued by an entity to itself to establish points of trust and to distribute a new signing public key.

- **Rollover certificates** — These certificates are issued by a CA to transition from an old public key to a new one.

Certificate Revocation Lists

Users check the certificate revocation list (CRL) to determine whether a digital certificate has been revoked. They check for the serial number of the signature. The CA signs the CRL for integrity and authentication purposes. A CRL is shown in Figure 6-7 for an X.509 version 2 certificate.

Version
Signature
Issuer
Thisupdate (Issue Date)
Nextupdate (Date by which the next CRL will be issued)
Revoked Certificates (List of Revoked Certificates)
CRLExtensions
SignatureAlgorithm
SignatureValue

Figure 6-7: CRL format (version 2)

The CA usually generates the CRLs for its population. If the CA generates the CRLs for its entire population, the CRL is called a *full CRL*.

Key Management

Obviously, when dealing with encryption keys, the same precautions must be used as with physical keys to secure the areas or the combinations to the safes. The following sections describe the components of key management.

Key Distribution

Because distributing secret keys in symmetric key encryption poses a problem, secret keys can be distributed using asymmetric key cryptosystems. Other means of distributing secret keys include face-to-face meetings to exchange keys, sending the keys by secure messenger, or some other secure alternate channel. Another method is to encrypt the secret key with another key, called a *key encryption key*, and send the encrypted secret key to the intended receiver. These key encryption keys can be distributed manually, but they need not be distributed often. The X9.17 Standard (ANSI X9.17 [Revised], "American National Standard for Financial Institution Key Management [Wholesale]," American Bankers Association, 1985) specifies key encryption keys as well as data keys for encrypting the plain-text messages.

Key distribution can also be accomplished by splitting the keys into different parts and sending each part by a different medium.

In large networks, key distribution can become a serious problem because in an N-person network, the total number of key exchanges is $N(N-1)/2$. Using public key cryptography or the creation and exchange of session keys that are valid only for a particular session and length of time are useful mechanisms for managing the key distribution problem.

Keys can be *updated* by generating a new key from an old key. If, for example, Alice and Bob share a secret key, they can apply the same transformation function (a hash algorithm) to their common secret key and obtain a new secret key.

Key Revocation

A digital certificate contains a timestamp or period for which the certificate is valid. Also, if a key is compromised or must be made invalid because of business- or personnel-related issues, it must be revoked. The CA maintains a CRL of all invalid certificates. Users should regularly examine this list.

Key Recovery

A system must be put in place to decrypt critical data if the encryption key is lost or forgotten. One method is *key escrow*. In this system, the key is subdivided into different parts, each of which is encrypted and then sent to a different trusted individual in an organization. Keys can also be escrowed onto smart cards.

Key Renewal

Obviously, the longer a secret key is used without changing it, the more it is subject to compromise. The frequency with which you change the key is a direct function of the value of the data being encrypted and transmitted. Also, if the same secret key is used to encrypt valuable data over a relatively long period of time, you risk compromising a larger volume of data when the key is broken. Another important concern if the key is not changed frequently is that an attacker can intercept and change messages and then send different messages to the receiver.

Key encryption keys, because they are not used as often as encryption keys, provide some protection against attacks. Typically, private keys used for digital signatures are not frequently changed and may be kept for years.

Key Destruction

Keys that have been in use for long periods of time and are replaced by others should be destroyed. If the keys are compromised, older messages sent with those keys can be read.

Keys that are stored on disks, EEPROMS, or flash memory should be overwritten numerous times. One can also destroy the disks by shredding and burning them. However, in some cases, it is possible to recover data from disks that were put into a fire. Any hardware device storing the key, such as an EPROM, should also be physically destroyed.

Older keys stored by the operating system in various locations in memory must also be searched out and destroyed.

Multiple Keys

Usually, an individual has more than one public/private key pair. The keys may be of different sizes for different levels of security. A larger key size may be used for digitally signing documents, whereas a smaller key size may be used for encryption. A person may also have multiple roles or responsibilities wherein they want to sign messages with a different signature. One key pair may be used for business matters, another for personal use, and another for some other activity, such as being a school board member.

Distributed versus Centralized Key Management

A CA is a form of centralized key management. It is a central location that issues certificates and maintains CRLs. An alternative is *distributed key management*, in which a "chain of trust" or "web of trust" is set up among users who know each other. Because they know each other, they can trust that each one's public key is valid. Some of these users may know other users and can thus verify their public key. The chain spreads outward from the original group. This arrangement results in an informal verification procedure that is based on people knowing and trusting each other.

Further Considerations

Additional mechanisms that can be applied to network connections to provide for secure cloud communications include the following:

- Layered security
- Segmentation of virtual local area networks and applications

- Clustering of DNS servers for fault tolerance
- Load balancers
- Firewalls

Microarchitectures

The term *computer architecture* refers to the organization of the fundamental elements composing the computer. From another perspective, it refers to the view a programmer has of the computing system when viewed through its instruction set. The main hardware components of a digital computer are the central processing unit (CPU), memory, and input/output devices. A basic CPU of a general-purpose digital computer consists of an arithmetic logic unit (ALU), control logic, one or more accumulators, multiple general-purpose registers, an instruction register, a program counter, and some on-chip local memory. The ALU performs arithmetic and logical operations on the binary words of the computer.

The design elements of the microprocessor hardware and firmware that provide for the implementation of the higher-level architecture are referred to as *microarchitecture*. As an example, a microarchitecture design might incorporate the following:

- **Pipelining** — Increases the performance of a computer by overlapping the steps of different instructions. For example, if the instruction cycle is divided into three parts — fetch, decode, and execute — instructions can be overlapped (as shown in Figure 6-8) to increase the execution speed of the instructions.

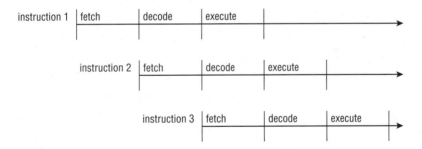

Figure 6-8: Instruction pipelining

- **Superscalar processor** — A processor that enables the concurrent execution of multiple instructions in both the same pipeline stage as well as different pipeline stages.
- **Very-long instruction word (VLIW) processor** — A processor in which a single instruction specifies more than one concurrent operation. For

example, the instruction might specify and concurrently execute two operations in one instruction. VLIW processing is illustrated in Figure 6-9.

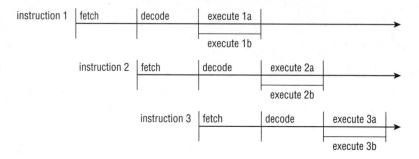

Figure 6-9: VLIW processing

- **Multi-programming** — Executes two or more programs simultaneously on a single processor (CPU) by alternating execution among the programs.

- **Multi-tasking** — Executes two or more subprograms or tasks at the same time on a single processor (CPU) by alternating execution among the tasks.

- **Multi-processing** — Executes two or more programs at the same time on multiple processors. In symmetric multi-processing, the processors share the same operating system, memory, and data paths, while in massively parallel multi-processing, large numbers of processors are used. In this architecture, each processor has its own memory and operating system but communicates and cooperates with all the other processors.

- **Multi-threading** — Concurrent tasks that share resources and run inside a process. In a multi-processing system, threads run in parallel.

- **Simultaneous multi-threading (SMT)** — Multiple threads running on a single core. SMT is especially valuable in enhancing the speed of RSA encryption computations that are widely used in securing cloud transactions.

Microarchitectures can be designed as hardware accelerators for functions such as encryption, arithmetic, and secure Web transactions to support cloud computing.

Identity Management and Access Control

Identity management and access control are fundamental functions required for secure cloud computing. The simplest form of identity management is logging on to a computer system with a user ID and password. However, true identity management, such as is required for cloud computing, requires more robust authentication, authorization, and access control. It should determine what resources are authorized to be accessed by a user or process by using technology such as biometrics or smart cards, and determine when a resource has been accessed by unauthorized entities.

Identity Management

Identification and authentication are the keystones of most access control systems. Identification is the act of a user professing an identity to a system, usually in the form of a username or user logon ID to the system. Identification establishes user accountability for the actions on the system. User IDs should be unique and not shared among different individuals. In many large organizations, user IDs follow set standards, such as first initial followed by last name, and so on. In order to enhance security and reduce the amount of information available to an attacker, an ID should not reflect the user's job title or function.

Authentication is verification that the user's claimed identity is valid, and it is usually implemented through a user password at logon. Authentication is based on the following three factor types:

- **Type 1** — Something you know, such as a personal identification number (PIN) or password
- **Type 2** — Something you have, such as an ATM card or smart card
- **Type 3** — Something you are (physically), such as a fingerprint or retina scan

Sometimes a fourth factor, something you do, is added to this list. Something you do might be typing your name or other phrases on a keyboard. Conversely, something you do can be considered something you are.

Two-factor authentication requires two of the three factors to be used in the authentication process. For example, withdrawing funds from an ATM machine requires two-factor authentication in the form of the ATM card (something you have) and a PIN number (something you know).

Passwords

Because passwords can be compromised, they must be protected. In the ideal case, a password should be used only once. This "one-time password," or OTP, provides maximum security because a new password is required for each new logon. A password that is the same for each logon is called a *static password*. A password that changes with each logon is termed a *dynamic password*. The changing of passwords can also fall between these two extremes. Passwords can be required to change monthly, quarterly, or at other intervals, depending on the criticality of the information needing protection and the password's frequency of use. Obviously, the more times a password is used, the more chance there is of it being compromised. A *passphrase* is a sequence of characters that is usually longer than the allotted number for a password. The passphrase is converted into a virtual password by the system.

In all these schemes, a front-end authentication device or a back-end authentication server, which services multiple workstations or the host, can perform the authentication.

Passwords can be provided by a number of devices, including tokens, memory cards, and smart cards.

Tokens

Tokens, in the form of small, hand-held devices, are used to provide passwords. The following are the four basic types of tokens:

- Static password tokens

  1. Owners authenticate themselves to the token by typing in a secret password.

  2. If the password is correct, the token authenticates the owner to an information system.

- Synchronous dynamic password tokens, clock-based

  1. The token generates a new, unique password value at fixed time intervals that is synchronized with the same password on the authentication server (this password is the time of day encrypted with a secret key).

  2. The unique password is entered into a system or workstation along with an owner's PIN.

  3. The authentication entity in a system or workstation knows an owner's secret key and PIN, and the entity verifies that the entered password is valid and that it was entered during the valid time window.

- Synchronous dynamic password tokens, counter-based

  1. The token increments a counter value that is synchronized with a counter in the authentication server.

  2. The counter value is encrypted with the user's secret key inside the token and this value is the unique password that is entered into the system authentication server.

3. The authentication entity in the system or workstation knows the user's secret key and the entity verifies that the entered password is valid by performing the same encryption on its identical counter value.

- Asynchronous tokens, challenge-response

   1. A workstation or system generates a random challenge string, and the owner enters the string into the token along with the proper PIN.

   2. The token performs a calculation on the string using the PIN and generates a response value that is then entered into the workstation or system.

   3. The authentication mechanism in the workstation or system performs the same calculation as the token using the owner's PIN and challenge string and compares the result with the value entered by the owner. If the results match, the owner is authenticated.

Memory Cards

Memory cards provide nonvolatile storage of information, but they do not have any processing capability. A memory card stores encrypted passwords and other related identifying information. A telephone calling card and an ATM card are examples of memory cards.

Smart Cards

Smart cards provide even more capability than memory cards by incorporating additional processing power on the cards. These credit-card-size devices comprise microprocessor and memory and are used to store digital signatures, private keys, passwords, and other personal information.

Biometrics

An alternative to using passwords for authentication in logical or technical access control is *biometrics*. Biometrics is based on the Type 3 authentication mechanism — something you are. Biometrics is defined as an automated means of identifying or authenticating the identity of a living person based on physiological or behavioral characteristics. In biometrics, identification is a one-to-many search of an individual's characteristics from a database of stored images. Authentication is a one-to-one search to verify a claim to an identity made by a person. Biometrics is used for identification in physical controls and for authentication in logical controls.

There are three main performance measures in biometrics:

- **False rejection rate (FRR) or Type I Error** — The percentage of valid subjects that are falsely rejected.

- **False acceptance rate (FAR) or Type II Error** — The percentage of invalid subjects that are falsely accepted.

- **Crossover error rate (CER)** — The percentage at which the FRR equals the FAR. The smaller the CER, the better the device is performing.

In addition to the accuracy of the biometric systems, other factors must be considered, including enrollment time, throughput rate, and acceptability. *Enrollment time* is the time that it takes to initially register with a system by providing samples of the biometric characteristic to be evaluated. An acceptable enrollment time is around two minutes. For example, in fingerprint systems the actual fingerprint is stored and requires approximately 250KB per finger for a high-quality image. This level of information is required for one-to-many searches in forensics applications on very large databases.

In finger-scan technology, a full fingerprint is not stored; rather, the features extracted from this fingerprint are stored by using a small template that requires approximately 500 to 1,000 bytes of storage. The original fingerprint cannot be reconstructed from this template. Finger-scan technology is used for one-to-one verification by using smaller databases. Updates of the enrollment information might be required because some biometric characteristics, such as voice and signature, might change over time.

The *throughput rate* is the rate at which the system processes and identifies or authenticates individuals. Acceptable throughput rates are in the range of 10 subjects per minute. *Acceptability* refers to considerations of privacy, invasiveness, and psychological and physical comfort when using the system. For example, a concern with retina scanning systems might be the exchange of body fluids on the eyepiece. Another concern would be disclosing the retinal pattern, which could reveal changes in a person's health, such as diabetes or high blood pressure.

Collected biometric images are stored in an area referred to as a *corpus*. The corpus is stored in a database of images. Potential sources of error include the corruption of images during collection, and mislabeling or other transcription problems associated with the database. Therefore, the image collection process and storage must be performed carefully with constant checking. These images are collected during the enrollment process and thus are critical to the correct operation of the biometric device.

The following are typical biometric characteristics that are used to uniquely authenticate an individual's identity:

- **Fingerprints** — Fingerprint characteristics are captured and stored. Typical CERs are 4–5%.

- **Retina scans** — The eye is placed approximately two inches from a camera and an invisible light source scans the retina for blood vessel patterns. CERs are approximately 1.4%.

- **Iris scans** — A video camera remotely captures iris patterns and characteristics. CER values are around 0.5%.

- **Hand geometry** — Cameras capture three-dimensional hand characteristics. CERs are approximately 2%.

- **Voice** — Sensors capture voice characteristics, including throat vibrations and air pressure, when the subject speaks a phrase. CERs are in the range of 10%.

- **Handwritten signature dynamics** — The signing characteristics of an individual making a signature are captured and recorded. Typical characteristics including writing pressure and pen direction. CERs are not published at this time.

Other types of biometric characteristics include facial and palm scans.

Implementing Identity Management

Realizing effective identity management requires a high-level corporate commitment and dedication of sufficient resources to accomplish the task. Typical undertakings in putting identity management in place include the following:

- Establishing a database of identities and credentials
- Managing users' access rights
- Enforcing security policy
- Developing the capability to create and modify accounts
- Setting up monitoring of resource accesses
- Installing a procedure for removing access rights
- Providing training in proper procedures

An identity management effort can be supported by software that automates many of the required tasks.

The Open Group and the World Wide Web Consortium (W3C) are working toward a standard for a global identity management system that would be interoperable, provide for privacy, implement accountability, and be portable. Identity management is also addressed by the XML-based eXtensible Name Service (XNS) open protocol for universal addressing. XNS provides the following capabilities:

- A permanent identification address for a container of an individual's personal data and contact information

- Means to verify whether an individual's contact information is valid

- A platform for negotiating the exchange of information among different entities

Access Control

Access control is intrinsically tied to identity management and is necessary to preserve the confidentiality, integrity, and availability of cloud data.

These and other related objectives flow from the organizational security policy. This policy is a high-level statement of management intent regarding the control of access to information and the personnel who are authorized to receive that information.

Three things that must be considered for the planning and implementation of access control mechanisms are threats to the system, the system's vulnerability to these threats, and the risk that the threats might materialize. These concepts are defined as follows:

- **Threat** — An event or activity that has the potential to cause harm to the information systems or networks

- **Vulnerability** — A weakness or lack of a safeguard that can be exploited by a threat, causing harm to the information systems or networks

- **Risk** — The potential for harm or loss to an information system or network; the probability that a threat will materialize

Controls

Controls are implemented to mitigate risk and reduce the potential for loss. Two important control concepts are *separation of duties* and the principle of *least privilege*. Separation of duties requires an activity or process to be performed by two or more entities for successful completion. Thus, the only way that a security policy can be violated is if there is collusion among the entities. For example, in a financial environment, the person requesting that a check be issued for payment should not also be the person who has authority to sign the check. Least privilege means that the entity that has a task to perform should be provided with the minimum resources and privileges required to complete the task for the minimum necessary period of time.

Control measures can be administrative, logical (also called technical), and physical in their implementation.

- Administrative controls include policies and procedures, security awareness training, background checks, work habit checks, a review of vacation history, and increased supervision.

- Logical or technical controls involve the restriction of access to systems and the protection of information. Examples of these types of controls are encryption, smart cards, access control lists, and transmission protocols.

- Physical controls incorporate guards and building security in general, such as the locking of doors, the securing of server rooms or laptops, the protection of cables, the separation of duties, and the backing up of files.

Controls provide accountability for individuals who are accessing sensitive information in a cloud environment. This accountability is accomplished through access control mechanisms that require identification and authentication, and through the audit function. These controls must be in accordance with and accurately represent the organization's security policy. Assurance procedures ensure that the control mechanisms correctly implement the security policy for the entire life cycle of a cloud information system.

In general, a group of processes that share access to the same resources is called a *protection domain,* and the memory space of these processes is isolated from other running processes.

Models for Controlling Access

Controlling access by a subject (an active entity such as an individual or process) to an object (a passive entity such as a file) involves setting up access rules. These rules can be classified into three categories or models.

Mandatory Access Control

The authorization of a subject's access to an object depends upon labels, which indicate the subject's *clearance*, and the *classification or sensitivity* of the object. For example, the military classifies documents as unclassified, confidential, secret, and top secret. Similarly, an individual can receive a clearance of confidential, secret, or top secret and can have access to documents classified at or below his or her specified clearance level. Thus, an individual with a clearance of "secret" can have access to secret and confidential documents with a restriction. This restriction is that the individual must have a *need to know* relative to the classified documents involved. Therefore, the documents must be necessary for that individual to complete an assigned task. Even if the individual is cleared for a classification level of information, the individual should not access the information unless there is a need to know. *Rule-based access control* is a type of mandatory access control because rules determine this access (such as the correspondence of clearance labels to classification labels), rather than the identity of the subjects and objects alone.

Discretionary Access Control

With discretionary access control, the subject has authority, within certain limitations, to specify what objects are accessible. For example, access control lists (ACLs) can be used. An access control list is a list denoting which users have what privileges to a particular resource. For example, a *tabular listing* would show the subjects or users who have access to the object, e.g., file X, and what privileges they have with respect to that file.

An *access control triple* consists of the user, program, and file, with the corresponding access privileges noted for each user. This type of access control is used in local, dynamic situations in which the subjects must have the discretion to specify what resources certain users are permitted to access. When a user within certain limitations has the right to alter the access control to certain objects, this is termed a *user-directed discretionary access control*. An identity-based access control is a type of discretionary access control based on an individual's identity. In some instances, a hybrid approach is used, which combines the features of user-based and identity-based discretionary access control.

Nondiscretionary Access Control

A central authority determines which subjects can have access to certain objects based on the organizational security policy. The access controls might be based on the individual's role in the organization (role-based) or the subject's responsibilities and duties (task-based). In an organization with frequent personnel changes, nondiscretionary access control is useful because the access controls are based on the individual's role or title within the organization. Therefore, these access controls don't need to be changed whenever a new person assumes that role.

Access control can also be characterized as *context-dependent* or *content-dependent*. Context-dependent access control is a function of factors such as location, time of day, and previous access history. It is concerned with the environment or context of the data. In content-dependent access control, access is determined by the information contained in the item being accessed.

Single Sign-On (SSO)

Single sign-on (SSO) addresses the cumbersome situation of logging on multiple times to access different resources. When users must remember numerous passwords and IDs, they might take shortcuts in creating them that could leave them open to exploitation. In SSO, a user provides one ID and password per work session and is automatically logged on to all the required applications. For SSO security, the passwords should not be stored or transmitted in the clear. SSO applications can run either on a user's workstation or on authentication servers. The advantages of SSO include having the ability to use stronger passwords, easier administration of changing or deleting the passwords, and less time to access resources. The major disadvantage of many SSO implementations is that once users obtain access to the system through the initial logon, they can freely roam the network resources without any restrictions.

Authentication mechanisms include items such as smart cards and magnetic badges. Strict controls must be enforced to prevent a user from changing configurations that another authority sets.

SSO can be implemented by using scripts that replay the users' multiple log-ins or by using authentication servers to verify a user's identity, and encrypted authentication tickets to permit access to system services.

Enterprise access management (EAM) provides access control management services to Web-based enterprise systems that include SSO. SSO can be provided in a number of ways. For example, SSO can be implemented on Web applications residing on different servers in the same domain by using nonpersistent, encrypted cookies on the client interface. This task is accomplished by providing a cookie to each application that the user wishes to access. Another solution is to build a secure credential for each user on a reverse proxy that is situated in front of the Web server. The credential is then presented each time a user attempts to access protected Web applications.

Autonomic Security

Autonomic computing refers to a self-managing computing model in which computer systems reconfigure themselves in response to changing conditions and are self-healing. The promise of autonomic computing will take a number of years to fully materialize, but it offers capabilities that can improve the security of information systems and cloud computing in particular. The ability of autonomic systems to collect and interpret data and recommend or implement solutions can go a long way toward enhancing security and providing for recovery from harmful events.

Autonomic Systems

Autonomic systems are based on the human autonomic nervous system, which is self-managing, monitors changes that affect the body, and maintains internal balances. Therefore, an autonomic computing system has the goal of performing self-management to maintain correct operations despite perturbations to the system. Such a system requires sensory inputs, decision-making capability, and the ability to implement remedial activities to maintain an equilibrium state of normal operation. Examples of events that would have to be handled autonomously include the following:

- Malicious attacks
- Hardware or software faults
- Excessive CPU utilization
- Power failures
- Organizational policies
- Inadvertent operator errors
- Interaction with other systems
- Software updates

IBM introduced the concept of autonomic computing and its eight defining characteristics[5] as follows:

- **Self-awareness** — An autonomic application/system "knows itself" and is aware of its state and its behaviors.

- **Self-configuring** — An autonomic application/system should be able configure and reconfigure itself under varying and unpredictable conditions.

- **Self-optimizing** — An autonomic application/system should be able to detect sub-optimal behaviors and optimize itself to improve its execution.

- **Self-healing** — An autonomic application/system should be able to detect and recover from potential problems and continue to function smoothly.

- **Self-protecting** — An autonomic application/system should be capable of detecting and protecting its resources from both internal and external attack and maintaining overall system security and integrity.

- **Context-aware** — An autonomic application/system should be aware of its execution environment and be able to react to changes in the environment.

- **Open** — An autonomic application/system must function in a heterogeneous world and should be portable across multiple hardware and software architectures. Consequently, it must be built on standard and open protocols and interfaces.

- **Anticipatory** — An autonomic application/system should be able to anticipate, to the extent possible, its needs and behaviors and those of its context, and be able to manage itself proactively.

The underlying concept of autonomic systems is self-management, whereby a computational system maintains proper operation in the face of changing external and internal conditions, evaluates the necessity for upgrades, installs software, conducts regression testing, performs performance tuning of middleware, and detects and corrects problem situations in general.

Autonomic Protection

Autonomic self-protection involves detecting a harmful situation and taking actions that will mitigate the situation. These systems will also be designed to predict problems from analysis of sensory inputs and initiate corrective measures.

An autonomous system security response is based on network knowledge, capabilities of connected resources, information aggregation, the complexity of the situation, and the impact on affected applications.

The decision-making element of autonomic computing, taking into account the current security posture and security context of the system to be protected, can take actions such as changing the strength of required authentications or modifying encryption keys. The security context is derived from information acquired from network and system supervising elements and then collected into a higher-level representation of the system security status.

An oft overlooked aspect of autonomic systems is that security vulnerabilities can be introduced by configuration changes and additional autonomous activities that are intended to address other computational areas.

Autonomous protection systems should, therefore, adhere to the following guidelines:

- Minimize overhead requirements.
- Be consistent with security policies.
- Optimize security-related parameters.
- Minimize impact on performance.
- Minimize potential for introducing new vulnerabilities.
- Conduct regression analysis and return to previous software versions if problems are introduced by changes.
- Ensure that reconfiguration processes are secure.

Autonomic Self-Healing

The process of diagnosing and repairing failures in IT systems can be difficult, time consuming, and usually requires intensive labor effort. Autonomic self-healing systems can provide the capability to detect and repair software problems and identify hardware faults without manual intervention.

The autonomic process would obtain logged and monitored information and perform an analysis to diagnose the problem area. This procedure is usually conducted by an autonomic manager that controls computing resource elements with well-defined interfaces that support the diagnostic and mitigation actions. The managed elements control their internal states and have defined performance characteristics and relationships with other computational elements.

The objective of the autonomous self-healing process is to keep the elements operating according to their design specifications.

Summary

Cloud computing security architecture is a critical element in establishing trust in the cloud computing paradigm. Confidence in using the cloud depends on trusted computing mechanisms, robust identity management and access control techniques, providing a secure execution environment, securing cloud communications, and supporting microarchitectures.

Autonomic computing can employ self-management, self-healing, and self-protection techniques to make cloud computing a more reliable, secure, and safe choice for the growing requirements for processing and storing large amounts of information in a cost-effective manner.

In Chapter 7, cloud computing life cycle issues are detailed, including responding to incidents, discussing cloud computing encryption issues, and cloud computing virtual machine retirement considerations.

Notes

1. NIST Special Publication 800-30, "Risk Management Guide for Information Technology Systems," July 2002.

2. NIST Special Publication 800-14, "Generally Accepted Principles and Practices for Securing Information Technology Systems," September 1996.

3. NIST Special Publication 800-14, "Generally Accepted Principles and Practices for Securing Information Technology Systems," September 1996.

4. Berger, S., Cáceres, R., Goldman, K.A., et al., "vTPM: Virtualizing the Trusted Platform Module," in Proceedings of the 15th USENIX Security Symposium, Vancouver, B.C., 2006.

5. Horn, P., "Autonomic Computing: IBM's Perspective on the State of Information Technology," http://www.research.ibm.com/autonomic/, IBM Corp., October 2001.

CHAPTER 7

Cloud Computing Life Cycle Issues

Any life truly lived is a risky business, and if one puts up too many fences against the risks one ends by shutting out life itself.
—Kenneth S. Davis

Commercial, industrial, military, and government IT operations are subject to a variety of regulatory and statutory requirements with regard to the security of sensitive data. Migration from a conventional IT server environment to a cloud paradigm poses new challenges and risks, and provides cost-saving opportunities.

IT organizations have relied on standards and guidelines from a number of organizations, including the National Institute of Standards and Technology (NIST), the International Organization for Standardization (ISO), the Open Web Applications Security Project (OWASP), the Organization for the Advancement of Structured Information Standards (OASIS), and the European Telecommunications Standards Institute (ETSI). These standards address life cycle issues, including requirements, architectures, implementation, deployment, and security.

In order for cloud computing to gain acceptance and trust, standards have to be developed for the cloud environment. In addition, important aspects of cloud security such as incident management and response, encryption, key management, and retirement of hardware and software must be addressed and incorporated into cloud computing implementations. This chapter covers these important topics.

Standards

There are a number of important guidelines and initiatives focusing on developing quality cloud security standards. However, at this time, there are no widely accepted standards or third-party certifications that cloud providers can profess to use to validate their security posture. The major initiatives in the cloud security standards arena are explored in this section.

Jericho Forum

The Jericho Forum is an international IT security association whose mission is the support of secure business in a global open-network environment. It is dedicated to the advancement of secure collaboration in appropriate business cloud configurations. In order to achieve these goals, the Forum is promoting standards that address the layers of business services desired, such as infrastructure, platform, and software process, as well as the best cloud formations to use.

To provide a basis for standardization, the Jericho Forum has defined a three-dimensional cube that specifies four criteria for categorizing cloud formations and their provisions in order to assist those making important decisions concerning projects to be placed in the cloud. The four criteria are illustrated in Figure 7-1 and summarized as follows:

- **Proprietary/open** — Specifies the state of ownership of the cloud components; and identifies the degree of portability between an organization's IT systems and other cloud systems without restrictions and constraints. Therefore, moving applications and data from a proprietary cloud might prove difficult and costly, whereas migrating from an open cloud, which uses nonproprietary technology, to another cloud form could be accomplished without restrictions.

- **Perimeterized/de-perimeterized** — Refers to the boundaries of IT operations. Perimeterized denotes functioning within traditional IT boundaries such as behind network firewalls. This mode of operation limits collaboration. De-perimeterized assumes that an IT system can collaborate securely as well as more freely with other entities without having to navigate multiple network layers and restrictions.

- **Insourced/outsourced** — Refers to the entity operating the cloud for the user. In an insourced cloud, the cloud service is provided by an organization's IT personnel under the control of the organization. Outsourced cloud operations denote that the cloud services are provided by a third-party organization.

- **Internal/external** — Describes where the data is physically located, either within or outside of an organization's boundary.

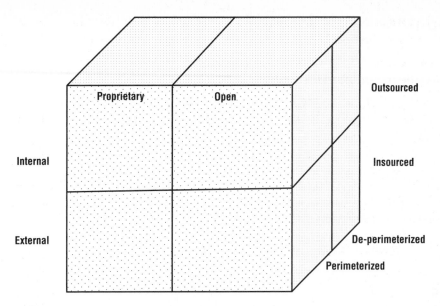

Figure 7-1: The 3D "cloud cube" model

This model is described in detail in the document "Cloud Cube Model: Selecting Cloud Formations for Secure Collaboration," located at `http://www.opengroup.org/jericho/cloud_cube_model_v1.0.pdf`.

The Distributed Management Task Force (DMTF)

The DMTF (`http://www.dmtf.org`) is an international organization comprising industry members that is dedicated to the development, adoption, and promotion of management standards that support multi-vendor interoperability.

Two major DMTF initiatives that are relevant to cloud computing are the DMTF Open Virtualization Format (OVF) and the Open Cloud Standards Incubator.

The DMTF Open Virtualization Format (OVF)

The Open Virtualization Format, DMTF Standard Specification DSP0243, defines an open, extensible format for virtual machine software packaging and distribution. The main characteristics of software meeting the OVF are described by the DMTF as follows:

- **Optimized for distribution** — Provides for software license management and integrity checking using public key cryptography
- **Optimized for a simple, automated user experience** — Enables validation of virtual machine components of the OVF during installation and

provides additional information to support the different phases of the installation process

- **Enable single and multiple VM configurations** — Supports installations on single or multiple, interdependent VMs

- **Portable VM packaging** — Provides for platform-specific upgrades while maintaining platform neutrality and the ability to incorporate future formats

- **Vendor and platform independent** — Maintains platform, vendor, and guest operating system independence

- **Open standard** — Designed to be an open standard for portable virtual machines

The DMTF Open Cloud Standards Incubator

The cloud incubator was initiated to promote cloud interoperability through the development of cloud resource packaging formats, security mechanisms, and resource management protocols. DMTF cloud incubation provides a basis for DMTF members to cooperate in developing specifications that can evolve in a rapid manner to standards development.

The International Organization for Standardization (ISO)

The ISO (http:/www.iso.org) has published a series of standards dedicated to the field of information system security and Web services interoperability that are applicable to cloud security and interoperability. The relevant standards are ISO 27001, 27002, 27003, 27004, 27005, 27006, 29361, 29362, and 29363.

The ISO has also formed Subcommittee (SC) 38 on Distributed Application Platforms and Services (DAPS) to work on the standardization of Web services, SOA, and cloud computing.

The ISO 27001–27006 and 29361–29363 standards, along with DAPS, are summarized in the following sections.

ISO 27001

The British Standards Institution (BSI) 7799-2 standard was the predecessor and basis for ISO 27001, which is the specification for an information security management system (ISMS). According to ISO, the standard is designed to "provide a model for establishing, implementing, operating, monitoring, reviewing, maintaining, and improving an information security management system."

ISO 27001 comprises the following topics:

- Management responsibility
- Internal audits
- ISMS improvement
- Annex A: Control objectives and controls
- Annex B: Organization for Economic Cooperation and Development (OECD) principles and this international standard
- Annex C: Correspondence between ISO 9001, ISO 14001, and this standard

ISO 27001 emphasizes developing an ISMS through an iterative plan-do-check-act (PDCA) cycle. The activities in each cycle component are summarized from the 27001 document as follows:

1. Plan
   - Establish scope.
   - Develop a comprehensive ISMS policy.
   - Conduct risk assessment.
   - Develop a risk treatment plan.
   - Determine control objectives and controls.
   - Develop a statement of applicability describing and justifying why the specific controls were selected and others not selected.

2. Do
   - Operate selected controls.
   - Detect and respond to incidents properly.
   - Conduct security awareness training.
   - Manage resources required to accomplish security tasks.

3. Check
   - Intrusion-detection operations.
   - Incident-handling operations.
   - Conduct internal ISMS audit.
   - Conduct a management review.

4. Act

- ▪ Implement improvements to the ISMS in response to items identified in the Check phase.

- ▪ Take corrective actions in response to items identified in the Check phase.

- ▪ Take preventive actions in response to items identified in the Check phase.

ISO 27002

ISO 27002, the "Code of Practice for Information Security Management," is a repackaged version of (ISO) 17779:2005. It is designed to serve as a single source for best practices in the field of information security and presents a range of controls applicable to most situations. It provides high-level, voluntary guidance for information security management.

ISO 27002 presents requirements for building, maintaining, and documenting ISMSs. As such, it lists recommendations for establishing an efficient information security management framework. ISO 27002 is also used as the basis of a certification assessment of an organization. It lists a variety of control measures that can be implemented according to practices outlined in ISO 27001. The areas covered in ISO 27002 are as follows:

- ▪ Structure
- ▪ Risk assessment and treatment
- ▪ Security policy
- ▪ Organization of information security
- ▪ Asset management
- ▪ Human resources security
- ▪ Physical security
- ▪ Communications and operations management
- ▪ Access control
- ▪ Information systems acquisition, development, maintenance
- ▪ Information security incident management
- ▪ Business continuity
- ▪ Compliance

ISO 27003

ISO 27003, "Information Technology — Security Techniques — Information Security Management System Implementation Guidance," is in draft form as of this writing. It uses the PDCA paradigm to provide recommendations and guidance in developing an ISMS.

The draft table of contents is as follows:

1. Introduction

2. Scope

3. Terms and Definitions

4. CSFs (Critical Success Factors)

5. Guidance on Process Approach

6. Guidance on Using PDCA

7. Guidance on Plan Processes

8. Guidance on Do Processes

9. Guidance on Check Processes

10. Guidance on Act Processes

11. Inter-Organization Co-operation

ISO 27004

ISO 27004, "Information Technology — Security Techniques — Information Security Management — Measurement," is in second final committee draft form as of this writing. According to ISO, the standard "provides guidance on the specification and use of measurement techniques for providing assurance as regards the effectiveness of information security management systems. It is intended to be applicable to a wide range of organizations with a correspondingly wide range of information security management systems."

ISO 27005

ISO 27005:2008, "Information Technology — Security Techniques — Information Security Risk Management," provides guidelines for information security risk management (ISRM) according to the requirements outlined in ISO 27001.

The main headings of ISO 27005 are as follows:

- Terms and Definitions
- Structure
- Background
- Overview of the ISRM Process
- Context Establishment
- Information Security Risk Assessment (ISRA)

- Information Security Risk Treatment
- Information security Risk Acceptance

ISO 27006

ISO 27006, "Information Technology — Security Techniques — Requirements for Bodies Providing Audit and Certification of Information Security Management Systems," provides guidelines for the accreditation of organizations that are concerned with certification and registration relating to ISMSs.

The main elements covered in the standard document are as follows:

- Scope
- References
- Terms
- Principles
- General requirements
- Structural requirements
- Resource requirements
- Information requirements
- Process requirements
- Management system requirements
- Information security risk communication
- Information security risk monitoring and review
- Annex A: Defining the scope of the process
- Annex B: Asset valuation and impact assessment
- Annex C: Examples of typical threats
- Annex D: Vulnerabilities and vulnerability assessment methods
- Annex E: Information security risk assessment (ISRA) approaches

International Organization for Standardization/International Electrotechnical Commission ISO/IEC 29361, ISO/IEC 29362, and ISO/IEC 29363 Standards

In July of 2008, three profiles of the Web Services Interoperability Organization (WS-I: http://www.ws-i.org) were made ISO/IEC standards. Basic Profile

Version 1.1, Attachments Profile Version 1.0, and Simple SOAP Binding Profile Version 1.0 are now ISO/IEC 29361:2008, ISO/IEC 29362:2008, and ISO/IEC 29363:2008 standards, respectively.

ISO/IEC 29361:2008 provides interoperability guidance for WSDL, SOAP, and UDDI nonproprietary Web services specifications. ISO/IEC 29362:2008 is a companion profile to ISO/IEC 29361:2008 and provides support for interoperable SOAP messages with attachments-based Web services. ISO/IEC 29363:2008 incorporates the Basic Profile requirements of ISO/IEC 29361:2008 related to the serialization of the envelope and its representation in the message.

Distributed Application Platforms and Services

As of this writing, the ISO has formed a study group to focus on the standardization of Web services, SOA, and cloud computing. The group is known as Subcommittee (SC) 38 on Distributed Application Platforms and Services (DAPS). Preliminary efforts of SC 38 will be to set up working groups in the following areas:

- Web Services
  - Maintenance of previously approved standards ISO/IEC 29361, ISO/IEC 29362 and ISO/IEC 29363.
  - Enhancements and maintenance of Web services inventory database and SOA standards
  - Exploration of any current related standards activities ongoing in Joint Technical Committee (JTC) 1 entities

- SOA
  - Exploration and coordination of relevant SOA standards efforts in JTC 1
  - Promulgation of SOA principles

- Cloud computing
  - Study market requirements for standardization.
  - Develop value proposition and terminology for cloud computing.
  - Determine business and market standardization requirements.
  - Evaluate current status of cloud computing standards under consideration by other entities.
  - Explore standardization collaboration with other mutually interested entities.

The European Telecommunications Standards Institute (ETSI)

The ETSI is a European standards organization that develops global standards for information and communications technologies. They have been particularly active in the area of grid computing standards. The GRID committee of ETSI has focused on developing a test framework for interoperable grid standards and works cooperatively with the Open Grid Forum (OGF), the DMTF, the Organization for the Advancement of Structured Information Standards (OASIS), the Storage Networking Industry Association (SNIA), and the Internet Engineering Task Force (IETF), among others.

The Organization for the Advancement of Structured Information Standards (OASIS)

OASIS develops global open standards in the areas of security, e-commerce, and Web services, in general. Oasis cloud-related standards efforts include SOA models, security access, data/import and export, identity management, registry, and directory.

Storage Networking Industry Association (SNIA)

The SNIA focuses on IT storage issues, technologies, specifications, and global storage-related standards. In the cloud computing arena, the SNIA has produced a public draft of a cloud storage standard titled "Cloud Data Management Interface (CDMI)," which can be reviewed at http://www.snia.org/cloud. In the standard, cloud storage is defined as "the delivery of virtualized storage on demand" and denoted by the formal term *Data Storage as a Service (DaaS)*. In addition, the word "container" is used as "an abstraction for storage space, grouping of data stored in the container, and a point of control for applying data services in the aggregate."

The Data Management Interface provides the following capabilities:

- Defines the functional interface that applications will use to generate, modify, and remove data from the cloud
- Provides information concerning the capabilities of the cloud storage function
- Provides the capability to manage data storage containers, associated security, and billing information
- Sets metadata on containers and their respective data
- Manages containers, accounts, security access, and monitoring/billing information, even for storage that is accessible by other protocols

Open Grid Forum (OGF)

The OGF (http://www.ogf.org) is an international organization committed to the development and adoption of standards for applied distributed computing technologies. OGF has established the Open Cloud Computing Interface (OCCI) Group with the objective of developing an open standard API for the cloud *Infrastructure as a Service (IaaS)* mode. The API effort will base its work on the Open Virtualization Format and address management of virtual machine life cycles as well as physical and virtual private servers. The open, free API is expected to provide the following benefits:

- Reduce the possibility of vendor lock-in.
- Support the emergence of hybrid cloud architectures that encompass multiple data centers and cloud services.
- Reduce migration costs among public clouds.
- Provide automated management of peak capacity.
- Use current Internet standards.
- Support the development of a servicers marketplace.
- Provide the customer with more cloud service options.
- Enhance interoperability of cloud computing.
- Encourage the development of new cloud applications.

The Open Web Application Security Project (OWASP)

The Open Web Application Security Project (OWASP) (www.owasp.org) is an open-source community that is dedicated to enhancing application software security. A number of its projects and documents can be directly applied to cloud system security, and support emerging standards. The principal OWASP efforts that can enhance cloud security are summarized in the following sections.

OWASP Top Ten Project

The Open Web Application Security Project (OWASP) Top Ten Project provides a minimum standard for Web application security and can be used to address cloud security. It summarizes the top ten Web application security vulnerabilities based on input from a variety of information system security experts. The results provide guidance regarding standards that can be used to address related cloud security weaknesses. The top ten vulnerabilities identified by OWASP are summarized in Table 7-1.

Table 7-1: OWASP Top Ten Web Application Vulnerabilities

A1 — Cross Site Scripting (XSS)
A2 — Injection Flaws
A3 — Malicious File Execution
A4 — Insecure Direct Object Reference
A5 — Cross Site Request Forgery (CSRF)
A6 — Information Leakage and Improper Error Handling
A7 — Broken Authentication and Session Management
A8 — Insecure Cryptographic Storage
A9 — Insecure Communications
A10 — Failure to Restrict URL Access

From OWASP Top Ten 2007 Website, `www.owasp.org/index.php/Top_10_2007`

OWASP Development Guide

Another document that can apply to cloud applications security is the OWASP Development Guide, version 3.0, which focuses on Web application security. The guide describes how to make Web applications self-defending. The chapters in the guide are organized into the following three sections:

- **Best practices** — Key features that should be included in applications
- **Secure patterns** — Optional security patterns that can be used as guides
- **Anti-patterns** — Patterns in code that increase vulnerability

Some of the topics addressed by the guide include the following:

- Secure coding principles
- Threat risk modeling
- Phishing
- AJAX and other "rich" interface technologies
- Session management
- Data validation
- Error handling, auditing, and logging
- Distributed computing
- Buffer overflows

- Cryptography
- Software quality assurance

OWASP Code Review Guide

The OWASP Code Review Guide defines secure code review as "the process of auditing code for an application on a line-by-line basis for its security quality. Code review is a way of ensuring that the application is developed in an appropriate fashion so as to be self defending in its given environment." Reviewing code for security is usually a manual effort, although some tools have been developed to assist in the process.

Secure code review comprises the following phases, according to the OWASP Code Review Guide:

- Discovery
- Transactional analysis
- Post-transaction analysis
- Procedure peer review
- Reporting and presentation
- Laying the groundwork

In secure code review, the following important items have to be considered:

- **Code** — The language and associated features used
- **Context** — Knowledge of the application
- **Audience** — The users of the application
- **Importance** — Criticality of the application's availability

OWASP has also identified the following "top nine" source code flaw categories:

- Input validation
- Source code design
- Information leakage and improper error handling
- Direct object reference
- Resource usage
- API usage
- Best practices violation
- Weak session management
- Using HTTP GET query strings

NIST SP 800-95

NIST Special Publication 800-95, "Guide to Secure Web Services," provides guidance on security Web services, and is useful in the cloud computing paradigm. It addresses the following issues:

- Functional integrity of Web services during transactions
- Confidentiality and integrity of data transmitted during Web services protocols
- Availability in the event of attacks, such as denial of service

The security techniques covered in NIST SP 800-35 are as follows:

- Confidentiality of Web services messages using XML Encryption
- Integrity of Web services messages using XML Signature
- Web service authentication and authorization using XML Signature
- Web Services (WS) Security
- Security for Universal Description, Discovery, and Integration (UDDI)

NIST SP 800-95 recommends that organizations consider the following security actions where applicable:

- Replicate data and services to improve availability.
- Use logging of transactions to improve nonrepudiation and accountability.
- Use threat modeling and secure software design techniques to protect from attacks.
- Use performance analysis and simulation techniques for end-to-end quality of service and quality of protection.
- Digitally sign UDDI entries to verify the author of registered entries.
- Enhance existing security mechanisms and infrastructure.

OWASP Testing Guide

The OWASP Testing Guide 2008, V3.0 (www.owasp.org/index.php /Category:OWASP_Testing_Project) defines testing as "a process of comparing the state of a system/application against a set of criteria." The testing techniques described in the guide are as follows:

- Manual inspections and reviews
- Threat modeling
- Code review
- Penetration testing

Testing is used to determine whether security controls are functioning as desired, validate security requirements, and determine threats and the root causes of vulnerabilities.

Common security tests that should be performed to evaluate security controls include the following:

- Authentication and access control
- Input validation and encoding
- Encryption
- User and session management
- Error and exception handling
- Auditing and logging

Open Cloud Consortium and Cloud Security Alliance are discussed in Chapter 8.

Incident Response

Incident response and management is critically important in the cloud computing arena. This capability has to be present in the organizations of both the cloud user and the cloud provider. An incident response resource must have the following two primary components:

- Creation and maintenance of intrusion detection systems (IDS) and processes for host and network monitoring and event notification
- Creation of a computer security incident response team (CSIRT) for the following:

    - Analysis of an event notification
    - Response to an incident if the analysis warrants it
    - Escalation path procedures
    - Resolution, post-incident follow-up, and reporting to the appropriate parties

NIST Special Publication 800-61

NIST Special Publication 800-61, "Computer Security Incident Handling Guide, Recommendations of the National Institute of Standards and Technology," January 2004, defines the incident response life cycle as follows:

1. Preparation
2. Detection and analysis

3. Containment, eradication, and recovery

4. Post-incident activity

Preparation

The preparation phase involves establishing an incident response capability as well as securing computing resources to prevent intrusions. A useful method for reducing the number of incidents is to conduct risk assessments to determine the risks posed by threats and vulnerabilities. NIST SP 800-61 recommends implementing patch management, host security, network security, malicious code prevention, and user awareness training to secure networks and minimize risks.

Detection and Analysis

NIST SP 800-61 also defines the following incident categories:

- **Denial of service** — An attack that prevents or impairs the authorized use of networks, systems, or applications by exhausting resources
- **Malicious code** — A virus, worm, Trojan horse, or other code-based malicious entity that infects a host
- **Unauthorized access** — Gaining logical or physical access without permission to a network, system, application, data, or other resource
- **Inappropriate usage** — Violating acceptable computing use policies
- **Multiple component** — A single incident that encompasses two or more incidents

In many instances, identifying a true incident is difficult. Some of the methods used to provide incident validation include the profiling of expected system activity in order to detect anomalous conditions, understanding normal system behavior, creating logs of activities, recording and analyzing system traffic, and correlating times of event occurrences.

If an incident has occurred or is suspected of being in progress, all the relevant information should be documented and preserved. If multiple incidents have occurred, the responses should be prioritized to address the most critical system resources. Table 7-2 provides examples of typical response times as a function of the predicted negative impact of a threat realized.

After an incident is detected and prioritized, it should be reported to the appropriate authorities in the organization. Typically, the incident should be reported to the chief security officer, the chief information officer, the system owner, the legal department, and, possibly, the public affairs department.

Table 7-2: Incident Response Times

CRITICALITY OF RESOURCES CURRENTLY IMPACTED OR LIKELY TO BE IMPACTED BY THE INCIDENT			
Current Impact Or Likely Future Impact Of The Incident	**High (E.G., Internet Connectivity, Public Web Servers, Firewalls, Customer Data)**	**Medium (E.G., System Administrator Workstations, File And Print Servers, XYZ Application Data)**	**Low (E.G., User Work-Stations)**
Root-level access	15 minutes	30 minutes	1 hour
Unauthorized data modification	15 minutes	30 minutes	2 hours
Unauthorized access to sensitive data	15 minutes	1 hour	1 hour
Unauthorized user-level access	30 minutes	2 hours	4 hours
Services unavailable	30 minutes	2 hours	4 hours
Annoyance	30 minutes	Local IT staff	Local IT staff

NIST SP 800-61, "Computer Security Incident Handling Guide, Recommendations of the National Institute of Standards and Technology," January 2004.

Containment, Eradication, and Recovery

It is important to contain an attack to prevent damage to the system and to keep an incident from spreading to other parts of the organization's computing resources. However, in some instances, containment can be postponed to allow the attacker to proceed into the system in order to track his or her activities for later use as evidence. Information about the attacker should be obtained only if it does not detract from containing and eradicating the incident. Information such as the attacker's true IP address, e-mail address, or Internet relay chat (IRC) name will provide leads to determine the attacker's identity and the source of the incident.

Following containment, the next step is to eradicate the components of the incident, such as removing viruses, and determining which user accounts have been compromised and disabling access to those accounts. In addition, files that are suspected of being breached or modified should be replaced from backup storage, new passwords should be issued, and appropriate patches should be installed.

Post-Incident Activity

An important component of incident response and management is to analyze the actions taken in the preparation, detection and analysis, and containment, eradication, and recovery phases and learn from those activities. Some typical questions to be asked, taken from NIST SP 800-61, include the following:

- Exactly what happened, and at what times?
- How well did staff and management perform in dealing with the incident? Were the documented procedures followed? Were they adequate?
- What information was needed sooner?
- Were any steps or actions taken that might have inhibited the recovery?
- What would the staff and management do differently the next time a similar incident occurs?
- What corrective actions can prevent similar incidents in the future?
- What additional tools or resources are needed to detect, analyze, and mitigate future incidents?

NIST Incident-Handling Summary

Table 7-3, from NIST 800-61, summarizes the important steps in incident handling.

Internet Engineering Task Force Incident-Handling Guidelines

Additional guidance on incident handling is provided by the Internet Engineering Task Force (IETF) RFC 2196, Site Security Handbook. The following approach, taken from the handbook, is recommended for the handling of incidents:

1. **Preparing and planning** — What are the goals and objectives in handling an incident?
2. **Notification** — Who should be contacted in the case of an incident?
   - Local managers and personnel
   - Law enforcement and investigative agencies
   - Computer security incident handling teams
   - Affected and involved sites
   - Internal communications
   - Public relations and press releases
3. **Identifying an incident** — Is it an incident and how serious is it?

4. **Handling** — What should be done when an incident occurs?

   - **Notification** — Who should be notified about the incident?
   - **Protecting evidence and activity logs** — What records should be kept from before, during, and after the incident?
   - **Containment** — How can the damage be limited?
   - **Eradication** — How [do we] eliminate the reasons for the incident?
   - **Recovery** — How [do we] reestablish service and systems?
   - **Follow Up** — What actions should be taken after the incident?

5. **Aftermath** — What are the implications of past incidents?

Table 7-3: Incident Handling Summary

DETECTION AND ANALYSIS
Prioritize handling the incident based on the business impact.
Identify which resources have been affected and forecast which resources will be affected.
Estimate the current and potential technical effect of the incident.
Find the appropriate cell(s) in the prioritization matrix, based on the technical effect and affected resources.
Report the incident to the appropriate internal personnel and external organizations.
CONTAINMENT, ERADICATION, AND RECOVERY
Acquire, preserve, secure, and document evidence.
Contain the incident.
Eradicate the incident.
Identify and mitigate all vulnerabilities that were exploited.
Remove malicious code, inappropriate materials, and other components.
Recover from the incident.
Return affected systems to an operationally ready state.
Confirm that the affected systems are functioning normally.
If necessary, implement additional monitoring to look for future related activity.
POST-INCIDENT ACTIVITY
Create a follow-up report.
Hold a lessons-learned meeting.

NIST SP 800-61, "Computer Security Incident Handling Guide, Recommendations of the National Institute of Standards and Technology," January 2004.

Layered Security and IDS

Computer security is most effective when multiple layers of security controls are used within an organization, and an intrusion detection system (IDS) is best utilized when implemented using a *layered security* approach. This means that multiple steps are taken to secure the data, thereby increasing the workload and time required for an intruder to penetrate the network. Although a firewall is an excellent perimeter security device, it is just one element of an effective security strategy. The more elements, or layers, of security that can be added to protect the data, the more secure the infrastructure will remain.

Elements of an effective layered security approach include the following:

- Security policies, procedures, standards, and guidelines, including a high-level security policy
- Perimeter security, such as routers, firewalls, and other edge devices
- Hardware and/or software host security products
- Auditing, monitoring, intrusion detection, and response

Each of these layers may be implemented independently of the others, yet they are interdependent when functioning. An IDS that alerts to unauthorized access attempts or port scanning is useless without a response plan to react to the problem. Since each layer provides elements of protection, the defeat of any one layer should not lead to a failure of protection.

Intrusion Detection

An intrusion detection system monitors network traffic and/or monitors host audit logs in order to determine whether any violations of an organization's security policy have taken place. An IDS can detect intrusions that have circumvented or passed through a firewall or that are occurring within the local area network behind the firewall.

A networked system's security policy should require that designated system and network administrators and response team members are trained in the use of intrusion response tools and environments. Also, the policy should require that the inventory of all applications software, operating systems, supporting tools, and hardware be kept up to date, and quick access to backups in an emergency is required, even if they are stored at a remote site. This may include defining procedures that give specific managers the responsibility to authorize such access.

Intrusion detection (ID) processes must be planned and implemented to help organizations detect and respond to incidents before they occur. It's important to respond to incidents in an efficient and effective manner. For example, the information system security officer (ISSO) must determine how the organization is going to monitor the intrusion detection system, who will monitor it, how alerts will be processed, and how the incident is remediated and with what level of response. The critical issues involved are as follows:

- Protecting assets that could be compromised

- Protecting resources that could be utilized more profitably if an incident did not require their services

- Complying with (government or other) regulations

- Preventing the use of your systems in attacks against other systems (which could cause you to incur legal liability)

- Minimizing the potential for negative exposure

The most common approaches to ID are *statistical anomaly detection* (also known as *behavior-based*) and *pattern-matching* (also known as *knowledge-based* or *signature-based*) *detection*. ID systems that operate on a specific host and detect malicious activity on that host only are called *host-based ID systems*. ID systems that operate on network segments and analyze that segment's traffic are called *network-based ID systems*. Because there are pros and cons for each, an effective IDS should use a combination of both network- and host-based intrusion detection systems. A truly effective IDS will detect common attacks as they occur, which includes distributed attacks.

Network-Based ID

Network-based ID systems commonly reside on a discrete network segment and monitor the traffic on that network segment. They usually consist of a network appliance with a network interface card (NIC) that is operating in promiscuous mode and is intercepting and analyzing the network packets in real time.

Network-based ID involves looking at the packets on the network as they pass by some sensor. The sensor can see only the packets that happen to be carried on its particular network segment. Network traffic on other segments cannot be monitored properly by a network-based IDS.

Packets are identified to be of interest if they match a signature. Three primary types of signatures are as follows:

- **String signatures** — String signatures look for a text string that indicates a possible attack.

- **Port signatures** — Port signatures watch for connection attempts to well-known, frequently attacked ports.

- **Header condition signatures** — Header signatures watch for dangerous or illogical combinations in packet headers.

A network-based IDS usually provides reliable, real-time information without consuming network or host resources because it is passive when acquiring data.

Because a network-based IDS reviews packets and headers, it can also detect denial-of-service (DoS) attacks. Furthermore, because this IDS is monitoring an attack in real time, it can also respond to an attack in progress, thereby limiting damage.

A problem with a network-based IDS system is that it will not detect attacks against a host made by an intruder who is logged in at the host's terminal. If a network IDS, along with some additional support mechanism, determines that an attack is being mounted against a host, it is usually not capable of determining the type or effectiveness of the attack being launched.

Host-Based ID

Host-based ID systems use small programs (intelligent agents) that reside on a host computer. They monitor the operating system for inappropriate activity, writing to log files and triggering alarms if anything is detected. Host-based systems look for activity only on the host computer; they do not monitor the entire network segment.

A host-based IDS can review the system and event logs to detect an attack on the host and determine whether the attack was successful. (It is also easier to respond to an attack from the host.) Detection capabilities of host-based ID systems are limited by the incompleteness of most host audit log capabilities.

In summary, host-based ID systems have the following characteristics:

- Monitor accesses and changes to critical system files and changes in user privileges.
- Detect trusted-insider attacks better than network-based IDS.
- Are relatively effective for detecting attacks from the outside.
- Can be configured to look at all network packets, connection attempts, or login attempts to the monitored machine, including dial-in attempts or other non-network-related communication ports.

An IDS detects an attack through one of two conceptual approaches: a signature-based ID or a statistical anomaly–based ID. These two mechanisms are also referred to as knowledge-based IDS and behavior-based IDS, respectively.

Signature-Based ID

In a signature-based (or knowledge-based) ID system, signatures or attributes that characterize an attack are stored for reference. When data about events is acquired from host audit logs or from network packet monitoring, this data is compared with the attack signature database. If there is a match, then a response is initiated.

These systems use a database of previous attacks and known system vulnerabilities to look for current attempts to exploit their vulnerabilities, and trigger an alarm if an attempt is found. These systems are more common than behavior-based ID systems. The advantages of signature-based ID systems are as follows:

- The system is characterized by low false-alarm rates (or positives).
- The alarms are standardized and clearly understandable by security personnel.

A weakness of a signature-based ID or knowledge-based approach is the failure to characterize slow attacks that extend over a long time period. To identify these types of attacks, large amounts of information must be held for extended time periods. Another issue with signature-based IDs is that only attack signatures that are stored in their database are detected. The main disadvantages of signature-based ID systems are as follows:

- The system is resource-intensive. The knowledge database continually needs maintenance and updating with new vulnerabilities and environments to remain accurate.
- Because knowledge about attacks is very focused (dependent on the operating system, version, platform, and application), new, unique, or original attacks often go unnoticed.

Statistical Anomaly–Based ID

Statistical anomaly- or behavior-based ID systems dynamically detect deviations from the learned patterns of user behavior and trigger an alarm when an exceptional (outside of normal system use) activity occurs. Behavior-based ID systems are less common than knowledge-based ID systems. Behavior-based ID systems learn normal or expected behavior of the system or the users and assume that an intrusion can be detected by observing deviations from this norm.

With this method, an IDS acquires data and defines a normal usage profile for the network or host that is being monitored. This characterization is accomplished by taking statistical samples of the system over a period of normal use. Typical characterization information used to establish a normal profile includes memory usage, CPU utilization, and network packet types. With this approach, new attacks can be detected because they produce abnormal system statistics. The advantages of behavior-based ID systems are as follows:

- The system can dynamically adapt to new, unique, or original vulnerabilities.
- A behavior-based ID system is not as dependent upon specific operating systems as a knowledge-based ID system.
- They help detect abuse of privileges types of attacks that do not actually involve exploiting any security vulnerability.

An important disadvantage of a statistical anomaly–based ID are that it will not detect an attack that does not significantly change the system operating characteristics, or it might falsely detect a non-attack event that caused a momentary anomaly in the system. Additional disadvantages of behavior-based ID systems are as follows:

- They are characterized by high false-alarm rates. Excessive positives are the most common failure of behavior-based ID systems and can create data noise that can make the system unusable or difficult to use.

- The activity and behavior of the users while in the networked system might not be static enough to effectively implement a behavior-based ID system.

- The network may experience an attack at the same time the intrusion detection system is learning the behavior.

IDS Issues

Many challenges confront the effective use of IDS, including the following:

- Increases in the types of intruder goals, intruder abilities, tool sophistication, and diversity, as well as the use of more complex, subtle, and new attack scenarios

- The use of encrypted messages to transport malicious information

- The need to interoperate and correlate data across infrastructure environments with diverse technologies and policies

- Ever-increasing network traffic

- The lack of widely accepted ID terminology and conceptual structures

- Volatility in the ID marketplace that makes the purchase and maintenance of ID systems difficult

- Risks inherent in taking inappropriate automated response actions

- Attacks on the ID systems themselves

- Unacceptably high levels of false positives and false negatives, making it difficult to determine true positives

- The lack of objective ID system evaluation and test information

- The fact that most computing infrastructures are not designed to operate securely

- Limited network traffic visibility resulting from switched local area networks; faster networks preclude effective real-time analysis of all traffic on large pipes

An issue with the implementation of intrusion detection systems is the performance of the IDS when the network bandwidth begins to reach saturation levels. This concern applies directly to cloud systems. Obviously, there is a limit to the number of packets a network intrusion detection sensor can accurately analyze in any given time period. The higher the network traffic level and the more complex the analysis, the more the IDS may experience high error rates, such as the premature discard of copied network packets.

Another issue with IDS is the proper implementation of IDS sensors in a switched environment. This issue arises from the basic differences between standard hubs and switches. Hubs exclude only the port the packet came in on, and echo every packet to every port on the hub. Therefore, in networks employing only hubs, IDS sensors can be placed almost anywhere in the infrastructure.

However, when a packet comes into a switch, a temporary connection in the switch is first made to the destination port and then the packets are forwarded. This means more care must be exerted when placing IDS sensors in a switched environment to ensure that the sensor is able to see all of the network traffic.

Some switches permit spanning port configuration, which configures the switch to behave like a hub only for a specific port. The switch can be configured to span the data from a specific port to the IDS port. Unfortunately, some switches cannot be guaranteed to pass all the traffic to the spanned port, and most switches allow only one port to be spanned at a time.

Another partial solution is to place a hub between the monitored connections, such as between two switches, a router and a switch, or a server and a switch. This allows traffic to flow between the switch and the target but with traffic copied off to the IDS. This solution, however, spells the beginning of the end for the switched network, and removes the benefits of a switched solution.

Computer Security and Incident Response Teams

As part of a structured program of intrusion detection and response, a computer security incident response team (CSIRT) may be created. The prime directive of every CSIRT is incident response management, which manages an organization's response to events that pose a risk to its computing environment. This management often consists of the following:

- Coordinating the notification and distribution of information pertaining to the incident to the appropriate parties (those with a need to know) through a predefined escalation path

- Mitigating risk to the enterprise by minimizing the disruptions to normal business activities and the costs associated with remediating the incident (including public relations)

- Assembling teams of technical personnel to investigate the potential vulnerabilities and to resolve specific intrusions

Additional examples of CSIRT activities are as follows:

- Management of the network logs, including collection, retention, review, and analysis of data

- Management of an incident's resolution, management of the remediation of a vulnerability, and post-event reporting to the appropriate parties

Numerous CSIRTs have formed to address the issue of coordination and communication in response to security incidents. These response teams provide a coordinated and organized method of data sharing in their sphere of influence. This coordination may include the detection, prevention, and handling of security incidents; understanding the current state of security; and identifying trends in activity within their constituency. Because the Internet is a cooperative network, there is no single entity with the authority or responsibility for its security. Instead, authority is scattered across logical domains.

CERT/CC

The CERT Coordination Center (CERT/CC) is a unit of the Carnegie Mellon University Software Engineering Institute (SEI). SEI is a federally funded research and development center. CERT's mission is to alert the Internet community to vulnerabilities and attacks and to conduct research and training in the areas of computer security, including incident response.

FedCIRC

The Federal Computer Incident Response Center "established a collaborative partnership of computer incident response, security and law enforcement professionals who work together to handle computer security incidents and to provide both proactive and reactive security services for the U.S. Federal government." The FedCIRC charter states: "FedCIRC provides assistance and guidance in incident response and provides a centralized approach to incident handling across agency boundaries." The mission of FedCIRC is to:

- Provide civil agencies with technical information, tools, methods, assistance, and guidance.

- Be proactive and provide liaison activities and analytical support.

- Encourage the development of quality products and services through collaborative relationships with federal civil agencies, Department of Defense, academia, and private industry.

- Promote the highest security profile for government information technology (IT) resources.

- Promote incident response and handling procedural awareness with the federal government.

FedCIRC was established in October 1996 by the National Institute for Science and Technology and was put under the General Services Administration (GSA) in October 1998. It then formed the initial nucleus of the US-CERT when the Department of Homeland Security (DHS) was formed in March 2003 (www.us-cert.gov). US-CERT is charged with providing response support and defense against computer intrusions for the Federal Civil Executive Branch and information sharing and collaboration with state and local government, industry and international partners.

Forum of Incident Response and Security Teams

The Forum of Incident Response and Security Teams (FIRST) (http://www.first.org/) brings together a variety of computer security incident response teams from government, commercial, and academic organizations. FIRST aims to foster cooperation and coordination in incident prevention, to prompt rapid reaction to incidents, and to promote information sharing among members and the community at large.

The goals of FIRST are as follows:

- To foster cooperation among information technology constituents in the effective prevention and detection of and recovery from computer security incidents

- To provide a means for the communication of alert and advisory information on potential threats and emerging incident situations

- To facilitate the actions and activities of the FIRST members, including research and operational activities

- To facilitate the sharing of security-related information, tools, and techniques

Security Incident Notification Process

All potential, suspected, or known information security incidents should be reported to a computer security and incident response team. The CSIRT then assigns personnel who will assemble all needed resources to handle the reported incident. The incident coordinator makes decisions as to the interpretation of policy, standards, and procedures when applied to the incident.

Law enforcement and investigative agencies are notified, as needed and required, by the CSIRT. In the event of an incident that has legal consequences, it is important to establish contact with investigative agencies such as the FBI as soon as possible. Local law enforcement should also be informed as appropriate. Legal counsel should be notified of an incident as soon as it is reported. At a minimum, legal counsel should be involved in protecting the legal and financial interests of an organization.

The security incident notification process should provide some escalation mechanisms. To define such a mechanism, the CSIRT should create an internal classification scheme for incidents. The appropriate procedures are associated with each level of incident. The following list is an example of various levels of incidents.

Priority One — Protect human life and people's safety; human life always has precedence over all other considerations.

Priority Two — Protect restricted and/or internal data. Prevent exploitation of restricted systems, networks, or sites. Inform affected restricted sensitive systems, networks, or sites about already occurred penetrations while abiding by any applicable government regulations.

Priority Three — Protect other data, including managerial, because loss of data is costly in terms of resources. Prevent exploitations of other systems, networks, or sites, and inform already affected systems, networks, or sites about successful penetrations.

Priority Four — Prevent damage to systems (e.g., loss or alteration of system files, damage to disk drives, etc.). Damage to systems can result in costly down time and recovery.

Priority Five — Minimize disruption of computing resources (including processes). It is better in many cases to shut a system down or disconnect from a network than to risk damage to data or systems. Each data and system owner must evaluate the trade-off between shutting down and disconnecting, and staying up. This decision must be made prior to an incident occurring. There may be service agreements in place that may require keeping the systems up even in light of further damage occurring. However, the damage and scope of an incident may be so extensive that service agreements may have to be overridden.

Automated Notice and Recovery Mechanisms

Automated notice and recovery mechanisms can provide capabilities in one or more of the following areas: intruder prevention, intruder detection, and damage assessment. A number of automated intruder responses have been implemented as part of intrusion detection systems. Some responses may be active, such as terminating processes, closing connections, and disabling accounts. Other responses are passive, such as sending an e-mail to the system administrator.

Damage assessment is normally performed after an attack. A number of vulnerability scanning tools, such as Tiger, may be used to perform damage assessment. Other tools, such as Tripwire, were specifically developed to aid in damage assessment. At Texas A&M, a prototype tool called the Automated Incident Response System (AIRS) was developed to perform damage control and damage assessment on individual hosts in a network.

The electronic quarantine concept requires the use of host-based intrusion detection systems, which perform real-time activity monitoring and maintain a suspicion level for each user as well as an overall suspicion level of the monitored host. Although not absolutely required, host-based intrusion detection systems have the important ability to cooperate and share information in order to track users as they connect to other monitored hosts.

Automated notice and recovery are appealing. Because they do not require continuous human oversight, they can act more rapidly than humans and can be tailored to, and will consistently follow, specified policies. Common automated response capabilities include session logging, session termination, posting events on the event console, and alerting personnel through e-mail, paging, and other means.

However, most often an IDS requires a human operator to be in the loop. Given the current maturity of IDS technology, the dangers of automated response are significant and outweigh the preceding advantages. With the frequency of false positives that exists in the current generation of ID systems, the potential for inappropriate response to misdiagnosis is too high. In addition, automated response could be exploited by a perpetrator whose aim is to induce denial of service by spoofing an attack from a legitimate user. Finally, many intrusion detection tools provide some form of automated intruder response, but few security tools perform any automated recovery.

CIDDS, the Common Intrusion Detection Director System (also known as CID Director), is a dedicated hardware/software/operating system platform supporting the Air Force Information Warfare Center's (AFIWC) Intrusion Detection Tools (IDT) program. AFIWC is the U.S. Air Force Office of Primary Responsibility for the IDT program. Within AFIWC, the Air Force Computer Emergency Response Team (AFCERT) is charged with the responsibility for day-to-day administration and network security operations involving the IDT program.

CIDDS receives near-real-time connections data and associated transcripts from Automated Security Incident Measurement (ASIM) Sensor host machines and selected other intrusion detection tools. It stores this data on a local database and allows for detailed (local, regional, or theater-wide) correlation and analysis by human analysts and automated tools.

Encryption and Key Management

The security of sensitive information being processed and stored in a cloud environment is one the major points of concern to cloud providers, users, and potential users. Some specific issues are as follows:

- Confidence in satisfying compliance and regulatory requirements
- Uncertainty as to the geographic location of cloud platforms and stored data
- Effectiveness and reliability of access control and authentication mechanisms
- Exposure caused by cloud multi-tenancy
- Quality of recovery mechanisms and customer support
- Effectiveness and duration of SLAs
- Encryption levels based on data location, criticality of data, and state of data (at rest or in transmission)
- Concentration of large amounts of sensitive information in a single, cloud environment

The strength of encryption protection can be enhanced by the proper use of VM architectures, appropriate countermeasures, and hardware and software protections as discussed in the following sections.

VM Architecture

The VM architecture of cloud systems and strong encryption are mitigating mechanisms against attacks and intrusions. The multiple virtual networks pose numerous targets for intruders to attempt to attack; and even if they penetrate a VM, strong encryption of the contained data will prevent the compromise of sensitive information. For encryption to be of maximum effectiveness, key management has to be carefully planned and implemented. There are two options for encryption key management:

- **Local key management** — Controls keys at the user's site, outside of the cloud facilities. This option provides enhanced key security and administration.
- **Cloud key management** — Performs encryption and key management at the cloud. This approach provides for ease of data sharing and interoperability among VMs. In this mode, the cloud provider must ensure that information is protected during transmission and storage. Because of cloud multi-tenancy, the possibility of key disclosure exists, so strict key security must be enforced. Also, the use of multiple keys for different VMs reduces the exposure if one key is compromised.

Another factor affecting the strength of encryption protection is the availability of quality random numbers. In order to generate a cryptographically strong key, a supply of good random numbers is necessary. VMs, which are software simulators, do not normally have access to a source of true random numbers. This weakness can potentially allow an attacker to eventually predict a cryptographic key used by a VM, enabling a successful attack.

Key Protection Countermeasures

Because cryptographic keys in active use need to be stored somewhere, they are an available and attractive target for attack. To counter these attacks, the paper "Lest We Remember: Cold Boot Attacks on Encryption Keys,[1]" proposes the following countermeasures and their limitations:

- **Scrubbing memory** — Software should overwrite keys when they are no longer needed, and it should attempt to prevent keys from being paged to disk. Runtime libraries and operating systems should clear memory proactively and at boot time, e.g., via a destructive power-on self test (POST) before loading the operating system. If the attacker cannot bypass the POST, they cannot image the computer's memory with local-executing software, but may still physically move the memory chips to another computer with a more permissive BIOS.

- **Limiting booting from network or removable media** — If an administrative password to boot from alternate devices is required, an attacker could still swap out the primary hard drive or reset the nonvolatile random access memory (NVRAM) to re-enable booting from an alternate device.

- **Suspending a system safely** — Screen-locking, suspending a computer's state ("sleeping"), and suspending a system to disk ("hibernating") do not protect the system's memory. Suspending can be made safe by requiring a password or other form of authentication, such as a biometric like a fingerprint reader, in order to reawaken the machines, and encrypting the contents of the memory using a key derived from a strong password.

- **Avoiding precomputation** — Using precomputation to speed cryptographic operations can make keys more vulnerable because it tends to lead to redundant storage of key information, helping an attacker reconstruct keys in the presence of bit errors. Avoiding precomputation will affect performance, but a compromise could involve caching precomputed values for a predetermined period of time, to be discarded if not reused.

- **Key expansion** — This involves applying a transform to the key as it is stored in memory in order to make it more difficult to reconstruct in the case of errors.

- **Physically protecting the memory** — DRAM chips could be locked in place inside the machine, or encased in an epoxy material to discourage attempts at removal. This method is similar to tamper-resistant hardware used in cryptographic modules.

- **Architectural changes** — Changes to the machine's architecture can be made, such as adding key-store hardware that is guaranteed to erase its state on power-up, reset, and shutdown; or routine encryption of memory contents. These solutions may prevent attacks as long as the encryption keys are destroyed on reset or power loss.

- **Encrypting in the disk controller** — Encrypting the data in the hard disk controller hardware, as in Full Disk Encryption (FDE) systems such as Seagate's Drive Trust technology[2] is an approach that uses a write-only *key register* in the disk controller that can hold the software key. To be secure, the system must ensure that the key register is erased whenever a new operating system is booted on the computer.

- **Trusted computing** — Trusted computing hardware in the form of trusted platform modules (TPMs) is now installed in some PCs. TPMs don't prevent the storage of the key in RAM in all cases.

Hardware Protection

One type of hardware-based protection is trusted platform modules (TPMs). Similar in intent to virtual machines (VMs) and sandboxes, TPMs use hardware to enforce VM-like isolation of processes, in terms of their interactions with other processes and their access to data and resources. TPMs can provide public/private-key Rivest-Shamir-Adleman (RSA) based encryption and decryption, along with a tamperproof on-chip memory for storing keys and passwords. In addition to the commercial TPMs available, the U.S. DoD Anti-Tamper/Software Protection Initiative is working to produce trustworthy, tamperproof hardware modules for hosting high-consequence software.

The most common hardware-based protection is a trusted, tamper-resistant processor. Tamper-resistant processors provide software license enforcement and intellectual property protection by deterring reverse engineering and illegal copying of software hosted on those processors. Tamper-resistant processors also deter unauthorized modification of that software, and thus provide a lower-assurance alternative to TPMs for protecting the integrity of trusted software.

During normal operation, the trusted processor checks and verifies every piece of hardware and software that requests to be run on a computer during the boot-up process. The processor is designed to guarantee integrity by checking every entity when the machine boots up, and every entity that will be run or used on that machine after it boots up. The hardware can store all of the keys necessary to verify digital signatures, decrypt licenses, decrypt software before running it, and encrypt messages for any online protocols it may need to run — for example, for updates with another trusted remote entity, such as the software publisher.

When software is downloaded onto the computer, it is stored encrypted on the hard drive, and is decrypted and executed by the hardware, which also encrypts and decrypts data it sends and receives to random access memory. The same software or media could be encrypted in a different way for each trusted processor that would execute it because each processor has a unique decryption key. This aids in preventing piracy because the disseminated software is tied to the processor itself.

Another hardware-based protection involves the use of a smart card, physically secure token, or hardware dongle. Typically, the token needs to be present in order for the software to run, to have certain functionality, for access to a media file, and so on. Defeating this type of protection usually means circumventing the requirement for the hardware, rather than duplicating the hardware. The difficulty of the circumvention depends on the role that the hardware-based protection plays in the protection. A device that outputs a serial number is vulnerable to a *replay attack*, whereby the serial number is replayed to the software, without the presence of the hardware device. Conversely, a smart card that uses a challenge-response protocol (authenticating with different information every use) prevents the replay attack but is still vulnerable, for example, to modification of the software interacting with the smart card. A device that can be more difficult to defeat is a hardware device such as a dongle that plugs into the computer through the USB port, and decrypts content or provides some essential feature of the application or media file.

Software-Based Protection

Software-based encryption protection uses encryption wrappers, which dynamically encrypt and decrypt critical portions (or all) of the software code at runtime. This approach has many advantages:

- It hinders at attacker's ability to statically analyze the software because the software is encrypted at rest.

- The attacker is then forced to perform more sophisticated types of dynamic attacks, which can significantly increase the amount of time needed to defeat the protection.

- At no time during execution is the entire software image in the clear; code decrypts just before it executes, leaving other parts of the application encrypted. Therefore, no single snapshot of memory can expose the whole decrypted application.

- It uses lightweight encryption to minimize the computational cost of executing the protected software. The encryption can be combined with compression (by compressing before encryption), resulting in a smaller footprint for the software (less storage space). The addition of compression also makes the encryption more difficult to defeat by cryptanalysis.

Disadvantages include the following:

- The attacker can expose the software by taking many snapshots of the decrypted application (e.g., through memory dumps), compare them, and piece them together to create the unencrypted image of the software.

- The attacker can attempt to discover the various decryption keys that are present in the software. To delay the attacker, defensive mechanisms can be implemented in the software to prevent the attacker from using runtime attack tools, such as an anti-debugger or anti-memory dump. The defensive mechanisms can make it more difficult for the attacker to run and analyze the program in a synthetic (virtual machine) environment. However, a determined attacker can typically defeat these protections through the use of virtual machines that perform faithful emulation of the computer, including rarely used instructions, cache behavior, etc.

- The software does not perform as well due to the performance penalty caused by the decryption overhead.

Data Deduplication

Data deduplication, which is also known as *deduping* and *single-instance storage (SIS)*, is a method for reducing the volume of backup data. This space-saving approach identifies duplicate blocks of data and, instead of storing all of them, saves one copy and generates pointers to the others. During retrieval, the single data block instance can be accessed by file requests using an index of the stored data blocks.

Deduplication can be classified into the categories of *source-side* and *target-side*. Source-side deduplication performs the single-instance storage function prior to transmitting the data to a backup resource. In this way, only new information will be transmitted without sending duplicate copies of files. Target-based deduplication performs processing to identify duplicate blocks and save a single instance plus pointers on the backup system. The latter method requires higher bandwidth communication links to the backup source because of the larger amount of data transmitted.

Deduplication can also occur within a file, so that multiple files with common data but some differences can be backed up to save only the different information.

Hashing

In order to determine whether two files or data blocks are identical, they have to be compared. Instead of doing a bit-by-bit comparison, which can be time-consuming for very large files, the files are put through a hash algorithm such as SHA (Secure Hash Algorithm) 512, SHA 384, SHA 256, or MD5. The hash function generates a unique, fixed-length message digest (MD) or signature for each different, variable-length input. Then the MDs of files are compared; and if the signatures are equal, the files are identical. As with all hash functions, there is still a possibility that two different files can generate the same message digest. If this occurs, then two different files are thought to be identical when they are not. This situation is known as a *hash collision*. Although the probability of collisions is very low, some organizations use a number of different hash algorithms on the data and then compare the MDs to ensure that the files are identical.

If the data is to be encrypted and/or compressed as well as deduped, the operations should be done in the following order:

1. Compress data.
2. Generate hash signature, conduct comparison, and determine whether the files match or not.
3. Encrypt data.

This sequence is important when encryption is employed with deduping. On the target side, deduping must be performed before encryption is applied. The reason for this sequence is that when a file or block of data is encrypted, it is accomplished with a unique encryption key. Thus, if two identical files are encrypted before deduping, each file is enciphered with a different key. Because the keys are different, the two identical encrypted files will be dissimilar. Then, when the two identical encrypted files are deduped and compared, their MDs will be different.

Source-side deduplication does not present the same challenge. On the source side, deduping is normally done before encryption, so there is no problem in identifying identical files or blocks of data.

An additional issue that has to be considered is the migration of deduped data from one cloud array to another cloud array. If cloud providers use different deduping algorithms and functions, moving deduped data from one cloud to another might present a vendor lock-in problem. It is desirable to move the data in its optimized deduped form, and not to have to "rehydrate" it back to its original form before moving it.

Retirement

The deployment of virtual machines (VMs) in a cloud system brings efficiencies in server utilization and reduction of hardware costs. Conversely, their expansive use can also result in poorly planned deployments, increased licensing costs, and end of life retirement issues. Thus, VM deployment requires a life cycle management process with particular attention to the retirement of hardware and software.

VM Life Cycle

A typical VM life cycle is illustrated in Figure 7-2.

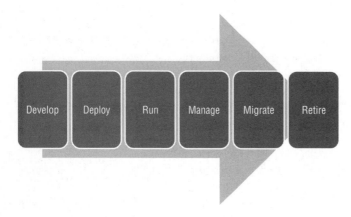

Figure 7-2: Typical VM life cycle

VM retirement requires knowledge of containers in memory and the interactions and dependencies of the VM with other VMs in the cloud. In particular, some of the important functions that have to be considered when deploying VMs in order to facilitate their orderly and efficient retirement at the end of their life cycle are summarized as follows:

- Identifying and cataloging of deployed VMs
- Tracking all containers
- Identifying installed VMs that do not conform to formal policies
- Ensuring that VMs were created from correct, trusted templates
- Identifying and managing progeny or relatives of a VM that might not be functioning properly, in order to take corrective action
- Having the capability to control and quarantine a VM

With this information and these capabilities in hand, an organization can formalize the VM retirement process by assigning an end-of-life date to a VM, including the capability to propagate this date to the VM's relatives or pre-defined groups of VMs. In addition, an alert can be programmed to remind the system administrator when the retirement date is approaching; and if the date is not changed, the VM will expire as assigned.

Policies and procedures addressing the end of life and disposal of hardware and software have to be developed, implemented, rehearsed, and reviewed. NIST SP 800-30, "Risk Management Guide for Information Technology Systems," states that "risk management activities are performed for system components that will be disposed of or replaced to ensure that the hardware and software are properly disposed of, that residual data is appropriately handled, and that system migration is conducted in a secure and systematic manner."

A critical aspect of end-of-life procedures in the cloud is the control and secure disposal of storage media. Media security controls should be designed to prevent the loss of sensitive information when the media are stored in a cloud outside of an organization's IT system. Some relevant definitions are as follows:

- **Logging** — Logging the use of data media provides accountability. Logging also assists in physical inventory control by preventing media from "walking away" and by facilitating their recovery process.

- **Access control** — Physical access control to the media is used to prevent unauthorized personnel from accessing it. This procedure is also a part of physical inventory control.

- **Proper disposal** — Proper disposal of the media after use is required to prevent data remanence. The process of removing information from used data media is called *sanitization*. Three techniques are commonly used for sanitization: overwriting, degaussing, and destruction.

Overwriting

Simply recopying new data to the media is not recommended because the application may not completely overwrite the old data properly; and strict configuration controls must be in place on both the operating system and the software itself. In addition, bad sectors on the media may not permit the software to overwrite old data properly.

To purge the media, the DoD requires overwriting with a pattern, then its complement, and finally with another pattern; for example, overwriting first with 0011 0101, followed by 1100 1010, then 1001 0111. To satisfy the DoD clearing requirement, a character must be written to all data locations in the disk.

The number of times an overwrite must be performed depends on the storage media, sometimes on its sensitivity, and sometimes on differing DoD component requirements, but seven times is most commonly recommended.

Degaussing

Degaussing is often recommended as the best method for purging most magnetic media. Degaussing is a process whereby the magnetic media are erased — that is, returned to the initial virgin state. Erasure via degaussing may be accomplished in two ways:

- In AC erasure, the media is degaussed by applying an alternating field that is reduced in amplitude over time from an initial high value (i.e., AC-powered)
- In DC erasure, the media is saturated by applying a unidirectional field (i.e., DC-powered or by employing a permanent magnet)

Degaussed magnetic hard drives generally require restoration of factory-installed timing tracks, so data purging is recommended.

Destruction

Paper reports and diskettes need to be physically destroyed before disposal. In addition, physical destruction of optical media (CD-ROM or WORM disks) is necessary. Destruction techniques include the following:

- Shredding
- Burning
- Physically breaking CD-ROMS and diskettes
- Destroying with acid

Care must be taken to limit access to reports prior to disposal and those stored for long periods. Paper reports should never be disposed of without shredding — for example, they should never be placed in a dumpster intact. They should be shredded by personnel with the proper level of security clearance. Some shredders cut in straight lines or strips; others cross-cut or disintegrate the material into pulp. Burning is also sometimes used to destroy paper reports, especially in the DoD.

In some cases, acid is used to destroy disk pack surfaces. Applying a concentration of hydriodic acid (55 to 58 percent solution) to the gamma ferric oxide disk surface is sometimes used as a method of media destruction. Of course, acid solutions should be used in a well-ventilated area only, and by qualified personnel.

Record Retention

Record retention refers to how long transactions and other types of records (legal, audit trails, e-mail, and so forth) should be retained according to management, legal, audit, or tax compliance requirements. An example of record retention could be the mandated retention periods for trial documentation or financial records. The retention of data media (tapes, diskettes, and backup media) can be based on one or more criteria, such as the number of days elapsed, number of days since creation, hold time, or other factors.

In the United States, organizations must also comply with e-discovery requirements established by the amended Federal Rules of Civil Procedure and various state court rules. *E-discovery* refers to the process in which electronic data is sought, located, secured, and searched with the intent of using it as evidence in the prosecution of a civil or criminal legal case.

Data Remanence

Data remanence refers to the data left on the media after the media has been erased. After erasure, there might be some physical traces left, which could enable the reconstruction of data that might contain sensitive material. Object reuse mechanisms ensure that system resources are allocated and reassigned among authorized users in a way that prevents the leakage of sensitive information, and that the authorized user of the system does not obtain residual information from system resources.

Object reuse has been defined as "the reassignment to some subject of a storage medium (e.g., page frame, disk sector, magnetic tape) that contained one or more objects. To be securely reassigned, no residual data can be available to the new subject through standard system mechanisms."[3]

Systems administrators and security administrators should be aware of the risks related to object reuse, declassification, destruction, and disposition of storage media.

Due Care and Due Diligence

The concepts of due care and due diligence require that an organization engage in good business practices relative to the organization's industry. Training employees in security awareness could be an example of due care, unlike simply creating a policy with no implementation plan or follow-up. Another example of due care is mandating employee statements that they have read and understood appropriate computer behavior.

Due diligence might be mandated by various legal requirements in the organization's industry or through compliance with governmental regulatory standards.

Due care and due diligence are becoming serious issues in computer operations today and in cloud systems in particular. In fact, the legal system has begun to hold major partners liable for the lack of due care in the event of a major security breach. Violations of security and privacy are hot-button issues confronting the Internet community, and standards covering best practices of due care are necessary for an organization's protection.

Documentation Control

A security system also needs documentation control. Documentation can include several things, such as security plans, contingency plans, risk analyses, and security policies and procedures. Most of this documentation must be protected from unauthorized disclosure; for example, printer output must be in a secure location. Disaster recovery documentation must also be readily available in the event of a disaster.

Summary

The life cycle of cloud software and VMs, as with other typical life cycles, ranges from design or development through deployment to maintenance and retirement. Currently, there are variations in each element of the life cycle because there are no commonly accepted cloud standards. As you have seen in this chapter, however, numerous groups, including open projects and international standards organizations and consortia, are addressing this problem by advancing basic principles and practices. These efforts are necessary if cloud computing is to grow and develop in a structured manner. In this chapter, the major efforts in standardization were reviewed and summarized in order to provide a roadmap to future developments.

Because security is a major concern of cloud providers and users, incident management and response are critical factors that affect the viability of cloud platforms. Both the client and the cloud provider must have effective and practiced incident management and response capabilities in place to ensure safe and protected cloud processing and data storage functions. In addition, encryption is an important tool that should be applied to affect the security of VMs and cloud information. Key management and countermeasures against cryptographic key attacks must be incorporated into the policies of both the cloud operators and the cloud users.

Finally, retirement of VMs, software in general, and hardware must follow rigorous policies and procedures in order to protect against the compromise of sensitive information. This includes approved methods for handling and disposal of storage media and paper documents, and being cognizant of legal, record retention, and other compliance requirements.

With an understanding of the cloud computing life cycle issues covered in this chapter, the next important steps are to determine how to take advantage of cloud computing benefits, what services should be moved to the cloud, and how to become involved in cloud computing information exchanges. These topics are discussed in Chapter 8.

Notes

1. Halderman, J. A., Schoen, S. D., Heninger, N., Clarkson, W., Paul, W., Calandrino, J. A., Feldman, A. J., Appelbaum, J., and Felten, E. W., "Lest We Remember: Cold Boot Attacks on Encryption Keys," Center for Information Technology Policy, Princeton University, 2008.

2. www.seagate.com/docs/pdf/whitepaper/TP564_DriveTrust_Oct06.pdf

3. NCSC-TG-018, "A Guide to Understanding Object Reuse in Trusted Systems." Light Blue Book (Rainbow Series), July, 1992.

CHAPTER 8

Useful Next Steps and Approaches

Removing the faults in a stage-coach may produce a perfect stage-coach, but it is unlikely to produce the first motor car.
—Edward de Bono

With the large volume of information on cloud computing and security presented in the previous chapters, it is valuable to use that information to make important decisions and find answers to common questions concerning the application of cloud computing in an organization.

This chapter focuses on exploring the questions to ask cloud providers when considering their services, the categories of applications that should be placed on the cloud, the type of cloud to be used, areas to obtain additional cloud information and assistance, and how to get started in cloud computing.

Getting Answers

Three common questions come up when an organization is considering using a cloud:

- What services should I move to the cloud?
- What questions should I ask the cloud provider?
- When should I use a public, private, or hybrid cloud?

These questions are addressed in the following sections.

What Services Should Be Moved to the Cloud?

One of the most important considerations in deciding which services should be placed on a cloud is cost. Cloud expenses include charges for storage, processing time, and bandwidth consumption. Bandwidth costs can be extremely high; therefore, a cloud application that involves a large amount of data being exchanged with a cloud over extended periods of time would not be a good cloud candidate. Also, applications that have a high degree of parallelism can be run more efficiently on cloud systems using available distributed processing frameworks such as Map/Reduce and Hadoop.

Another important consideration, especially for companies involved in e-commerce, is availability and resilience. Critical applications that can affect an organization's mission should not be placed on the cloud, and the cloud provider should demonstrate that its system exhibits resiliency in the event of system crashes and unexpected events.

Applications should be designed such that they can be moved from one cloud provider to another, in order to avoid being locked in to a particular vendor. In addition, some laws and regulations require that critical data be kept on the organization's site and under its control.

Cloud computing can also be used to provide cost-effective backup services and to handle overflow tasks during periods of peak activity such as seasonal work.

BACKUP SERVICES

A cloud can deliver protections against disasters by providing online data backup at an alternate location. This approach avoids large investments in redundant hardware and software and enables a cloud user to recover rapidly from a harmful event. Cloud computing provides this business continuity and disaster recovery through the use of dynamically scalable and virtualized resources.

The following additional points are useful in evaluating whether or not an application is a good candidate for cloud deployment:

- If an application has speed and response-time requirements, it is probably not practical to place it on a cloud.

- If a cloud provider requires an application to be written in a certain language and has restrictions such as no VPNs, it might not be cost effective to rewrite applications and make other related changes in order to migrate to a cloud.

- Some regulations such as HIPAA require that sensitive data be managed and controlled in-house.

- If gearing up internally to develop a product or service is going to take many months, and time to market is a consideration, moving applications to a cloud might be an effective solution.

- If an application can run more effectively on a parallelized system or in a virtualized environment, then it is a good candidate for migration to the cloud.

- If an application incorporates multi-tenancy, it is a good candidate for the cloud.

- Very critical applications and highly sensitive data that are essential to the survival of an organization are better kept in-house.

- In general, if an entire process is currently being run well in-house and there are no compelling maintenance, staffing, and other resource issues, there is no need to partition it out to a cloud.

- Selected applications that involve serious liability issues might be better kept inside an organization's IT system.

What Questions Should You Ask Your Cloud Provider?

There are numerous questions that can be asked of a cloud provider, including concerns about security, performance, cost, control, availability, resiliency, and vendor lock-in. Some of the critical questions that should be asked that address these concerns are as follows:

- Do I have any control or choice over where my information will be stored? Where will my data reside and what are the security and privacy laws in effect in those locations?

- Are your cloud operations available for physical inspection?

- Can you provide an estimate of historical downtimes at your operation?

- Are there any exit charges or penalties for migrating from your cloud to another vendor's cloud operation? Do you delete all my data from your systems if I move to another vendor? How do you prove to me that you have completely removed all my data from your cloud system?

- Can you provide documentation about your disaster recovery policies and procedures and how they are implemented?

- What are your organization's privacy policies and policies addressing ownership of client data?

- Will you provide a sample of your log files so that the types of data being recorded are available for review?

- What are your policies concerning my sensitive information when a law enforcement agency presents a subpoena for that data? What protections for my information can you provide in this event?

- Will you provide samples of your SLA?

If an application involves real-time streaming media, it is important to ask the cloud provider if its load-balancing approach supports *direct server return (DSR)*. In DSR, server data is sent directly to the client without having to go through intermediate, delay-inducing processing, such as a load balancer.

An obvious question is "How can the client determine if an instance of an application is available and if multiple instances have been unnecessarily launched?" Superfluous instances can result in higher costs; and, conversely, a client should have the assurance that an instance will be relaunched after a system failure.

It is also important to determine the cloud provider's auditing practices and liability protections, as well as authentication, authorization, and other security processes. For example, does the vendor encrypt the client's data both in storage and during transmission? What types of encryption technologies are employed? Are employees vetted to ensure they will not compromise critical data on the cloud?

The user has to understand how the cloud provider implements the provisioning and de-provisioning of resources and if these functions can be accomplished on demand and in an automated fashion. The provider should also be asked to explain its fail-over policies and capabilities.

While there are probably many more areas that have to be examined, the answers to these questions and concerns will give a potential cloud user a fairly good picture of the cloud provider's capabilities, responsibilities, and approaches to protecting client data.

When Should You Use a Public, Private, or Hybrid Cloud?

Recall that a private cloud is owned and controlled by a single party whose services are provided on a private network. The hardware and software are purchased by the private organization; and it may be housed on or off the organization's premises, and could be managed by the organization or a third party. Following are the principal advantages of using a private cloud:

- Delivery of cloud economic and flexibility benefits inside an organization

- Means to develop and debug new applications and then eventually transfer them to a public cloud

- Means to meet regulatory and legal requirements without having to interact with a cloud provider

- Path to leveraging existing investments in computational resources, such as virtualization software
- Utilization of other available resources in proximity to the private cloud
- Ability to directly control security, sensitive applications, and data
- Capability to develop and implement desired privacy policies
- Means to control hardware characteristics and provisioning
- Ability to reduce operational costs and increase server utilization
- Opportunity to increase use of automation and standards

A public cloud, which provides a shared computing environment through the Internet, is more efficient because of common resources, but it poses more security risks. A public cloud is a good choice if the following conditions exist:

- Budget limitations on capital expenditures for computing resources.
- Application code has to be developed and tested.
- Preference for a pay-as-you-go model.
- Desire to reduce IT operational and maintenance staff.
- Additional computing resources are needed on an intermittent basis, such as for seasonal workloads.
- Availability of large Internet bandwidth.
- It's necessary to support a large number of collaborative projects.
- SaaS applications can be provided by a trusted vendor.
- Applications are widely used and better implemented off-site, such as e-mail.

In general, a private cloud provides control and a more secure environment for sensitive applications and data, while a public cloud is more cost effective and provides increased flexibility and scalability. The confluence of these characteristics leads to consideration of a hybrid cloud, which is a combination of a public and private cloud. A hybrid cloud involves multiple providers and a plurality of platforms to manage and protect. A hybrid cloud is useful in the following situations:

- An organization uses a public cloud to communicate and exchange information with clients and partners, but protects associated data on an internal, private cloud.
- An organization has policies and means in place to manage and control movement of work projects in and out of the cloud.

- An organization has the ability to make decisions about where to run applications depending on changes in cost structures and services.

- An organization has the means and policies in place to ensure that regulatory and legal requirements are met when moving applications between private and public cloud environments.

- An organization needs secure SaaS applications and uses a private cloud provided by a cloud vendor.

Getting Help

Several working groups and forums have been established both to support the exchange of information among cloud users and potential users and to advance the development of cloud computing standards. These organizations welcome new participants and encourage discussions on topics of interest to the cloud community. A few of the prominent groups are summarized in the following sections.

Cloud Security Alliance

The stated mission of the Cloud Security Alliance (`http://www.cloudsecurity-alliance.org/`) is "to promote the use of best practices for providing security assurance within Cloud Computing, and provide education on the uses of Cloud Computing to help secure all other forms of computing." The Alliance has published a document titled "Security Guidance for Critical Areas of Focus in Cloud Computing," which can be viewed at `http://www.cloudsecurity-alliance.org/guidance/csaguide.pdf`. The document defines the following 15 domains that are critical in cloud security:

- Cloud Architecture
  - Domain 1: Cloud Computing Architectural Framework
- Governing in the Cloud
  - Domain 2: Governance and Enterprise Risk Management
  - Domain 3: Legal
  - Domain 4: Electronic Discovery
  - Domain 5: Compliance and Audit
  - Domain 6: Information Lifecycle Management
  - Domain 7: Portability and Interoperability

- Operating in the Cloud
  - Domain 8: Traditional Security, Business Continuity and Disaster Recovery
  - Domain 9: Data Center Operations
  - Domain 10: Incident Response, Notification and Remediation
  - Domain 11: Application Security
  - Domain 12: Encryption and Key Management
  - Domain 13: Identity and Access Management
  - Domain 14: Storage
  - Domain 15: Virtualization

Interested parties can obtain a complimentary membership in the Alliance through their LinkedIn location at `http://www.linkedin.com/groups?gid=1864210`. Current members include HP, AT&T, Dell, MacAfee, and Microsoft.

In addition, industry groups and not-for-profit groups can become affiliates of the Cloud Security Alliance. Information on the affiliates program is available at `affiliates@cloudsecurityalliance`.

Cloud Computing Google Groups

Google Groups provides the means for individuals and organizations to set up a Group site devoted to a special interest or topic. Having done so, group members can communicate through the Web or e-mail to exchange information on their subjects of interest.

The Cloud Computing Google Group website is located at `http://groups.google.com/group/cloud-computing`. Google Group rules allow the following interactions with the website:

- Anybody can view group content.
- Only managers can view a group's members list.
- People can request an invitation to join.
- Members can create and edit pages.
- Only managers can upload files.
- Only members can post.
- All messages are held for moderation.
- Messages from new members are moderated.

Anyone wishing to join the Cloud Computing Google Group can apply at `http://www.linkedin.com/e/gis/61513/6213F13BB1AA`.

Cloud Computing Interoperability Forum

The Cloud Computing Interoperability Forum (CCIF) (`http://www.cloud forum.org`) defines its mission as follows: "CCIF is an open, vendor neutral, open community of technology advocates, and consumers dedicated to driving the rapid adoption of global cloud computing services. CCIF shall accomplish this by working through the use of open forums (physical and virtual) focused on building community consensus, exploring emerging trends, and advocating best practices/reference architectures for the purposes of standardized cloud computing."

CCIF members include Intel, Cisco, Sun, IBM, and RSA.

The motivation for the CCIF was to define a common cloud computing interface and uniform definitions to support interoperability among cloud vendors.

The CCIF conducts meetings and workshops to involve the broad cloud computing community in the determination of appropriate standards and best practices and to develop vendor-neutral approaches.

Open Cloud Consortium

The Open Cloud Consortium (OCC) (`opencloudconsortium.org/`) comprises universities and vendors, and is focused on standards and open frameworks to promote cloud interoperability. OCC members include Cisco, Northwestern University, Johns Hopkins University, the University of Chicago, and the California Institute for Telecommunications and Information Technology (Calit2). The stated goals of the OCC are as follows:

- Manage and operate an open cloud testbed.

- Generate cloud computing benchmarks.

- Develop cloud computing standards and frameworks to promote interoperability.

- Conduct workshops relating to cloud computing.

The Open Cloud Consortium is organized into the following four working groups:

- **Working Group on Standards and Interoperability for Large Data Clouds** — Develops standards for interoperability among large data clouds such as Hadoop Map/Reduce and distributed file systems. Hadoop Map/Reduce is a software framework for developing applications that parallel process terabytes of data on large numbers of computing nodes.

■ **The Open Cloud Testbed Working Group** — Operates the Open Cloud Testbed. Membership is restricted to participants that can contribute resources to the testbed.

■ **The Open Science Data Cloud (OSDC) Working Group** — Operates a large data cloud to support research. Members of this group include the Institute for Genomics and Systems Biology at the University of Chicago, Johns Hopkins University, the Laboratory for Advanced Computing at the University of Illinois at Chicago, and Northwestern University.

■ **Intercloud Testbed Working Group** — Operates a testbed to explore the services of the Interface to Metadata Access Point (IF-MAP) protocol. IF-MAP supports integrated security by providing the capability for security mechanisms such as intrusion detection systems to acquire and share information that can be evaluated by MAP for security breaches.

Membership information for the consortium can be found at `http://opencloudconsortium.org/membership-documents/`.

Getting Started

Fortunately, it's easy to get started in cloud computing; unfortunately, it's a problem if your IT department isn't prepared. Remember that just because this technology now has the word "cloud" in front of it, it doesn't mean that traditional information systems security standards don't apply.

This is especially important when an organization begins to shift to virtual all-cloud operations. Now the lion's share of your computing systems may move under the control of a third-party provider. Your task is to not only acquire cloud services that can fit with your internal systems, but also guarantee that the new cloud services interoperate with your traditional infrastructure.

Cloud computing can make it difficult for security professionals to implement best practices, both in-house and when using Cloud Service Providers (CSPs). In this section, we'll take a high view, and give you some pointers on the best way to start your cloud computing security journey.

Top Ten List

We've given you a ton of information and advice throughout the book, so here we'll try to condense it down to just a few points to get you started. Okay, there's more than just ten items here, but it's easier to digest if you create a hierarchical system.

1. Assess Your Data's Sensitivity

You need to know how much security is enough, and to do that you need to know the security needs of your data. Therefore, companies should assess the sensitivity of the data they are considering moving to the cloud.

There's several ways to approach this determination. You might be subject to various compliance regulations that will require data sensitivity classification, such as the following:

- BASEL II
- DoD Directive 8500.1
- FISMA
- Gramm-Leach-Bliley
- HIPAA
- NERC
- Payment Card Industry (PCI) Data Security Standard
- Sarbanes-Oxley

You might decide to identify your information data assets and then institute data classification security management practices. That means classifying your organization's assets and rating their vulnerabilities so that effective security controls can be implemented.

The Information Classification Process

The information that an organization processes must be classified according to the organization's sensitivity to its loss or disclosure. The information system owner is responsible for defining the sensitivity level of the data. Classification according to a defined classification scheme enables the security controls to be properly implemented.

Implementing information classification has several clear benefits to an organization, such as:

- It demonstrates an organization's commitment to security protections.
- Classification helps identify which information is the most sensitive or vital to an organization.
- It supports the tenets of confidentiality, integrity, and availability as it pertains to data.
- It also helps identify which protections apply to which information.
- Classification might be required for regulatory, compliance, or legal reasons.

The following classification terms are often used in the private sector:

- **Public** — Information that is similar to unclassified information; all of a company's information that does not fit into any of the next categories can be considered public. While its unauthorized disclosure may be against policy, it is not expected to impact seriously or adversely the organization, its employees, and/or its customers.

- **Sensitive** — Information that requires a higher level of classification than public data. This information is protected from a loss of confidentiality as well as from a loss of integrity due to an unauthorized alteration. This classification applies to information that requires special precautions to ensure the integrity of the information by protecting it from unauthorized modification or deletion. It is information that requires a higher than normal assurance of accuracy and completeness.

- **Private** — This classification applies to personal information that is intended for use within the organization. Its unauthorized disclosure could seriously and adversely impact the organization and/or its employees. For example, salary levels and medical information are considered private.

- **Confidential** — This classification applies to the most sensitive business information that is intended strictly for use within the organization. Its unauthorized disclosure could seriously and adversely impact the organization, its stockholders, its business partners, and/or its customers. This information is exempt from disclosure under the provisions of the Freedom of Information Act or other applicable federal laws or regulations. For example, information about new product development, trade secrets, and merger negotiations is considered confidential.

In all of these categories, in addition to having the appropriate clearance to access the information, an individual or process must have a "need to know" the information. Thus, individuals cleared for high data classification levels may still not be authorized to access classified material at that same level if it is determined that access to that material is not needed for them to perform their assigned job functions. Table 8-1 shows a simple data classification scheme for the private sector. This is a very high level scheme, and is used to begin the classification process.

Table 8-1: Private/Commercial Sector Information Classification Scheme

DEFINITION	DESCRIPTION
Public Use	Information that is safe to disclose publicly
Internal Use Only	Information that is safe to disclose internally but not externally
Company Confidential	The most sensitive need-to-know information

Alternatively, an organization may use the high, medium, or low classification scheme based upon its data sensitivity needs and whether it requires high, medium, or low protective controls. For example, a system and its information may require a high degree of integrity and availability, yet have no need for confidentiality.

The designated owners of information are responsible for determining data classification levels, subject to executive management review. Table 8-2 shows a simple H/M/L data classification for sensitive information.

Table 8-2: H/M/L Data Classification

CATEGORY	DESCRIPTION
High	Could cause loss of life, imprisonment, major financial loss, or require legal remediation if the information is compromised
Medium	Could cause noticeable financial loss if the information is compromised
Low	Would cause only minor financial loss or require minor administrative action for correction if the information is compromised

(Source: NIST Special Publication 800-26, "Security Self-Assessment Guide for Information Technology Systems.")

Classification Criteria

Several criteria may be used to determine the classification of an information object:

- **Value** — Value is the number one commonly used criteria for classifying data in the private sector. If the information is valuable to an organization or its competitors, it needs to be classified.

- **Age** — The classification of information might be lowered if the information's value decreases over time. In the Department of Defense, for example, some classified documents are automatically declassified after a predetermined time period has passed.

- **Useful life** — If the information has been made obsolete due to new information, substantial changes in the company, or other reasons, the information can often be declassified.

- **Personal association** — If information is personally associated with specific individuals or is addressed by a privacy law, it might need to be classified. For example, investigative information that reveals informant names might need to remain classified.

Information Classification Procedures

There are several steps in establishing a classification system. These are the steps in priority order:

1. Identify the administrator and data custodian.

2. Specify the criteria for classifying and labeling the information.

3. Classify the data by its owner, who is subject to review by a supervisor.

4. Specify and document any exceptions to the classification policy.

5. Specify the controls that will be applied to each classification level.

6. Specify the termination procedures for declassifying the information or for transferring custody of the information to another entity.

7. Create an enterprise awareness program about the classification controls.

2. Analyze the Risks vs. Benefits of Cloud Computing

It's also very important to consider the risks and benefits of cloud computing. This can be done by executing a traditional risk assessment, while focusing it on the risk/benefit of exploiting the cloud.

Risk Management

Adopting a flexible risk management process can be a big help, if you don't do this already. RM is the identification, analysis, control, and minimization of loss that is associated with events. RM's main function is to mitigate risk. Mitigating risk means reducing risk until it reaches a level that is acceptable to an organization.

The risk management process minimizes the impact of threats realized and provides a foundation for effective management decision making. As defined in NIST SP 800-30, risk management is composed of three processes:

- Risk assessment
- Risk mitigation
- Evaluation and assessment

The RM task process has several elements, primarily including the following: performing a risk analysis; including the cost-benefit analysis of protections; and implementing, reviewing, and maintaining protections.

To enable this process, you need to determine some properties of the various elements, such as the value of assets, threats, and vulnerabilities, and the likelihood of events. A primary part of the RM process is assigning values to threats and estimating how often (or how likely) that threat might occur.

The identification of risk to an organization entails defining the following basic elements:

- The actual threat
- The possible consequences of the realized threat
- The probable frequency of the occurrence of a threat
- Confidence level that the threat will happen

Many formulas and processes are designed to help provide some certainty when answering these questions. Of course, because these threats are constantly evolving, it is impossible to consider every possibility. Risk management is an attempt to anticipate, to the extent possible, future threats, and to lower the possibility of their occurrence (and subsequent impact on the company).

It's important to remember that the risk to an enterprise can never be totally eliminated; that would entail ceasing operations. Risk management means finding out what level of risk the enterprise can safely tolerate and still continue to function effectively.

Trade-off Analysis

As you consider security management controls, a cost versus benefit analysis is a very important process. The need for, or value of, a particular security control must be weighed against its impact on resource allocation. A company can have exemplary security with a seemingly infinite budget, but there is always a point of diminishing returns, when the security demands interfere with the primary business. Making the financial case to upper management for various security controls is a very important part of a security manager's function.

A trade-off analysis can be formal or informal, depending upon the audience and the intent of the analysis. If the audience of the TOA is higher management or a client, often a formalized TOA, supported by objective evidence, documentation, and reports, will be necessary. If the TOA will be examined by internal staff or departments, often it can be less formal; but the fundamental concepts and principles still apply in either case.

Cloud Cube Model

The Jericho Forum's Cloud Cube model we described in Chapter 4 is a good starting point for determining the value of a cloud-based technology; it can help you get a better handle on the security issues associated with a specific flavor of cloud.

The Cloud Cube models suggests you ask four fundamental questions about your proposed cloud implementation:

- Is it an internal or external cloud?
- Does it use proprietary or open technology?

- Is the cloud service outsourced or done in-house?

- Does the cloud work within the company's security perimeter, such as a network firewall, or outside it?

Answering these four questions will help you to determine the necessary security controls.

3. Define Business Objectives

Early in the requirements process, approach cloud security from a higher level in the organization. That is, initially define business objectives, not technical objectives. Consider the following four aspects of any business objectives:

- **Business** — What are the vendor integration challenges? How important is data portability? Which data should remain in house?

- **Financial** — Build it or buy it? What are the costs of data loss? What should be part of a disaster recovery plan?

- **Legal and regulatory** — Key regulations include HIPAA and state data protection laws.

- **Technical** — These issues include authentication, data integrity, data flow, and privacy assessment.

4. Understand the Underlying Structure of Your Network

By creating application and network diagrams of the security architecture, you will understand the underlying cloud structure better and be better able to reach your security control objectives.

The network diagram should cover how the data travels through your network (data in motion), where it's stored (data at rest), and who's using it and how (data in use). You'll also need to know how cloud vendors are interacting with your applications, as this will affect security concerns.

INSTITUTE A LAYERED SECURITY ARCHITECTURE

In order to create a sound security architecture, consider a layered approach to addressing threats or reducing vulnerabilities. For example, using a packet-filtering router in conjunction with an application gateway and an intrusion detection system increases the amount of effort an attacker must expend to successfully attack your system.

5. Implement Traditional Best Practice Security Solutions

To preserve security of your private cloud-based virtual infrastructure, enact security best practices at both the traditional IT and virtual cloud layers. Traditional computer security best practices that translate directly to virtual environments include the following:

- **Encryption** — Use encryption wisely and make it well-focused. The sensitivity of the data may require that the network traffic to and from the VM be encrypted, and full disk encryption might also be required, using encryption at the host OS or hypervisor level. However, encryption isn't a panacea for a poorly designed security architecture; use it sparingly and examine your options for file encryption, volume encryption, and disk encryption carefully.

- **Physical security** — Sometimes the most obvious risk is the most serious and often overlooked. Keep the virtual system (and cloud management hosts) safe and secure behind carded doors, and environmentally safe.

- **Authentication and access control** — Authentication and access control lie at the foundation of a successful security program. The authentication capabilities within your virtual system should mimic the way your other physical systems authenticate. Two-factor authentication, one-time passwords, and biometrics should all be implemented in the same manner.

- **Separation of duties** — As systems get more complex, misconfiguration is more likely. Lack of expertise coupled with insufficient communication can make this more likely. Be sure to enforce least privileges with access controls and accountability.

- **Configuration, change control, and patch management** — This is very important, and sometimes overlooked in smaller organizations. Configuration and change control, patch management, and update processes need to be maintained in the virtual world as well as the physical world.

- **Intrusion detection and prevention** — As mentioned in Chapter 5, know what's coming into and going out of your network. A host-based intrusion prevention system coupled with a hypervisor-based solution could examine both virtual network traffic and traffic to the box.

6. Employ Virtualization Best Practices

A virtualized system also requires its own set of best practices, above and beyond the traditional physical IT security best practices (BPs) already described. Remember that these best security practices involve both processes and technologies; don't get so caught up in a shiny, magic bullet that you overlook processes and procedures. These best practices include the following:

- Enforce least privileges.
- Harden access controls.
- Monitor virtual traffic.
- Don't combine in-scope and out-of-scope VMs.
- Implement one primary function per VM.
- Track VM migrations.
- Include offline VMs in the patching process.
- Decommission VMs when they are no longer needed.
- Implement VM life cycle management.
- Bind sensitive VMs to separate physical network interfaces.
- Monitor VM snapshots and rollback.
- Scan and audit VMs prior to deployment.

7. Prevent Data Loss with Backups

Always backup, backup, and backup again. Computers fail, so plan for failure through redundancy and backups. Some cloud vendors provide backup services or data export processes, enabling companies to create their own backups. Other cloud vendors require you to use a custom solution or provide your own third-party application.

In addition, ensure that the backup stream traversing the cloud is encrypted, and that the physical backup location and media transfer and storage are also secure. In any event, know how your backup is being performed, and schedule regular restore tests. Be sure you know how to access the cloud vendor for the restore procedure if you've suffered a catastrophic failure.

8. Monitor and Audit

Monitor continually and audit frequently. Your cloud vendor must be able to guarantee that it can monitor who has accessed your data. Even though you may not control vulnerability monitoring in a public cloud scenario, you're still accountable for risk to the enterprise. Therefore, you'll need to assess the efficacy of the vendor's auditing program. Cloud vendors are going to be improving in this area, as each vendor seeks to be differentiated from the pack.

9. Seek Out Advice

Sometime a little knowledge can be a dangerous thing. Fortunately, a wealth of information is beginning to be disseminated about cloud security. In addition, the following three main resources are useful in securing your virtual infrastructure:

- **Cloud Security Alliance (CSA)** — We've described them before, and can't mention them enough. The CSA published its first security guideline in April 2009: "Security Guidance for Areas of Focus in Cloud Computing." There is now a Version 2.1 (`www.cloudsecurityalliance.org/guidance/csaguide.v2.1.pdf`) that continues its mission to "create and apply best practices to secure cloud computing." The CSA recognizes that a secure cloud is a "shared responsibility," and as such, the guidance it provides applies to both users and providers.

- **European Network and Information Security Agency (ENISA)** — In November 2009, the European Network and Information Security Agency (ENISA) brought together more than two dozen contributors to prepare and publish its "Cloud Computing: Benefits, Risks and Recommendations for Information Security." The contents of the ENISA cloud computing guide include detailed discussions on the benefits, risks, and vulnerabilities of cloud computing

- **National Institute of Science and Technology (NIST)** — NIST is the grand-daddy of computer security documents, and has recently begun creating guidelines for secure cloud computing (`http://csrc.nist.gov/groups/SNS/cloud-computing`). Expect much more from this organization soon.

CLOUD DATA MANAGEMENT INTERFACE (CDMI)

The Storage Networking Industry Association (SNIA) (`http://cdmi.snia-cloud.com`) **has generated the open Cloud Data Management Interface (CDMI) standard, version 1.0. The CDMI is designed to manage access to and storage of data on the cloud, and is based on the model of on-demand delivery of virtualized storage. This standard is important because it supports interoperability of the cloud storage mechanism among different cloud service providers.**

The CDMI standard builds on the existing functional and management cloud interfaces and offers an interface model that can be used as the basis for future cloud storage interfaces.

As stated in the standard document, "the SNIA Cloud Data Management Interface (CDMI) is the functional interface that applications may use to create, retrieve, update, and delete data elements from the cloud. As part of this interface, the client will be able to discover the capabilities of the cloud storage offering and to use this interface to manage containers and the data that is placed in them."[1]

> An important characteristic of this interface is that it can be used in a complementary fashion with existing propriety interfaces. The CDMI specification employs Representational State Transfer (RESTful) principles in its design. These principles embody features similar to those of the World Wide Web, whereby clients and servers interact and transfer data among each other. The RESTful principles were developed by Roy Fielding and described in the context of HTTP in his doctoral dissertation (see `http://www.ics.uci.edu/~fielding/pubs/dissertation/top.htm`). CDMI employs a variety of security mechanisms, including encryption, authorization, access controls, transport security, and media sanitization.

10. Employ Deception

A *honeypot* is a networked environment created solely for the purpose of identifying hackers and their activity. Usually, honeypots are impractical in the traditional IT world because of their expense, and therefore aren't employed routinely. If you aren't familiar with the concept of honeypots, we'd recommend reading the very entertaining 1989 book written by Clifford Stoll, *The Cuckoo's Egg: Tracking a Spy Through the Maze of Computer Espionage.*

A virtual machine honeypot, however, can be quickly set up and torn down in the DMZ, therefore reducing ownership costs. Also, the traffic can be isolated from the rest of the network, and heavy-duty IDS and monitoring can be employed.

Parting Words

Secure cloud delivery lives in a changing, challenging world, but the following benefits of virtualization can easily outweigh the risks:

- Major savings in initial capital outlay
- Important power savings, particularly now when electricity is expensive and lines are limited
- More efficient use of space in the data center
- Easier workload balancing through dynamic provisioning
- Faster deployment, rollback, and decommissioning of server farms
- Faster disaster recovery by mounting a snapshot image

We hope that this book, in addition to clearing up any cloud concerns you may have had, has given you some great new ideas and the confidence to jump into the cloud!

Notes

1. SNIA Cloud Storage Technical Working Group, `http://cdmi.sniacloud.com/`

Glossary of Terms and Acronyms

1000BaseT — 1,000 Mbps (1 Gbps) baseband Ethernet using twisted pair wire.

100BaseT — 100 Mbps baseband Ethernet using twisted pair wire.

10Base2 — 802.3 IEEE Ethernet standard for 10 Mbps Ethernet using coaxial cable (thinnet) rated to 185 meters.

10Base5 — 10 Mbps Ethernet using coaxial cable (thicknet) rated to 500 meters.

10BaseF — 10 Mbps baseband Ethernet using optical fiber.

10BaseT — 10 Mbps UTP Ethernet rated to 100 meters.

10Broad36 — 10 Mbps broadband Ethernet rated to 3,600 meters.

3DES — Triple Data Encryption Standard.

802.10 — IEEE standard that specifies security and privacy access methods for LANs.

802.11 — IEEE standard that specifies 1 Mbps and 2 Mbps wireless connectivity. Defines aspects of frequency hopping and direct-sequence spread spectrum (DSSS) systems for use in the 2.4 MHz ISM (industrial, scientific, medical) band. Also refers to the IEEE committee responsible for setting wireless LAN standards.

802.11a — Specifies high-speed wireless connectivity in the 5 GHz band using orthogonal frequency division multiplexing (OFDM) with data rates up to 54 Mbps.

802.11b — Specifies high-speed wireless connectivity in the 2.4 GHz ISM band up to 11 Mbps.

802.15 — Specification for Bluetooth LANs in the 2.4–2.5 GHz band.

802.2 — Standard that specifies the LLC (logical link control).

802.3 — Ethernet bus topology using carrier sense medium access control/carrier detect (CSMA/CD) for 10 Mbps wired LANs. Currently, it is the most popular LAN topology.

802.4 — Specifies a token-passing bus access method for LANs.

802.5 — Specifies a token-passing ring access method for LANs.

acceptance inspection — The final inspection to determine whether a facility or system meets specified technical and performance standards. Note: This inspection is held immediately after facility and software testing and is the basis for commissioning or accepting the information system.

acceptance testing — A type of testing used to determine whether the network is acceptable to the actual users.

access — A specific type of interaction between a subject and an object that results in the flow of information from one to the other.

access control — The process of limiting access to system resources only to authorized programs, processes, or other systems (on a network). This term is synonymous with controlled access and limited access.

access control mechanism — Hardware or software features, operating procedures, management procedures, and various combinations thereof that are designed to detect and prevent unauthorized access and to permit authorized access in an automated system.

access level — The hierarchical portion of the security level that is used to identify the sensitivity of data and the clearance or authorization of users. Note: The access level, in conjunction with the nonhierarchical categories, forms the sensitivity label of an object. See category, security level, and sensitivity label.

access list — A list of users, programs, and/or processes and the specifications of access categories to which each is assigned; a list denoting which users have what privileges to a particular resource.

access period — A segment of time, generally expressed on a daily or weekly basis, during which access rights prevail.

access point (AP) — A wireless LAN transceiver interface between the wireless network and a wired network. Access points forward frames between wireless devices and hosts on the LAN.

access port — A logical or physical identifier that a computer uses to distinguish different terminal input/output data streams.

access type — The nature of an access right to a particular device, program, or file (for example, read, write, execute, append, modify, delete, or create).

accountability — Property that allows auditing of IT system activities to be traced to persons or processes that may then be held responsible for their actions. Accountability includes authenticity and nonrepudiation.

accreditation — A formal declaration by the designated approving authoring (DAA) that the AIS is approved to operate in a particular security mode by using a prescribed set of safeguards. Accreditation is the official management authorization for operation of an AIS and is based on the certification process as well as other management considerations. The accreditation statement affixes security responsibility with the DAA and shows that due care has been taken for security.

accreditation authority — Synonymous with designated approving authority (DAA).

ACK — Acknowledgment; a short-return indication of the successful receipt of a message.

acknowledged connectionless service — A datagram-style service that includes error-control and flow-control mechanisms.

ACO — Authenticated ciphering offset.

acquisition organization — The government organization that is responsible for developing a system.

adaptive routing — A form of network routing whereby the path data packets traverse from a source to a destination node, depending upon the current state of the network, by calculating the best path through the network.

add-on security — The retrofitting of protection mechanisms implemented by hardware or software.

Address Resolution Protocol (ARP) — A TCP/IP protocol that binds logical (IP) addresses to physical addresses.

administrative security — The management constraints and supplemental controls established to provide an acceptable level of protection for data. Synonymous with procedural security.

Advanced Encryption Standard (AES) (Rijndael) — A symmetric block cipher with a block size of 128 bits in which the key can be 128, 192, or 256 bits. The Advanced Encryption Standard replaces the Date Encryption Standard (DES) and was announced on November 26, 2001, as Federal Information Processing Standard Publication (FIPS PUB 197).

AIS — Automated information system.

analog signal — An electrical signal with an amplitude that varies continuously.

Application Layer — The top layer of the OSI reference model, which is concerned with application programs. It provides services such as file transfer and e-mail to the network's end users.

application process — An entity, either human or software, that uses the services offered by the Application Layer of the OSI reference model.

application program interface — A software interface provided between a specialized communications program and an end-user application.

application software — Software that accomplishes functions such as database access, electronic mail, and menu prompts.

architecture — As refers to a computer system, an architecture describes the type of components, interfaces, and protocols the system uses and how they fit together. The configuration of any equipment or interconnected system or subsystems of equipment that is used in the automatic acquisition, storage, manipulation, management, movement, control, display, switching, interchange, transmission, or reception of data or information; includes computers, ancillary equipment, and services, including support services and related resources.

assurance — A measure of confidence that the security features and architecture of an AIS accurately mediate and enforce the security policy. Grounds for confidence that an IT product or system meets its security objectives. See Defense Information Technology Systems Certification and Accreditation Process (DITSCAP).

asymmetric (public) key encryption — Cryptographic system that employs two keys, a public key and a private key. The public key is made available to anyone wishing to send an encrypted message to an individual holding the corresponding private key of the public-private key pair. Any message encrypted with one of these keys can be decrypted with the other. The private key is always kept private. It should not be possible to derive the private key from the public key.

Asynchronous Transfer Mode — A cell-based connection-oriented data service offering high-speed data communications. ATM integrates circuit and packet switching to handle both constant and burst information at rates up to 2.488 Gbps. Also called cell relay.

asynchronous transmission — Type of communications data synchronization with no defined time relationship between transmission of data frames. See synchronous transmission.

attachment unit interface (AUI) — A 15-pin interface between an Ethernet Network Interface Card and a transceiver.

attack — The act of trying to bypass security controls on a system. An attack can be active, resulting in data modification, or passive, resulting in the release of data. Note: The fact that an attack is made does not necessarily mean that it will succeed. The degree of success depends on the vulnerability of the system or activity and the effectiveness of existing countermeasures.

audit trail — A chronological record of system activities that is sufficient to enable the reconstruction, reviewing, and examination of the sequence of environments and activities surrounding or leading to an operation, a procedure, or an event in a transaction — from its inception to its final result.

authenticate — (1) To verify the identity of a user, device, or other entity in a computer system, often as a prerequisite to allowing access to system resources.

(2) To verify the integrity of data that has been stored, transmitted, or otherwise exposed to possible unauthorized modification.

authentication — Generically, the process of verifying "who" is at the other end of a transmission.

authentication device — A device whose identity has been verified during the lifetime of the current link based on the authentication procedure.

authenticator — The means used to confirm the identity or verify the eligibility of a station, originator, or individual.

authenticity — The property that allows the ability to validate the claimed identity of a system entity.

authorization — The granting of access rights to a user, program, or process.

automated data processing security — Synonymous with automated information systems security.

automated information system (AIS) — An assembly of computer hardware, software, and/or firmware that is configured to collect, create, communicate, compute, disseminate, process, store, and/or control data or information.

automated information system security — Measures and controls that protect an AIS against Denial of Service (DoS) and unauthorized (accidental or intentional) disclosure, modification, or destruction of AISs and data. AIS security includes consideration of all hardware and/or software functions, characteristics, and/or features; operational procedures, accountability procedures, and access controls at the central computer facility, remote computers and terminal facilities; management constraints; physical structures and devices; and personnel and communication controls that are needed to provide an acceptable level of risk for the AIS and the data and information contained in the AIS. It includes the totality of security safeguards needed to provide an acceptable protection level for an AIS and for data handled by an AIS.

automated security monitoring — The use of automated procedures to ensure that security controls are not circumvented.

availability — Timely, reliable access to data and information services for authorized users.

availability of data — The condition in which data is in the place needed by the user, at the time the user needs it, and in the form needed by the user.

backbone network — A network that interconnects other networks.

back door — Synonymous with trapdoor.

backup plan — Synonymous with contingency plan.

bandwidth — Specifies the amount of the frequency spectrum that is usable for data transfer. In other words, bandwidth identifies the maximum data rate a signal can attain on the medium without encountering significant attenuation (loss of power). Also, the amount of information one can send through a connection.

baud rate — The number of pulses of a signal that occurs in one second. Thus, baud rate is the speed at which the digital signal pulses travel. Also, the rate at which data is transferred.

benign environment — A nonhostile environment that might be protected from external hostile elements by physical, personnel, and procedural security countermeasures.

between-the-lines entry — Unauthorized access obtained by tapping the temporarily inactive terminal of a legitimate user. See piggyback.

binary digit — See bit.

biometrics — Access control method in which an individual's physiological or behavioral characteristics are used to determine that individual's access to a particular resource.

BIOS — Basic Input/Output System; the BIOS is the first program to run when the computer is started. BIOS initializes and tests the computer hardware, loads and runs the operating system, and manages setup for making changes in the computer.

bit — Short for binary digit. A single-digit number in binary (0 or 1).

bit rate — The transmission rate of binary symbol 0s and 1s. Bit rate is equal to the total number of bits transmitted in one second.

Blackbox test — Testing design method in which an ethical hacking team has no knowledge of the target network.

Blackhat hacker — A hacker who conducts unethical and illegal attacks against information systems to gain unauthorized access to sensitive information.

blind signature — A form of digital signature whereby the signer is not privy to the content of the message.

block cipher — A symmetric key algorithm that operates on a fixed-length block of plaintext and transforms it into a fixed-length block of ciphertext. A block cipher is obtained by segregating plaintext into blocks of n characters or bits and applying the same encryption algorithm and key to each block.

Bluetooth — An open specification for wireless communication of data and voice, based on a low-cost, short-range radio link facilitating protected ad hoc connections for stationary and mobile communication environments.

bridge — A network device that provides internetworking functionality by connecting networks. Bridges can provide segmentation of data frames and can be used to connect LANs by forwarding packets across connections at the media access control (MAC) sublayer of the OSI model's Data Link Layer.

broadband — A transmission system in which signals are encoded and modulated into different frequencies and then transmitted simultaneously with other signals (that is, of a different frequency). A LAN broadband signal is commonly analog.

browsing — The act of searching through storage to locate or acquire information without necessarily knowing the existence or the format of the information being sought.

BSI ISO/IEC 17799:2000, BS 7799-I — 2000, Information technology — Code of practice for information security management, British Standards Institution, London, UK.

A standard intended to "provide a comprehensive set of controls comprising best practices in information security." ISO refers to the International Organization for Standardization, and IEC is the International Electrotechnical Commission.

bus topology — A type of network topology wherein all nodes are connected to a single length of cabling with a terminator at each end.

Business Software Alliance (BSA) — An international organization representing leading software and e-commerce developers in 65 countries around the world. BSA efforts include educating computer users about software copyrights; advocating for public policy that fosters innovation and expands trade opportunities; and fighting software piracy.

byte — A set of bits, usually eight, that represent a single character.

C&A — Certification and Accreditation.

CA — Certification Authority/Agent. See certification authority.

callback — A procedure for identifying a remote terminal. In a callback, the host system disconnects the caller and then dials the authorized telephone number of the remote terminal in order to reestablish the connection. Synonymous with dialback.

capability — A protected identifier that both identifies the object and specifies the access rights allowed to the accessor who possesses the capability. In a capability-based system, access to protected objects (such as files) is granted if the would-be accessor possesses a capability for the object.

Carnivore — A device used by the U.S. FBI to monitor ISP traffic ("Independent Technical Review of the Carnivore System — Draft report," U.S. Department of Justice Contract # 00-C-328 IITRI, CR-022-216, November 17, 2000).

carrier current LAN — A LAN that uses power lines within the facility as a medium for data transport.

carrier sense multiple access (CSMA) — The technique used to reduce transmission contention by listening for contention before transmitting.

carrier sense multiple access/collision detection (CSMA/CD) — The most common Ethernet cable access method.

category — A restrictive label that has been applied to classified or unclassified data as a means of increasing the protection of the data and further restricting its access.

category 1 twisted pair wire — Used for early analog telephone communications; not suitable for data.

category 2 twisted pair wire — Rated for 4 Mbps and used in 802.5 token ring networks.

category 3 twisted pair wire — Rated for 10 Mbps and used in 802.3 10Base-T Ethernet networks.

category 4 twisted pair wire — Rated for 16 Mbps and used in 802.5 token ring networks.

category 5 twisted pair wire — Rated for 100 Mbps and used in 100BaseT Ethernet networks.

CBC — See cipher block chaining.

CC — See Common Criteria.

Centronics — A de facto, standard 36-pin parallel 200 Kbps asynchronous interface for connecting printers and other devices to a computer.

CERT Coordination Center (CERT/CC) — A unit of the Carnegie Mellon University Software Engineering Institute (SEI). SEI is a federally funded R&D center. CERT's mission is to alert the Internet community to vulnerabilities and attacks and to conduct research and training in the areas of computer security, including incident response.

certification — The comprehensive evaluation of the technical and nontechnical security features of an AIS and other safeguards, made in support of the accreditation process, that establishes the extent to which a particular design and implementation meets a specified set of security requirements.

certification authority (CA) — The official responsible for performing the comprehensive evaluation of the technical and nontechnical security features of an IT system and other safeguards, made in support of the accreditation process, to establish the extent to which a particular design and implementation meet a set of specified security requirements.

cipher — A cryptographic transformation that operates on characters or bits.

cipher block chaining (CBC) — An encryption mode of the Data Encryption Standard (DES) that operates on plaintext blocks 64 bits in length.

ciphertext or cryptogram — An unintelligible encrypted message.

circuit-switched — The application of a network wherein a dedicated line is used to transmit information; contrast with packet-switched.

client — A computer that accesses a server's resources.

client/server architecture — A network system design in which a processor or computer designated as a file server or database server provides services to other client processors or computers. Applications are distributed between a host server and a remote client.

closed security environment — An environment in which both of the following conditions hold true:

(1) Application developers (including maintainers) have sufficient clearances and authorizations to provide an acceptable presumption that they have not introduced malicious logic, and (2) Configuration control provides sufficient assurance that applications and equipment are protected against the introduction of malicious logic prior to and during the operation of system applications.

closed shop — Data processing area using physical access controls to limit access to authorized personnel.

cloudburst — The term cloudburst has two meanings, one negative and one positive:

- Cloudburst (negative) — The failure of a cloud computing environment due to an inability to handle a spike in demand

- Cloudburst (positive) — The dynamic deployment of a software application that runs on internal organizational compute resources to a public cloud to address a spike in demand

cloudstorming — The act of connecting multiple cloud computing environments.

cloudware — A general term referring to a variety of software, typically at the infrastructure level, that enables building, deploying, running, or managing applications in a cloud computing environment.

cloud enabler — A general term that refers to organizations (typically vendors) who are not cloud providers per se, but make available technology, such as cloudware, that enables cloud computing.

cloud operating system (COS) — The COS manages the cloud infrastructure in an elastic and dynamic operating mode.

cloud-oriented architecture (COA) — An architecture for IT infrastructure and software applications that is optimized for use in cloud computing environments. The term is not yet in wide use, and like the term *cloud computing* itself, there is no common or generally accepted definition or specific description of a cloud-oriented architecture.

cloud portability — The ability to move applications (and often their associated data) across cloud computing environments from different cloud providers, as well as across private or internal cloud and public or external clouds.

cloud service architecture (CSA) — Coined by Jeff Barr, chief evangelist at Amazon Web Services, this term describes an architecture in which applications and application components act as services on the cloud, serving other applications within the same cloud environment.

cloud service provider (CSP) — An organization that makes a cloud computing environment available to others, such as an external or public cloud.

cloudsourcing — Leveraging services in the network cloud to provide external computing capabilities, often to replace more expensive local IT capabilities. Cloudsourcing can theoretically provide significant economic benefits, along with some attendant trade-offs. These trade-offs can include security and performance.

cloud spanning — Running an application in such a way that its components straddle multiple cloud environments (which could be any combination of internal/private and external/public clouds. Unlike cloudbursting, which refers strictly to expanding the application to an external cloud to handle spikes in demand, cloud spanning includes scenarios in which an application's components are continuously distributed across multiple clouds.

clustering — Situation in which a plaintext message generates identical ciphertext messages using the same transformation algorithm but with different cryptovariables or keys.

coaxial cable (coax) — Type of transmission cable consisting of a hollow outer cylindrical conductor that surrounds a single inner wire conductor for current flow. Because the shielding reduces the amount of electrical noise interference, coax can extend much greater lengths than twisted pair wiring.

code division multiple access (CDMA) — A spread spectrum digital cellular radio system that uses different codes to distinguish users.

codes — Cryptographic transformations that operate at the level of words or phrases.

collision detection — The detection of simultaneous transmissions on the communications medium.

Common Criteria — A standard for specifying and evaluating the features of computer products and systems.

Common Object Model (COM) — A model that enables two software components to communicate with each other independent of their platforms' operating systems and languages of implementation. As in the object-oriented paradigm, COM works with encapsulated objects.

Common Object Request Broker Architecture (CORBA) — A standard that uses the Object Request Broker (ORB) to implement exchanges among objects in a heterogeneous, distributed environment.

Communications Assistance for Law Enforcement Act (CALEA) of 1994 — An act that required all communications carriers to make wiretaps possible in ways approved by the FBI.

communications security (COMSEC) — Measures and controls taken to deny unauthorized persons information derived from telecommunications and to ensure the authenticity of such telecommunications. Communications security includes cryptosecurity, transmission security, emission security, and physical security of COMSEC material and information.

compartment — A class of information that has need-to-know access controls beyond those normally provided for access to confidential, secret, or top-secret information.

compartmented security mode — See modes of operation.

compensating controls — A combination of controls, such as physical and technical, or technical and administrative (or all three).

composition model — An information security model that investigates the resulting security properties when subsystems are combined.

compromise — A violation of a system's security policy such that unauthorized disclosure of sensitive information might have occurred.

compromising emanations — Unintentional data-related or intelligence-bearing signals that, when intercepted and analyzed, disclose the information transmission that is received, handled, or otherwise processed by any information processing equipment. See TEMPEST.

COMPUSEC — See computer security.

computer abuse — The misuse, alteration, disruption, or destruction of data-processing resources. The key is that computer abuse is intentional and improper.

computer cryptography — The use of a crypto-algorithm in a computer, microprocessor, or microcomputer to perform encryption or decryption in order to protect information or to authenticate users, sources, or information.

computer facility — The physical structure housing data processing operations.

computer forensics — Information collection from and about computer systems that is admissible in a court of law.

computer fraud — Computer-related crimes involving deliberate misrepresentation, alteration, or disclosure of data in order to obtain something of value (usually for monetary gain). A computer system must have been involved in the perpetration or cover-up of the act or series of acts. A computer system might have been involved through improper manipulation of input data, output or results, applications programs, data files, computer operations, communications, computer hardware, systems software, or firmware.

computer security (COMPUSEC) — Synonymous with automated information systems security.

computer security subsystem — A device designed to provide limited computer security features in a larger system environment.

Computer Security Technical Vulnerability Reporting Program (CSTVRP) — A program that focuses on technical vulnerabilities in commercially available hardware, firmware, and software products acquired by the DoD. CSTVRP provides for the reporting, cataloging, and discrete dissemination of technical vulnerability and corrective measure information to DoD components on a need-to-know basis.

computing environment — The total environment in which an automated information system, network, or component operates. The environment includes physical, administrative, and personnel procedures, as well as communication and networking relationships with other information systems.

COMSEC — See communications security.

concealment system — A method of achieving confidentiality in which sensitive information is hidden by embedding it inside irrelevant data.

confidentiality — Assurance that information is not disclosed to unauthorized persons, processes, or devices. The concept of holding sensitive data in confidence, limited to an appropriate set of individuals or organizations.

configuration control — The process of controlling modifications to the system's hardware, firmware, software, and documentation to provide sufficient assurance that the system is protected against the introduction of improper modifications prior to, during, and after system implementation. Compare with configuration management.

configuration management — The management of security features and assurances through control of changes made to a system's hardware, software, firmware, documentation, test, test fixtures, and test documentation throughout the development and operational life of the system. Compare with configuration control.

configuration manager — The individual or organization responsible for configuration control or configuration management.

confinement — The prevention of the leaking of sensitive data from a program.

confinement channel — Synonymous with covert channel.

confinement property — Synonymous with star property (* property).

connection-oriented service — Service that establishes a logical connection that provides flow control and error control between two stations that need to exchange data.

connectivity — A path through which communications signals can flow.

connectivity software — A software component that provides an interface between the networked appliance and the database or application software located on the network.

containment strategy — A strategy for stopping the spread of a disaster, and the identification of the provisions and processes required to contain the disaster.

contamination — The intermixing of data at different sensitivity and need-to-know levels. The lower-level data is said to be contaminated by the higher-level data; thus, the contaminating (higher-level) data might not receive the required level of protection.

contingency management — Establishing actions to be taken before, during, and after a threatening incident.

contingency plan — A plan for emergency response, backup operations, and post-disaster recovery maintained by an activity as a part of its security program; this plan ensures the availability of critical resources, and facilitates the continuity of operations in an emergency situation. Synonymous with disaster plan and emergency plan.

continuity of operations — Maintenance of essential IP services after a major outage.

control zone — The space, expressed in feet of radius, surrounding equipment processing sensitive information that is under sufficient physical and technical control to preclude an unauthorized entry or compromise.

controlled access — See access control.

controlled sharing — The condition that exists when access control is applied to all users and components of a system.

Copper Data Distributed Interface (CDDI) — A version of FDDI specifying the use of unshielded twisted pair wiring.

cost-risk analysis — The assessment of the cost of providing data protection for a system versus the cost of losing or compromising the data.

COTS — Commercial off-the-shelf. Typically refers to readily available computer hardware and software.

countermeasure — Any action, device, procedure, technique, or other measure that reduces the vulnerability of, or threat to, a system.

countermeasure/safeguard — An entity that mitigates the potential risk to an information system.

covert channel — A communications channel that enables two cooperating processes to transfer information in a manner that violates the system's security policy. Synonymous with confinement channel.

covert storage channel — A covert channel that involves the direct or indirect writing of a storage location by one process and the direct or indirect reading of the storage location by another process. Covert storage channels typically involve a finite resource (for example, sectors on a disk) shared by two subjects at different security levels.

covert timing channel — A covert channel in which one process signals information to another by modulating its own use of system resources (for example, CPU time) in such a way that this manipulation affects the real response time observed by the second process.

CPU — The central processing unit of a computer.

criteria — See DoD Trusted Computer System Evaluation Criteria.

CRL — Certificate Revocation List.

cryptanalysis — Refers to the ability to "break" the cipher so that the encrypted message can be read. Cryptanalysis can be accomplished by exploiting weaknesses in the cipher or somehow determining the key.

crypto-algorithm — A well-defined procedure, sequence of rules, or steps used to produce a key stream or ciphertext from plaintext, and vice versa. A step-by-step procedure that is used to encipher plaintext and decipher ciphertext. Also called a cryptographic algorithm.

cryptographic algorithm — See crypto-algorithm.

cryptographic application programming interface (CAPI) — An interface to a library of software functions that provide security and cryptography services. CAPI is designed for software developers to call functions from the library, which makes it easier to implement security services.

cryptography — The principles, means, and methods for rendering information unintelligible and for restoring encrypted information to intelligible form. The word cryptography comes from the Greek *kryptos*, meaning "hidden," and *graphein*, meaning "to write."

cryptosecurity — The security or protection resulting from the proper use of technically sound cryptosystems.

cryptosystem — A set of transformations from a message space to a ciphertext space. This system includes all cryptovariables (keys), plaintexts, and ciphertexts associated with the transformation algorithm.

cryptovariable — See key.

CSMA/CA — Carrier sense multiple access/collision avoidance, commonly used in 802.11 Ethernet and LocalTalk.

CSMA/CD — Carrier sense multiple access/collision detection, used in 802.3 Ethernet.

CSTVRP — See Computer Security Technical Vulnerability Reporting Program.

cyclic redundancy check (CRC) — A common error-detection process. A mathematical operation is applied to the data when transmitted. The result is appended to the core packet. Upon receipt, the same mathematical operation is performed and checked against the CRC. A mismatch indicates a very high probability that an error has occurred during transmission.

DAA — See designated approving authority.

DAC — See discretionary access control.

data dictionary — A database that comprises tools to support the analysis, design, and development of software and to support good software engineering practices.

Data Encryption Standard (DES) — A cryptographic algorithm for the protection of unclassified data, published in Federal Information Processing Standard (FIPS) 46. The DES, which was approved by the National Institute of Standards and Technology (NIST), is intended for public and government use.

data flow control — See information flow control.

data integrity — The attribute of data that is related to the preservation of its meaning and completeness, the consistency of its representation(s), and its correspondence to what it represents. When data meets a prior expectation of quality.

Data Link Layer — The OSI level that performs the assembly and transmission of data packets, including error control.

data mart — A database that comprises data or relations that have been extracted from the data warehouse. Information in the data mart is usually of interest to a particular group of people.

data mining — The process of analyzing large data sets in a data warehouse to find non-obvious patterns.

data scrubbing — Maintenance of a data warehouse by deleting information that is unreliable or no longer relevant.

data security — The protection of data from unauthorized (accidental or intentional) modification, destruction, or disclosure.

Data service unit/channel service unit (DSU/CSU) — A set of network components that reshape data signals into a form that can be effectively transmitted over a digital transmission medium, typically a leased 56 Kbps or T1 line.

data warehouse — A subject-oriented, integrated, time-variant, non-volatile collection of data in support of management's decision-making process.

database — A persistent collection of data items that form relations among each other.

database shadowing — A data redundancy process that uses the live processing of remote journaling but creates even more redundancy by duplicating the database sets to multiple servers.

datagram service — A connectionless form of packet switching whereby the source does not need to establish a connection with the destination before sending data packets.

DB-9 connector — A standard 9-pin connector commonly used with RS-232 serial interfaces on portable computers. The DB-9 connector does not support all RS-232 functions.

DB-15 connector — A standard 15-pin connector commonly used with RS-232 serial interfaces, Ethernet transceivers, and computer monitors.

DB-25 connector — A standard 25-pin connector commonly used with RS-232 serial interfaces. The DB-25 connector supports all RS-232 functions.

de facto standard — A standard based on broad usage and support but not directly specified by the IEEE.

decipher — To unscramble the encipherment process in order to make a message human readable.

declassification of AIS storage media — An administrative decision or procedure to remove or reduce the security classification of the subject media.

DeCSS — A program that bypasses the Content Scrambling System (CSS) software used to prevent the viewing of DVD movie disks on unlicensed platforms.

dedicated security mode — See modes of operation.

default — A value or option that is automatically chosen when no other value is specified.

default classification — A temporary classification reflecting the highest classification being processed in a system. The default classification is included in the caution statement that is affixed to the object.

defense information infrastructure (DII) — The DII is the seamless web of communications networks, computers, software, databases, applications, data, security services, and other capabilities that meets the information processing and transport needs of DoD users in peace and in all crises, conflict, humanitarian support, and wartime roles.

(DITSCAP) — Establishes for the defense entities a standard process, set of activities, general task descriptions, and management structure to certify and accredit IT systems that will maintain the required security posture. The process is designed to certify that the IT system meets the accreditation requirements and that the system will maintain the accredited security posture throughout the system life cycle. The four phases to the DITSCAP are Definition, Verification, Validation, and Post Accreditation.

degauss — To degauss a magnetic storage medium is to remove all the data stored on it by demagnetization. A degausser is a device used for this purpose.

Degausser Products List (DPL) — A list of commercially produced degaussers that meet National Security Agency (NSA) specifications. This list is included in the NSA Information Systems Security Products and Services Catalogue and is available through the Government Printing Office.

degraded fault tolerance — Specifies which capabilities the TOE will still provide after a system failure. Examples of general failures are flooding of the computer room, short-term power interruption, breakdown of a CPU or host, software failure, or buffer overflow. Only functions specified must be available.

Denial of Service (DoS) — Any action (or series of actions) that prevents any part of a system from functioning in accordance with its intended purpose. This includes any action that causes unauthorized destruction, modification, or delay of service. Synonymous with interdiction.

DES — See Data Encryption Standard.

Descriptive Top-Level Specification (DTLS) — A top-level specification that is written in a natural language (for example, English), an informal design notation, or a combination of the two.

designated approving authority — The official who has the authority to decide on accepting the security safeguards prescribed for an AIS, or the official who might be responsible for issuing an accreditation statement that records the decision to accept those safeguards.

developer — The organization that develops the information system.

dialback — Synonymous with callback.

dial-up — The service whereby a computer terminal can use the telephone to initiate and effect communication with a computer.

diffusion — A method of obscuring redundancy in plaintext by spreading the effect of the transformation over the ciphertext.

Digital Millennium Copyright Act (DMCA) of 1998 — In addition to addressing licensing and ownership information, the DMCA prohibits trading, manufacturing, or selling in any way that is intended to bypass copyright protection mechanisms.

DII — See defense information infrastructure.

Direct-sequence spread spectrum (DSSS) — A method used in 802.11b to split the frequency into 14 channels, each with a frequency range, by combining a data signal with a chipping sequence. Data rates of 1, 2, 5.5, and 11 Mbps are obtainable. DSSS spreads its signal continuously over this wide-frequency band.

disaster — A sudden, unplanned, calamitous event that produces great damage or loss; any event that prevents an organization from providing critical business functions for some undetermined period of time.

disaster plan — Synonymous with contingency plan.

disaster recovery plan — A procedure for emergency response, extended backup operations, and post-disaster recovery when an organization suffers a loss of computer resources and physical facilities.

discovery — In the context of legal proceedings and trial practice, a process in which the prosecution presents information it has uncovered to the defense. This information may include potential witnesses, reports resulting from the investigation, evidence, and so on. During an investigation, discovery refers to both the process undertaken by investigators to acquire evidence needed for prosecution of a case, and a step in the computer forensic process.

discretionary access control — A means of restricting access to objects based on the identity and need-to-know of the user, process, and/or groups to which they belong. The controls are discretionary in the sense that a subject that has certain access permissions and is capable of passing that permission (perhaps indirectly) on to any other subject. Compare with mandatory access control.

disk image backup — A bit-level, sector-by-sector copy of a disk that enables the examination of slack space; undeleted clusters; and, possibly, deleted files.

Distributed Component Object Model (DCOM) — A distributed object model that is similar to the Common Object Request Broker Architecture (CORBA). DCOM is the distributed version of COM; it supports remote objects as if the objects resided in the client's address space. A COM client can access a COM object through the use of a pointer to one of the object's interfaces and then invoke methods through that pointer.

Distributed Queue Dual Bus (DQDB) — The IEEE 802.6 standard that provides full-duplex 155 Mbps operation between nodes in a metropolitan area network.

distributed routing — A form of routing wherein each router on the network periodically identifies neighboring nodes, updates its routing table, and, with this information, sends its routing table to all of its neighbors. Because each node follows the same process, complete network topology information propagates through the network and eventually reaches each node.

DITSCAP — See Defense Information Technology Systems Certification and Accreditation Process.

DNS enumeration — Gathering information on DNS servers.

DoD — U.S. Department of Defense.

DoD Trusted Computer System Evaluation Criteria (TCSEC) — A document published by the National Computer Security Center containing a uniform set of basic requirements and evaluation classes for assessing degrees of assurance regarding the effectiveness of hardware and software security controls built into systems. These criteria are intended for use in the design and evaluation of systems that process and/or store sensitive or classified data. This document is Government Standard DoD 5200.28-STD and is frequently referred to as "The Criteria" or "The Orange Book."

DoJ — U.S. Department of Justice.

domain — The unique context (for example, access control parameters) in which a program is operating; in effect, the set of objects that a subject has the ability to access. See process and subject.

dominate — Security level S1 is said to dominate security level S2 if the hierarchical classification of S1 is greater than or equal to that of S2 and if the nonhierarchical categories of S1 include all those of S2 as a subset.

DoS attack — Denial of Service attack.

DPL — Degausser Products List.

DT — Data terminal.

due care — The care that an ordinary, prudent person would exercise under the same or similar circumstances. The terms due care and reasonable care are used interchangeably.

Dynamic Host Configuration Protocol (DHCP) — A protocol that issues IP addresses automatically within a specified range to devices such as PCs when they are first powered on. The device retains the use of the IP address for a specific license period that the system administrator can define.

EAP — Extensible Authentication Protocol. This is a Cisco proprietary protocol for enhanced user authentication and wireless security management.

EBCDIC — Extended Binary-Coded Decimal Interchange Code. An 8-bit character representation developed by IBM in the early 1960s.

ECC — Elliptic curve cryptography.

ECDSA — Elliptic curve digital signature algorithm.

Echelon — A cooperative, worldwide signal intelligence system that is run by the NSA of the United States, the Government Communications Head Quarters (GCHQ) of England, the Communications Security Establishment (CSE) of Canada, the Australian Defense Security Directorate (DSD), and the General Communications Security Bureau (GCSB) of New Zealand.

elastic computing — Provides the means to dynamically tailor computational resources such as storage, memory, and processing capability to address varying demand over time.

Electronic Communications Privacy Act (ECPA) of 1986 — An act that prohibited eavesdropping or the interception of message contents without distinguishing between private or public systems.

Electronic Data Interchange (EDI) — A service that provides communications for business transactions. ANSI standard X.12 defines the data format for EDI.

electronic vaulting — The transfer of backup data to an offsite location. This process is primarily a batch process of dumping the data through communications lines to a server at an alternate location.

Electronics Industry Association (EIA) — A U.S. standards organization that represents a large number of electronics firms.

emanations — See compromising emanations.

embedded system — A system that performs or controls a function, either in whole or in part, as an integral element of a larger system or subsystem.

emergency plan — Synonymous with contingency plan.

emission(s) security (EMSEC) — The protection resulting from all measures taken to deny unauthorized persons information of value derived from the intercept and analysis of compromising emanations from crypto-equipment or an IT system.

EMSEC — See emissions security.

encipher — To make a message unintelligible to all but its intended recipients.

end-to-end encryption — Encrypted information sent from the point of origin to the final destination. In symmetric key encryption, this process requires the sender and the receiver to have the identical key for the session.

Enhanced Hierarchical Development Methodology — An integrated set of tools designed to aid in creating, analyzing, modifying, managing, and documenting program specifications and proofs. This methodology includes a specification parser and typechecker, a theorem prover, and a multilevel security checker. Note: This methodology is not based upon the Hierarchical Development Methodology.

entrapment — The deliberate planting of apparent flaws in a system for the purpose of detecting attempted penetrations.

Enumeration — Gathering detailed information about a target information system.

environment — The aggregate of external procedures, conditions, and objects that affect the development, operation, and maintenance of a system.

erasure — A process by which a signal recorded on magnetic media is removed. Erasure is accomplished in two ways: (1) by alternating current erasure, whereby which the information is destroyed when an alternating high and low magnetic field is applied to the media; or (2) by direct current erasure, whereby the media is saturated by applying a unidirectional magnetic field.

Ethernet — An industry-standard local area network media access method that uses a bus topology and CSMA/CD. IEEE 802.3 is a standard that specifies Ethernet.

Ethernet repeater — A component that provides Ethernet connections among multiple stations sharing a common collision domain. Also referred to as a shared Ethernet hub.

Ethernet switch — More intelligent than a hub, with the capability to connect the sending station directly to the receiving station.

Ethical hacker — Trusted individual who performs penetration tests without malicious intent.

ETL — Endorsed Tools List.

ETSI — European Telecommunications Standards Institute.

evaluation — Assessment of an IT product or system against defined security functional and assurance criteria, performed by a combination of testing and analytic techniques.

Evaluation Assurance Level (EAL) — In the Common Criteria, the degree of examination of the product to be tested. EALs range from EA1 (functional testing) to EA7 (detailed testing and formal design verification). Each numbered package represents a point on the CCs predefined assurance scale. An EAL can be considered a level of confidence in the security functions of an IT product or system.

evolutionary program strategies — Generally characterized by design, development, and deployment of a preliminary capability that includes provisions for the evolutionary addition of future functionality and changes as requirements are further defined (DoD Directive 5000.1).

executive state — One of several states in which a system can operate and the only one in which certain privileged instructions can be executed. Such instructions cannot be executed when the system is operating in other (for example, user) states. Synonymous with supervisor state.

exigent circumstances doctrine — Specifies that a warrantless search and seizure of evidence can be conducted if there is probable cause to suspect criminal activity or destruction of evidence.

expert system shell — An off-the-shelf software package that implements an inference engine, a mechanism for entering knowledge, a user interface, and a system to provide explanations of the reasoning used to generate a solution. It provides the fundamental building blocks of an expert system and supports the entering of domain knowledge.

exploitable channel — Any information channel that is usable or detectable by subjects that are external to the trusted computing base, whose purpose is to violate the security policy of the system. See covert channel.

exposure — An instance of being exposed to losses from a threat.

external cloud — A cloud computing environment that is external to the boundaries of the organization. Although it often is, an external cloud is not necessarily a public cloud. Some external clouds make their cloud infrastructure available to specific other organizations and not to the public at large.

fail over — Operations automatically switching over to a backup system when one system/application fails.

fail-safe — Describes the automatic protection of programs and/or processing systems to maintain safety when a hardware or software failure is detected.

fail-secure — Describes a system that preserves a secure state during and after identified failures occur.

fail-soft — Describes the selective termination of affected nonessential processing when a hardware or software failure is detected in a system.

failure access — An unauthorized and usually inadvertent access to data resulting from a hardware or software failure in the system.

failure control — The methodology that is used to detect and provide fail-safe or fail-soft recovery from hardware and software failures in a system.

fault — A condition that causes a device or system component to fail to perform in a required manner.

fault-resilient systems — Systems designed without redundancy; in the event of failure, they result in a slightly longer down time.

FCC — Federal Communications Commission.

FDMA — Frequency division multiple access. A spectrum-sharing technique whereby the available spectrum is divided into a number of individual radio channels.

FDX — Full-duplex.

Federal Intelligence Surveillance Act (FISA) of 1978 — An act that limited wiretapping for national security purposes, enacted as a result of the Nixon Administration's history of using illegal wiretaps.

fetch protection — A system-provided restriction to prevent a program from accessing data in another user's segment of storage.

Fiber-Distributed Data Interface (FDDI) — An ANSI standard for token-passing networks. FDDI uses optical fiber and operates at 100 Mbps in dual, counter-rotating rings.

Fiestel cipher — An iterated block cipher that encrypts by breaking a plaintext block into two halves and, with a subkey, applying a "round" transformation to one of the halves. The output of this transformation is then XOR'd with the remaining half. The round is completed by swapping the two halves.

FIFO — First in, first out.

file server — A computer that provides network stations with controlled access to sharable resources. The network operating system (NOS) is loaded on the file server, and most sharable devices, including disk subsystems and printers, are attached to it.

file protection — The aggregate of all processes and procedures in a system designed to inhibit unauthorized access, contamination, or elimination of a file.

file security — The means by which access to computer files is limited to authorized users only.

File Transfer Protocol (FTP) — A TCP/IP protocol for file transfer.

FIPS — Federal Information Processing Standard.

firewall — A network device that shields the trusted network from unauthorized users in the untrusted network by blocking certain specific types of traffic. Many types of firewalls exist, including packet filtering and stateful inspection.

firmware — Executable programs stored in nonvolatile memory.

flaw hypothesis methodology — A systems analysis and penetration technique in which specifications and documentation for the system are analyzed and then hypotheses are made regarding flaws in the system. The list of hypothesized flaws is prioritized on the basis of the estimated probability that a flaw exists, on the ease of exploiting it if it does exist, and on the extent of control or compromise that it would provide. The prioritized list is used to direct a penetration attack against the system.

flow control — See information flow control.

frequency modulation (FM) — A method of transmitting information over a radio wave by changing frequencies.

Footprinting — Gathering information in both active and passive modes.

formal access approval — Documented approval by a data owner to allow access to a particular category of information.

Formal development methodology — A collection of languages and tools that enforces a rigorous method of verification. This methodology uses the Ina Jo specification language for successive stages of system development, including identification and modeling of requirements, high-level design, and program design.

formal proof — A complete and convincing mathematical argument presenting the full logical justification for each proof step for the truth of a theorem or set of theorems.

formal security policy model — A mathematically precise statement of a security policy. To be adequately precise, such a model must represent the initial state of a system, the way in which the system progresses from one state to another, and a definition of a secure state of the system.

To be acceptable as a basis for a TCB, the model must be supported by a formal proof that if the initial state of the system satisfies the definition of a secure state and if all assumptions required by the model hold, then all future states of the system will be secure. Some formal modeling techniques include state transition models, denotational semantics models, and algebraic specification models. See Bell-LaPadula model.

Formal Top-Level Specification (FTLS) — A top-level specification that is written in a formal mathematical language to enable theorems showing the correspondence of the system specification to its formal requirements to be hypothesized and formally proven.

formal verification — The process of using formal proofs to demonstrate the consistency between a formal specification of a system and a formal security policy model (design verification), or between the formal specification and its high-level program implementation (implementation verification).

fractional T-1 — A 64 Kbps increment of a T1 frame.

frame relay — A packet-switching interface that operates at data rates of 56 Kbps to 2 Mbps. Frame relay is minus the error control overhead of X.25, and it assumes that a higher-layer protocol will check for transmission errors.

frequency division multiple access (FDMA) — A digital radio technology that divides the available spectrum into separate radio channels. Generally used in conjunction with time division multiple access (TDMA) or code division multiple access (CDMA).

frequency hopping multiple access (FHMA) — A system using frequency hopping spread spectrum (FHSS) to permit multiple, simultaneous conversations or data sessions by assigning different hopping patterns to each.

frequency hopping spread spectrum (FHSS) — A method used to share the available bandwidth in 802.11b WLANs. FHSS takes the data signal and modulates it with a carrier signal that hops from frequency to frequency on a cyclical basis over a wide band of frequencies. FHSS in the 2.4 GHz frequency band will hop between 2.4 GHz and 2.483 GHz. The receiver must be set to the same hopping code.

frequency shift keying (FSK) — A modulation scheme for data communications using a limited number of discrete frequencies to convey binary information.

front-end security filter — A security filter, implemented in hardware or software, which is logically separated from the remainder of the system in order to protect the system's integrity.

functional programming — A programming method that uses only mathematical functions to perform computations and solve problems.

functional testing — The segment of security testing in which the advertised security mechanisms of the system are tested, under operational conditions, for correct operation.

gateway — A network component that provides interconnectivity at higher network layers.

gigabyte (GB, GByte) — A unit of measure for memory or disk storage capacity; usually 1,073,741,824 bytes.

gigahertz (GHz) — A measure of frequency; one billion hertz.

Global System for Mobile (GSM) communications — The wireless analog of the ISDN landline system.

GOTS — Government off-the-shelf software.

governing security requisites — Those security requirements that must be addressed in all systems. These requirements are set by policy, directive, or common practice set — for example, by EO, OMB, the OSD, a military service, or a DoD agency. These requirements are typically high-level. Although implementation varies from case to case, those requisites are fundamental and shall be addressed.

Gramm-Leach-Bliley (GLB) Act of November 1999 — An act that removes Depression-era restrictions on banks that limited certain business activities, mergers, and affiliations. It repeals the restrictions on banks affiliating with securities firms contained in Sections 20 and 32 of the Glass-Steagall Act. GLB became effective on November 13, 2001. GLB also requires health plans and insurers to protect member and subscriber data in electronic and other formats. These health plans and insurers fall under new state laws and regulations that are being passed to implement GLB because GLB explicitly assigns enforcement of the health plan and insurer regulations to state insurance authorities (15 U.S.C. §6805). Some of the privacy and security requirements of Gramm-Leach-Bliley are similar to those of HIPAA.

grand design program strategies — Characterized by acquisition, development, and deployment of the total functional capability in a single increment, reference (i).

granularity — An expression of the relative size of a data object; for example, protection at the file level is considered coarse granularity, whereas protection at the field level is considered to be of a finer granularity.

Graybox test — Test in which the ethical hacking team has partial knowledge of the target information system.

Grayhat hacker — A hacker who normally performs ethical hacking but sometimes reverts to malicious, blackhat hacking.

grid computing — Grid computing applies multiple computational resources (a computing grid) to the solution of a single, defined problem.

guard — A processor that provides a filter between two disparate systems operating at different security levels or between a user terminal and a database in order to filter out data that the user is not authorized to access.

handshaking procedure — A dialogue between two entities (e.g., a user and a computer, a computer and another computer, or a program and another program) for the purpose of identifying and authenticating the entities to one another.

HDX — Half-duplex.

Hertz (Hz) — A unit of frequency measurement; one cycle of a periodic event per second. Used to measure frequency.

Hierarchical Development Methodology — A methodology for specifying and verifying the design programs written in the SPECIAL specification language. The tools for this methodology include the SPECIAL specification processor, the Boyer-Moore theorem prover, and the Feiertag information flow tool.

high-level data link control — An ISO protocol for link synchronization and error control.

HIPAA — See Kennedy-Kassebaum Act of 1996.

host — A time-sharing computer accessed via terminals or terminal emulation; a computer to which an expansion device attaches.

host to front-end protocol — A set of conventions governing the format and control of data that is passed from a host to a front-end machine.

HTTP — Hypertext Transfer Protocol.

hybrid cloud — A computing environment combining both private (internal) and public (external) cloud computing environments. It may be either on a continuous basis or in the form of a "cloudburst."

Hypertext Markup Language (HTML) — A standard used on the Internet for defining hypertext links between documents.

hypervisor — The hypervisor is a virtualization mechanism, usually software, which supports multiple operating systems running on single host computer.

I&A — Identification and authentication.

IA — Information Assurance.

IAC — Inquiry access code; used in inquiry procedures. The IAC can be one of two types: a dedicated IAC for specific devices or a generic IAC for all devices.

IaaS (Infrastructure-as-a-Service) — IaaS provides for the delivery of Web-based computational resources and storage on the cloud.

IAW — In accordance with.

ICV — Integrity check value; In WEP encryption, the frame is run through an integrity algorithm, and the generated ICV is placed at the end of the encrypted data in the frame. Then the receiving station runs the data through its integrity algorithm and compares it to the ICV received in the frame. If it matches, the unencrypted frame is passed to the higher layers. If it does not match, the frame is discarded.

ID — Common abbreviation for "identifier" or "identity."

identification — The process that enables a system to recognize an entity, generally by the use of unique machine-readable user names.

Identity-Based Encryption (IBE) — The IBE concept proposes that any string can be used as an individual's public key, including his or her e-mail address.

IDS — Intrusion detection system.

IETF — Internet Engineering Task Force.

IKE — Internet key exchange.

impersonating — Synonymous with spoofing.

incomplete parameter checking — A system design flaw that results when not all parameters have been fully examined for accuracy and consistency, thus making the system vulnerable to penetration.

incremental program strategies — Characterized by acquisition, development, and deployment of functionality through a number of clearly defined system "increments" that stand on their own.

individual accountability — The ability to positively associate the identity of a user with the time, method, and degree of access to a system.

industrial, scientific, and medicine (ISM) bands — Radio frequency bands authorized by the Federal Communications Commission (FCC) for wireless LANs. The ISM bands are located at 902 MHz, 2.400 GHz, and 5.7 GHz. The transmitted power is commonly less than 600 mw, but no FCC license is required.

inference engine — A component of an artificial intelligence system that takes inputs and uses a knowledge base to infer new facts and solve a problem.

information category — The term used to bound information and tie it to an information security policy.

information flow control — A procedure undertaken to ensure that information transfers within a system are not made from a higher security level object to an object of a lower security level. See covert channel, simple security property, and star property (* property). Synonymous with data flow control and flow control.

information flow model — Information security model in which information is categorized into classes, and rules define how information can flow between the classes.

information security policy — The aggregate of public law, directives, regulations, and rules that regulate how an organization manages, protects, and distributes information. For example, the information security policy for financial data processed on DoD systems may be in U.S.C., E.O., DoD Directives, and local regulations. The information security policy lists all the security requirements applicable to specific information.

information system (IS) — Any telecommunications or computer-related equipment, or interconnected systems or subsystems of equipment, that is used in the acquisition, storage, manipulation, management, movement, control, display, switching, interchange, transmission, or reception of voice and/or data; includes software, firmware, and hardware.

information system security officer (ISSO) — The person who is responsible to the DAA for ensuring that security is provided for and implemented throughout the life cycle of an AIS, from the beginning of the concept development plan through its design, development, operation, maintenance, and secure disposal. In C&A, the person responsible to the DAA for ensuring the security of an IT system is approved, operated, and maintained throughout its life cycle in accordance with the SSAA.

information technology (IT) — The hardware, firmware, and software used as part of the information system to perform DoD information functions.

This definition includes computers, telecommunications, automated information systems, and automatic data processing equipment. IT includes any assembly of computer hardware, software, and/or firmware configured to collect, create, communicate, compute, disseminate, process, store, and/or control data or information.

information technology security (ITSEC) — Protection of information technology against unauthorized access to or modification of information, whether in storage, processing, or transit, and against the denial of service to authorized users, including those measures necessary to detect, document, and counter such threats. Protection and maintenance of confidentiality, integrity, availability, and accountability.

INFOSEC — Information System Security.

infrared (IR) light — Light waves that range in length from about 0.75 to 1,000 microns; this is a lower frequency than the spectral colors but a higher frequency than radio waves.

infrastructure-centric — A security management approach that considers information systems and their computing environment as a single entity.

inheritance (in object-oriented programming) — When all the methods of one class, called a superclass, are inherited by a subclass. Thus, all messages understood by the superclass are understood by the subclass.

Institute of Electrical and Electronic Engineers (IEEE) — A U.S.-based standards organization participating in the development of standards for data transmission systems. The IEEE has made significant progress in the establishment of standards for LANs — namely, the IEEE 802 series.

Integrated Services Digital Network (ISDN) — A collection of CCITT standards specifying WAN digital transmission services. The overall goal of ISDN is to provide a single physical network outlet and transport mechanism for the transmission of all types of information, including data, video, and voice.

integration testing — Testing process used to verify the interface among network components as the components are installed. The installation crew should integrate components into the network one-by-one and perform integration testing when necessary to ensure proper gradual integration of components.

integrator — An organization or individual that unites, combines, or otherwise incorporates information system components with another system(s).

integrity — (1) A term that refers to a sound, unimpaired, or perfect condition.

(2) Quality of an IT system reflecting the logical correctness and reliability of the operating system; the logical completeness of the hardware and software implementing the protection mechanisms; and the consistency of the data structures and occurrence of the stored data. It is composed of data integrity and system integrity.

interdiction — See Denial of Service.

Interface Definition Language (IDL) — A standard interface language that is used by clients to request services from objects.

internal cloud — A cloud-computing-like environment within the boundaries of an organization and typically available for exclusive use by said organization.

internal security controls — Hardware, firmware, and software features within a system that restrict access to resources (hardware, software, and data) to authorized subjects only (persons, programs, or devices).

International Standards Organization (ISO) — A non-treaty standards organization active in the development of international standards, such as the Open System Interconnection (OSI) network architecture.

International Telecommunications Union (ITU) — An intergovernmental agency of the United States responsible for making recommendations and standards regarding telephone and data communications systems for public and private telecommunication organizations and for providing coordination for the development of international standards.

International Telegraph and Telephone Consultative Committee (CCITT) — Part of the ITU, this international standards organization is dedicated to establishing effective and compatible telecommunications among members of the United Nations. The CCITT develops the widely used V Series and X Series standards and protocols.

Internet — The largest network in the world. The successor to ARPANET, the Internet includes other large internetworks. The Internet uses the TCP/IP protocol suite and connects universities, government agencies, and individuals around the world.

Internet Protocol (IP) — The Internet standard protocol that defines the Internet datagram as the information unit passed across the Internet. IP provides the basis of a best-effort packet delivery service. The Internet protocol suite is often referred to as TCP/IP because IP is one of the two fundamental protocols, the other being the Transfer Control Protocol.

Internetwork Packet Exchange (IPX) — NetWare protocol for the exchange of message packets on an internetwork. IPX passes application requests for network services to the network drives and then to other workstations, servers, or devices on the internetwork.

IPSec — Secure Internet Protocol.

IS — See information system.

isochronous transmission — Type of synchronization whereby information frames are sent at specific times.

isolation — The containment of subjects and objects in a system in such a way that they are separated from one another as well as from the protection controls of the operating system.

ISP — Internet service provider.

ISSE — Information systems security engineering/engineer.

ISSO — See information system security officer.

IT — See information technology.

ITA — Industrial Telecommunications Association.

ITSEC — See information technology security.

IV — Initialization vector; for WEP encryption.

Kennedy Kassebaum Act — Kennedy-Kassebaum Health Insurance Portability and Accountability Act (HIPAA) of 1996. A set of regulations that mandates the use of standards in health care record keeping and electronic transactions. The act requires that health care plans, providers, insurers, and clearinghouses do the following:

- Provide for restricted access by the patient to personal healthcare information.
- Implement administrative simplification standards.
- Enable the portability of health insurance.
- Establish strong penalties for healthcare fraud.

Kerberos — A trusted, third-party authentication protocol that was developed under Project Athena at MIT. In Greek mythology, Kerberos is a three-headed dog that guards the entrance to the underworld. Using symmetric key cryptography, Kerberos authenticates clients to other entities on a network to which a client requires services.

key — Information or sequence that controls the enciphering and deciphering of messages. Also known as a *cryptovariable*. Used with a particular algorithm to encipher or decipher the plaintext message.

key clustering — A situation in which a plaintext message generates identical ciphertext messages by using the same transformation algorithm but with different cryptovariables.

key schedule — A set of subkeys derived from a secret key.

kilobyte (KB, Kbyte) — A unit of measurement of memory or disk storage capacity; a data unit of 210 (1,024) bytes.

kilohertz (kHz) — A unit of frequency measurement equivalent to 1,000 hertz.

knowledge acquisition system — The means of identifying and acquiring the knowledge to be entered into an expert system's knowledge base.

knowledge base — Refers to the rules and facts of the particular problem domain in an expert system.

least privilege — The principle that requires each subject to be granted the most restrictive set of privileges needed for the performance of authorized tasks. The application of this principle limits the damage that can result from accident, error, or unauthorized use.

legacy information system — An operational information system that existed before the implementation of the DITSCAP.

Light-emitting diode (LED) — Used in conjunction with optical fiber, an LED emits incoherent light when current is passed through it. Its advantages include low cost and long lifetime, and it is capable of operating in the Mbps range.

limited access — Synonymous with access control.

limited fault tolerance — Specifies the type of failures against which the Target of Evaluation (TOE) must be resistant. Examples of general failures are flooding of the computer room, short-term power interruption, breakdown of a CPU or host, software failure, or buffer overflow. Requires all functions to be available if a specified failure occurs.

Link Access Procedure — An ITU error correction protocol derived from the HDLC standard.

link encryption — Each entity has keys in common with its two neighboring nodes in the chain of transmission. Thus, a node receives the encrypted message from its predecessor neighboring node, decrypts it, and re-encrypts it with another key that is common to the successor node. Then, the encrypted message is sent on to the successor node, where the process is repeated until the final destination is reached. Obviously, this mode provides no protection if the nodes along the transmission path are subject to compromise.

list-oriented — A computer protection system in which each protected object has a list of all subjects that are authorized to access it. Compare ticket-oriented.

LLC — Logical Link Control; the IEEE Layer 2 protocol.

local area network (LAN) — A network that interconnects devices in the same office, floor, building, or close buildings.

lock-and-key protection system — A protection system that involves matching a key or password with a specific access requirement.

logic bomb — A resident computer program that triggers the perpetration of an unauthorized act when particular states of the system are realized.

Logical Link Control layer — The highest layer of the IEEE 802 reference model; provides similar functions to those of a traditional data link control protocol.

loophole — An error of omission or oversight in software or hardware that permits circumventing the system security policy.

LSB — Least-significant bit.

MAC — Mandatory access control if used in the context of a type of access control; MAC also refers to the media access control address assigned to a network interface card on an Ethernet network.

magnetic remanence — A measure of the magnetic flux density that remains after removal of the applied magnetic force. Refers to any data remaining on magnetic storage media after removal of the power.

mail gateway — A type of gateway that interconnects dissimilar e-mail systems.

maintainer — The organization or individual that maintains the information system.

maintenance hook — Special instructions in software to enable easy maintenance and additional feature development. These instructions are not clearly defined during access for design specification. Hooks frequently enable entry into the code at unusual points or without the usual checks, so they are serious security risks if they are not removed prior to live implementation. Maintenance hooks are special types of trapdoors.

maintenance organization — The organization that keeps an IT system operating in accordance with prescribed laws, policies, procedures, and regulations. In the case of a contractor-maintained system, the maintenance organization is the government organization responsible for, or sponsoring the operation of, the IT system.

malicious logic — Hardware, software, or firmware that is intentionally included in a system for an unauthorized purpose (for example, a Trojan horse).

MAN — Metropolitan area network.

management information base (MIB) — A collection of managed objects residing in a virtual information store.

mandatory access control (MAC) — A means of restricting access to objects based on the sensitivity (as represented by a label) of the information contained in the objects, and the formal authorization (i.e., clearance) of subjects to access information of such sensitivity. Compare discretionary access control.

MAPI — Microsoft's mail application programming interface.

mashup — Refers to a Web-based application that combines items such as data or capability from a number of sources to develop new capabilities or services.

masquerading — See spoofing.

media access control (MAC) — An IEEE 802 standards sublayer used to control access to a network medium, such as a wireless LAN. Also deals with collision detection. Each computer has its own unique MAC address.

Medium access — The Data Link Layer function that controls how devices access a shared medium. IEEE 802.11 uses either CSMA/CA or contention-free access modes. Also, a data link function that controls the use of a common network medium.

Megabits per second (Mbps) — One million bits per second.

Megabyte (MB, Mbyte) — A unit of measurement for memory or disk storage capacity; usually 1,048,576 bytes.

Megahertz (MHz) — A measure of frequency equivalent to one million cycles per second.

middleware — An intermediate software component located on the wired network between the wireless appliance and the application or data residing on the wired network. Middleware provides appropriate interfaces between the appliance and the host application or server database.

mimicking — See spoofing.

mission — The assigned duties to be performed by a resource.

Mobile IP — A protocol developed by the IETF that enables users to roam to parts of the network associated with an IP address other than the one loaded in the user's appliance. Also refers to any mobile device that contains the IEEE 802.11 MAC and physical layers.

modes of operation — A description of the conditions under which an AIS functions, based on the sensitivity of data processed and the clearance levels and authorizations of the users. Four modes of operation are authorized:

Dedicated mode — An AIS is operating in the dedicated mode when each user who has direct or indirect individual access to the AIS, its peripherals, remote terminals, or remote hosts has all of the following:

- A valid personnel clearance for all information on the system

- Formal access approval; furthermore, the user has signed nondisclosure agreements for all the information stored and/or processed (including all compartments, subcompartments, and/or special access programs)

- A valid need-to-know for all information contained within the system

System-high mode — An AIS is operating in the system-high mode when each user who has direct or indirect access to the AIS, its peripherals, remote terminals, or remote hosts has all of the following:

- A valid personnel clearance for all information on the AIS

- Formal access approval, and signed nondisclosure agreements, for all the information stored and/or processed (including all compartments, subcompartments, and/or special access programs)

- A valid need-to-know for some of the information contained within the AIS

Compartmented mode — An AIS is operating in the compartmented mode when each user who has direct or indirect access to the AIS, its peripherals, remote terminals, or remote hosts has all of the following:

- A valid personnel clearance for the most restricted information processed in the AIS

- Formal access approval, and signed nondisclosure agreements, for that information which he or she will be able to access

- A valid need-to-know for that information which he or she will be able to access

Multilevel mode — An AIS is operating in the multilevel mode when all of the following statements are satisfied concerning the users who have direct or indirect access to the AIS, its peripherals, remote terminals, or remote hosts:

- Some do not have a valid personnel clearance for all the information processed in the AIS.

- All have the proper clearance and the appropriate formal access approval for that information to which they are to have access.

- All have a valid need-to-know for that information to which they are to have access.

modulation — The process of translating the baseband digital signal to a suitable analog form. Any of several techniques for combining user information with a transmitter's carrier signal.

MSB — Most significant bit.

multicore processor — An integrated circuit to which two or more processors have been attached for enhanced performance, reduced power consumption, and more efficient simultaneous processing of multiple tasks.

multilevel device — A device that is used in a manner that permits it to simultaneously process data of two or more security levels without risk of compromise. To accomplish this, sensitivity labels are normally stored on the same physical medium and in the same form (for example, machine-readable or human-readable) as the data being processed.

multilevel secure — A class of system containing information with different sensitivities that simultaneously permits access by users with different security clearances and needs-to-know but that prevents users from obtaining access to information for which they lack authorization.

multilevel security mode — See modes of operation.

multipath — The signal variation caused when radio signals take multiple paths from transmitter to receiver.

multipath fading — A type of fading caused by signals taking different paths from the transmitter to the receiver and consequently interfering with each other.

multiple access rights terminal — A terminal that can be used by more than one class of users — for example, users who have different access rights to data.

multiple inheritance — In object-oriented programming, a situation where a subclass inherits the behavior of multiple superclasses.

multiplexer — A network component that combines multiple signals into one composite signal in a form suitable for transmission over a long-haul connection, such as leased 56 Kbps or T1 circuits.

Multi-station access unit (MAU) — A multiport wiring hub for token-ring networks.

multiuser mode of operation — A mode of operation designed for systems that process sensitive, unclassified information in which users might not have a need-to-know for all information processed in the system. This mode is also used for microcomputers processing sensitive unclassified information that cannot meet the requirements of the stand-alone mode of operation.

Musical Instrument Digital Interface (MIDI) — A standard protocol for the interchange of musical information between musical instruments and computers.

mutually suspicious — A state that exists between interacting processes (subsystems or programs) in which neither process can expect the other process to function securely with respect to some property.

MUX — Multiplexing sublayer; a sublayer of the L2CAP layer.

NACK or NAK — Negative acknowledgement. This can be a deliberate signal that the message was received in error or it can be inferred by a timeout.

National Computer Security Center (NCSC) — Originally named the DoD Computer Security Center, the NCSC is responsible for encouraging the widespread availability of trusted computer systems throughout the federal government. A branch of the National Security Agency (NSA), it also initiates research and develops and publishes standards and criteria for trusted information systems.

National Information Assurance Certification and Accreditation Process (NIACAP) — Provides a standard set of activities, general tasks, and a management structure to certify and accredit systems that will maintain the information assurance and security posture of a system or site. The NIACAP is designed to certify that the information system meets documented accreditation requirements and continues to maintain the accredited security posture throughout the system life cycle.

National Security Decision Directive 145 (NSDD 145) — Signed by President Ronald Reagan in 1984, this directive provides initial objectives, policies, and an organizational structure to guide the conduct of national activities for safeguarding systems that process, store, or communicate sensitive information; establishes a mechanism for policy development; and assigns implementation responsibilities.

National Telecommunications and Information System Security Directives (NTISSD) — NTISS directives establish national-level decisions relating to NTISS policies, plans, programs, systems, or organizational delegations of authority. NTISSDs are promulgated by the executive agent of the government for telecommunications and information systems security or by the chairman of the NTISSC when so delegated by the executive agent. NTISSDs are binding upon all federal departments and agencies.

National Telecommunications and Information Systems Security Advisory Memoranda/Instructions (NTISSAM, NTISSI) — Provides advice, assistance, or information on telecommunications and systems security that is of general interest to applicable federal departments and agencies. NTISSAMs/NTISSIs are promulgated by the National Manager for Telecommunications and Automated Information Systems Security and are recommendatory.

NCSC — See National Computer Security Center.

NDI — See non-developmental item.

need-to-know access — The level of access to, knowledge of, or possession of specific information that is required to carry out official duties.

Network Basic Input/Output System (NetBIOS) — A standard interface between networks and PCs that enables applications on different computers to communicate within a LAN. NetBIOS was created by IBM for its early PC network, was adopted by Microsoft, and has since become a de facto industry standard. It is not routable across a WAN.

network file system (NFS) — A distributed file system enabling a set of dissimilar computers to access each other's files in a transparent manner.

network front end — A device that implements the necessary network protocols, including security-related protocols, to enable a computer system to be attached to a network.

network interface card (NIC) — A network adapter inserted into a computer that enables the computer to be connected to a network.

network monitoring — A form of operational support enabling network management to view the network's inner workings. Most network-monitoring equipment is non-obtrusive and can be used to determine the network's utilization and locate faults.

network reengineering — A structured process that can help an organization proactively control the evolution of its network. Network reengineering consists of continually identifying factors influencing network changes, analyzing network modification feasibility, and performing network modifications as necessary.

network service access point (NSAP) — A point in the network where OSI network services are available to a transport entity.

NIACAP — See National Information Assurance Certification and Accreditation Process.

NIAP — National Information Assurance Partnership.

NIST — National Institute of Standards and Technology.

node — Any network-addressable device on the network, such as a router or network interface card. Also any network station.

NSA — National Security Agency.

NSDD 145 — See National Security Decision Directive 145.

NSTISS — National Security Telecommunications and Information Systems Security.

NTISSC — The National Telecommunications and Information Systems Security Committee.

Number Field Sieve (NFS) — A general-purpose factoring algorithm that can be used to factor large numbers.

object — A passive entity that contains or receives information. Access to an object potentially implies access to the information that it contains. Examples of objects include records, blocks, pages, segments, files, directories, directory trees, and programs, as well as bits, bytes, words, fields, processors, video displays, keyboards, clocks, printers, and network nodes.

Object Request Broker (ORB) — The fundamental building block of the Object Request Architecture (ORA), which manages the communications among the ORA entities. The purpose of the ORB is to support the interaction of objects in heterogeneous, distributed environments. The objects may be on different types of computing platforms.

object reuse — The reassignment and reuse of a storage medium (e.g., page frame, disk sector, and magnetic tape) that once contained one or more objects. To be securely reused and assigned to a new subject, storage media must contain no residual data (data remanence) from the object(s) that were previously contained in the media.

object services — Services that support the ORB in creating and tracking objects as well as performing access control functions.

OFDM — Orthogonal frequency division multiplexing; a set of frequency-hopping codes that never use the same frequency at the same time. Used in IEEE 802.11a for high-speed data transfer.

OMB — Office of Management and Budget.

one-time pad — Encipherment operation performed using each component of the key, K, only once to encipher a single character of the plaintext. Therefore, the key has the same length as the message. The popular interpretation of one-time pad is that the key is used only once and never used again. Ideally, the components of the key are truly random and have no periodicity or predictability, making the ciphertext unbreakable.

Open Database Connectivity (ODBC) — A standard database interface enabling interoperability between application software and multivendor ODBC-compliant databases.

Open Data-Link Interface (ODI) — Novell's specification for Network Interface Card device drivers, enabling simultaneous operation of multiple protocol stacks.

open security environment — An environment that includes those systems in which at least one of the following conditions holds true: 1) application developers (including maintainers) do not have sufficient clearance or authorization to provide an acceptable presumption that they have not introduced malicious logic, and 2) configuration control does not provide sufficient assurance that applications are protected against the introduction of malicious logic prior to and during the operation of system applications.

Open Shortest Path First (OSPF) — A TCP/IP routing protocol that bases routing decisions on the least number of hops from source to destination.

open system authentication — The IEEE 802.11 default authentication method, which is a very simple, two-step process: First, the station that wants to authenticate with another station sends an authentication management frame containing the sending station's identity. Then the receiving station sends back a frame indicating whether it recognizes the identity of the authenticating station.

Open System Interconnection (OSI) — An ISO standard specifying an open system capable of enabling communications between diverse systems. OSI has the following seven layers of distinction: Physical, Data Link, Network, Transport, Session, Presentation, and Application. These layers provide the functions that enable standardized communications between two application processes.

operations security — Controls over hardware, media, and operators who have access; protects against asset threats, baseline, or selective mechanisms.

Operations Security (OPSEC) — An analytical process by which the U.S. government and its supporting contractors can deny to potential adversaries information about capabilities and intentions by identifying, controlling, and protecting evidence of the planning and execution of sensitive activities and operations.

operator — An individual who supports system operations from the operator's console, monitors execution of the system, controls the flow of jobs, and mounts input/output volumes.

OPSEC — See Operations Security.

Orange Book — Alternate name for DoD Trusted Computer Security Evaluation Criteria.

original equipment manufacturer (OEM) — A manufacturer of products for integration in other products or systems.

OS — Commonly used abbreviation for "operating system."

OSD — Office of the Secretary of Defense.

other program strategies — Strategies intended to encompass variations and/or combinations of the grand design, incremental, evolutionary, or other program strategies (DoD Directive 5000.1).

overt channel — A path within a computer system or network that is designed for the authorized transfer of data. Compare with covert channel.

overwrite procedure — A stimulation to change the state of a bit followed by a known pattern. See magnetic remanence.

PaaS (Platform-as-a-Service) — PaaS provides a comprehensive application development environment accessed through subscription service.

packet — A basic message unit for communication across a network. A packet usually includes routing information, data, and (sometimes) error-detection information.

packet-switched — Describes: (1) A network that routes data packets based on an address contained in the data packet. Multiple data packets can share the same network resources. (2) A communications network that uses shared facilities to route data packets from and to different users. Unlike a circuit-switched network, a packet-switched network does not set up dedicated circuits for each session.

PAD — Packet assembly/disassembly.

partitioned security mode — A mode of operation wherein all personnel have the clearance but not necessarily the formal access approval and need-to-know for all information contained in the system. Not to be confused with compartmented security mode.

password — A protected/private character string that is used to authenticate an identity.

PCMCIA — Personal Computer Memory Card International Association. The industry group that defines standards for PC cards (and the name applied to the cards themselves). These roughly credit card–sized adapters for memory and modem cards are available in three thicknesses: 3.3, 5, and 10.5 mm.

PDN — Public data network.

PED — Personal electronic device.

Peer-to-peer network — A network in which a group of devices can communicate among a group of equal devices. A peer-to-peer LAN does not depend upon a dedicated server but allows any node to be installed as a nondedicated server and share its files and peripherals across the network.

pen register — A device that records all the numbers dialed from a specific telephone line.

penetration — The successful act of bypassing a system's security mechanisms.

penetration signature — The characteristics or identifying marks that might be produced by a penetration.

penetration study — A study to determine the feasibility and methods for defeating the controls of a system.

penetration testing — The portion of security testing in which the evaluators attempt to circumvent the security features of a system. The evaluators might be assumed to use all system design and implementation documentation, which can include listings of system source code, manuals, and circuit diagrams. Evaluators work under the same constraints that are applied to ordinary users.

performance modeling — The use of simulation software to predict network behavior, enabling developers to perform capacity planning. Simulation makes it possible to model the network and impose varying levels of utilization to observe the effects.

performance monitoring — Activity that tracks network performance during normal operations. Performance monitoring includes real-time monitoring, during which metrics are collected and compared against thresholds; recent-past monitoring, in which metrics are collected and analyzed for trends that may lead to performance problems; and historical data analysis, in which metrics are collected and stored for later analysis.

periods processing — The processing of various levels of sensitive information at distinctly different times. Under periods processing, the system must be purged of all information from one processing period before transitioning to the next, when there are different users who have differing authorizations.

permissions — A description of the type of authorized interactions that a subject can have with an object. Examples of permissions types include read, write, execute, add, modify, and delete.

permutation — A method of encrypting a message, also known as transposition; operates by rearranging the letters of the plaintext.

personnel security — Describes: (1) The procedures that are established to ensure that all personnel who have access to sensitive information possess the required authority as well as appropriate clearances. (2) Procedures to ensure a person's background; provides assurance of necessary trustworthiness.

PGP — Pretty Good Privacy; a form of encryption.

Physical Layer (PHY) — The layer of the OSI model that provides the transmission of bits through a communication channel by defining electrical, mechanical, and procedural specifications. It establishes protocols for voltage and data transmission timing and rules for "handshaking."

physical security — The application of physical barriers and control procedures as preventive measures or countermeasures against threats to resources and sensitive information.

piconet — A collection of devices connected via Bluetooth technology in an ad hoc fashion. A piconet starts with two connected devices, such as a portable PC and a cellular phone, and can grow to eight connected devices.

piggyback — Gaining unauthorized access to a system via another user's legitimate connection. See between-the-lines entry.

pipelining — In computer architecture, a design in which the decode and execution cycles of one instruction are overlapped in time with the fetch cycle of the next instruction.

PKI — Public key infrastructure.

plain old telephone system (POTS) — The original analog telephone system, which is still in widespread use today.

plaintext — Message text in clear, human-readable form.

Platform for Privacy Preferences (P3P) — Proposed standards developed by the World Wide Web Consortium (W3C) to implement privacy practices on websites.

Point-to-Point Protocol (PPP) — A protocol that provides router-to-router and host-to-network connections over both synchronous and asynchronous circuits. PPP is the successor to SLIP.

portability — Defines network connectivity that can be easily established, used, and then dismantled.

port scanning — Connecting to UDP and TCP ports in order to determine the services and applications running on the target host.

PRBS — Pseudorandom bit sequence.

Presentation Layer — The layer of the OSI model that negotiates data transfer syntax for the Application Layer and performs translations between different data types, if necessary.

print suppression — Eliminating the displaying of characters in order to preserve their secrecy; for example, not displaying a password as it is keyed at the input terminal.

private cloud — A cloud-computing-like environment within the boundaries of an organization and typically for its exclusive use, typically hosted on an enterprise's private network.

private key encryption — See symmetric (private) key encryption.

privileged instructions — A set of instructions (e.g., interrupt handling or special computer instructions) to control features such as storage protection features that are generally executable only when the automated system is operating in the executive state.

PRNG — Pseudorandom number generator.

procedural language — Implies sequential execution of instructions based on the von Neumann architecture of a CPU, memory, and input/output device. Variables are part of the sets of instructions used to solve a particular problem; therefore, the data is not separate from the statements.

procedural security — Synonymous with administrative security.

process — A program in execution. See domain and subject.

program manager — The person ultimately responsible for the overall procurement, development, integration, modification, operation, and maintenance of the IT system.

Protected Health Information (PHI) — Individually identifiable health information that is

- Transmitted by electronic media
- Maintained in any medium described in the definition of electronic media (under HIPAA)
- Transmitted or maintained in any other form or medium

protection philosophy — An informal description of the overall design of a system that delineates each of the protection mechanisms employed. A combination, appropriate to the evaluation class, of formal and informal techniques is used to show that the mechanisms are adequate to enforce the security policy.

Protection Profile (PP) — In the Common Criteria, an implementation-independent specification of the security requirements and protections of a product that could be built.

protection-critical portions of the TCB — Those portions of the TCB whose normal function is to deal with access control between subjects and objects. Their correct operation is essential to the protection of the data on the system.

protocols — A set of rules and formats, semantic and syntactic, that permits entities to exchange information.

prototyping — A method of determining or verifying requirements and design specifications. The prototype normally consists of network hardware and software that support a proposed solution. The approach to prototyping is typically a trial-and-error experimental process.

pseudoflaw — An apparent loophole deliberately implanted in an operating system program as a trap for intruders.

PSTN — Public-switched telephone network; the general phone network.

public cloud — A cloud computing environment that is open for use to the general public, whether individuals, corporations, or other types of organizations. Amazon Web Services is an example of a public cloud. The public cloud service is often provided to customers on a pay-as-you-go basis.

public key cryptography — See asymmetric key encryption.

Public Key Cryptography Standards (PKCS) — A set of public key cryptography standards that supports algorithms such as Diffie-Hellman and RSA, as well as algorithm-independent standards.

Public Law 100-235 (P.L. 100-235) — Also known as the Computer Security Act of 1987, this law creates a means for establishing minimum acceptable security practices for improving the security and privacy of sensitive information in federal computer systems. This law assigns responsibility to the National Institute of Standards and Technology for developing standards and guidelines for federal computer systems processing unclassified data. The law also requires establishment of security plans by all operators of federal computer systems that contain sensitive information.

purge — The removal of sensitive data from an AIS, AIS storage device, or peripheral device with storage capacity, at the end of a processing period. This action is performed with an assurance, proportional to the sensitivity of the data, that the data cannot be reconstructed. An AIS must be disconnected from any external network before a purge. After a purge, the medium can be declassified by observing the review procedures of the respective agency.

RADIUS — Remote Authentication Dial-In User Service.

RC4 — RSA cipher algorithm 4.

read — A fundamental operation that results only in the flow of information from an object to a subject.

read access — Permission to read information.

recovery planning — The advance planning and preparations that are necessary to minimize loss and to ensure the availability of the critical information systems of an organization.

recovery procedures — The actions necessary to restore a system's computational capability and data files after a system failure or outage/disruption.

Reduced Instruction Set Computer (RISC) architecture — A computer architecture designed to reduce the number of cycles required to execute an instruction. A RISC architecture uses simpler instructions but makes use of other features, such as optimizing compilers and large numbers of general-purpose registers in the processor and data caches, to reduce the number of instructions required.

reference-monitor concept — An access-control concept that refers to an abstract machine that mediates all access to objects by subjects.

reference-validation mechanism — An implementation of the reference monitor concept. A security kernel is a type of reference-validation mechanism.

reliability — The probability of a given system performing its mission adequately for a specified period of time under expected operating conditions.

remote bridge — A bridge connecting networks separated by longer distances. Organizations use leased 56 Kbps circuits, T1 digital circuits, and radio waves to provide such long-distance connections among remote sites.

remote journaling — Refers to the parallel processing of transactions to an alternate site, as opposed to a batch dump process such as electronic vaulting. A communications line is used to transmit live data as it occurs. This enables the alternate site to be fully operational at all times and introduces a very high level of fault tolerance.

repeater — A network component that provides internetworking functionality at the Physical Layer of a network's architecture. A repeater amplifies network signals, extending the distance they can travel.

residual risk — The portion of risk that remains after security measures have been applied.

residue — Data left in storage after processing operations are complete but before degaussing or rewriting has taken place.

resource encapsulation — The process of ensuring that a resource not be directly accessible by a subject but that it be protected so that the reference monitor can properly mediate access to it.

restricted area — Any area to which access is subject to special restrictions or controls for reasons of security or safeguarding of property or material.

RFC — Request for comment.

RFP — Request for proposal.

ring topology — A topology in which a set of nodes are joined in a closed loop.

risk — (1) A combination of the likelihood that a threat will occur, the likelihood that a threat occurrence will result in an adverse impact, and the severity of the resulting impact. (2) The probability that a particular threat will exploit a particular vulnerability of the system.

risk analysis — The process of identifying security risks, determining their magnitude, and identifying areas needing safeguards. Risk analysis is a part of risk management. Synonymous with risk assessment.

risk assessment — Process of analyzing threats to an IT system, vulnerabilities of a system, and the potential impact that the loss of information or capabilities of a system would have on security. The resulting analysis is used as a basis for identifying appropriate and effective measures.

risk index — The disparity between the minimum clearance or authorization of system users and the maximum sensitivity (for example, classification and categories) of data processed by a system. See the publications CSC-STD-00385 and CSC-STD-004-85 for a complete explanation of this term.

risk management — The total process of identifying, controlling, eliminating, or minimizing uncertain events that might affect system resources. It includes risk analysis, cost-benefit analysis, selection, implementation, tests, a security evaluation of safeguards, and an overall security review.

ROM — Read-only memory.

router — A network component that provides internetworking at the Network Layer of a network's architecture by allowing individual networks to become part of a WAN. A router works by using logical and physical addresses to connect two or more separate networks. It determines the best path by which to send a packet of information.

Routing Information Protocol (RIP) — A common type of routing protocol. RIP bases its routing path on the distance (number of hops) to the destination. RIP maintains optimum routing paths by sending out routing update messages if the network topology changes.

RS-232 — (1) A serial communications interface. (2) The ARS-232n EIA standard that specifies up to 20 Kbps, 50-foot, serial transmission between computers and peripheral devices. Serial communication standards are defined by the Electronic Industries Association (EIA).

RS-422 — An EIA standard specifying electrical characteristics for balanced circuits (i.e., both transmit and return wires are at the same voltage above ground). RS-422 is used in conjunction with RS-449.

RS-423 — An EIA standard specifying electrical characteristics for unbalanced circuits (i.e., the return wire is tied to the ground). RS-423 is used in conjunction with RS-449.

RS-449 — An EIA standard specifying a 37-pin connector for high-speed transmission.

RS-485 — An EIA standard for multipoint communications lines.

S/MIME — A protocol that adds digital signatures and encryption to Internet MIME (Multipurpose Internet Mail Extensions).

safeguards — See security safeguards.

sandbox — An access control–based protection mechanism. It is commonly applied to restrict the access rights of mobile code that is downloaded from a website as an applet. The code is set up to run in a "sandbox" that blocks its access to the local workstation's hard disk, thus preventing the code from malicious activity. The sandbox is usually interpreted by a virtual machine such as the Java Virtual Machine (JVM). Also describes a security mechanism for safely running programs, often used to execute untested code, or untrusted programs from unverified third-parties, suppliers, and untrusted users.

SaaS (Software-as-a-Service) — SaaS provides access to software applications remotely as a Web-based service.

SAS 70 — SAS 70, or Statement on Auditing Standard # 70, "Service Organizations" Type II Audit evaluates a service organization's internal controls to determine whether accepted best practices are being applied to protect client information.

SBU — Sensitive but unclassified; an information designation.

scalar processor — A processor that executes one instruction at a time.

scanning — Actively connecting to a system to obtain a response.

scavenging — Searching through object residue to acquire unauthorized data.

SCI — Sensitive Compartmented Information.

SDLC — Synchronous data link control.

secure configuration management — The set of procedures that are appropriate for controlling changes to a system's hardware and software structure for the purpose of ensuring that changes will not lead to violations of the system's security policy.

secure state — A condition in which no subject can access any object in an unauthorized manner.

secure subsystem — A subsystem that contains its own implementation of the reference monitor concept for those resources it controls. The secure subsystem, however, must depend on other controls and the base operating system for the control of subjects and the more primitive system objects.

security — Measures and controls that ensure the confidentiality, integrity, availability, and accountability of the information processed and stored by a computer.

security critical mechanisms — Those security mechanisms whose correct operation is necessary to ensure that the security policy is enforced.

security evaluation — An evaluation to assess the degree of trust that can be placed in a system for the secure handling of sensitive information. One type, a *product evaluation*, is performed on the hardware and software features and assurances of a computer product from a perspective that excludes the application environment. The other type, a *system evaluation*, is made for the purpose of assessing a system's security safeguards with respect to a specific operational mission; it is a major step in the certification and accreditation process.

security fault analysis — A security analysis, usually performed on hardware at the gate level, to determine the security properties of a device when a hardware fault is encountered.

security features — The security-relevant functions, mechanisms, and characteristics of system hardware and software. Security features are a subset of system security safeguards.

security filter — A trusted subsystem that enforces a security policy on the data that passes through it.

security flaw — An error of commission or omission in a system that might enable protection mechanisms to be bypassed.

security flow analysis — A security analysis performed on a formal system specification that locates the potential flows of information within the system.

security functional requirements — Requirements, preferably from the Common Criteria, Part 2, that when taken together specify the security behavior of an IT product or system.

security inspection — Examination of an IT system to determine compliance with security policy, procedures, and practices.

security kernel — The hardware, firmware, and software elements of a Trusted Computer Base (TCB) that implement the reference monitor concept. The security kernel must mediate all accesses, must be protected from modification, and must be verifiable as correct.

security label — A piece of information that represents the security level of an object.

security level — The combination of a hierarchical classification and a set of nonhierarchical categories that represents the sensitivity of information.

security measures — Elements of software, firmware, hardware, or procedures that are included in a system for the satisfaction of security specifications.

security objective — A statement of intent to counter specified threats and/or satisfy specified organizational security policies and assumptions.

security perimeter — The boundary where security controls are in effect to protect assets.

security policy — The set of laws, rules, and practices that regulates how an organization manages, protects, and distributes sensitive information.

security policy model — A formal presentation of the security policy enforced by the system. It must identify the set of rules and practices that regulate how a system manages, protects, and distributes sensitive information. See formal security policy model.

security process — The series of activities that monitor, evaluate, test, certify, accredit, and maintain the system accreditation throughout the system life cycle.

security range — The highest and lowest security levels that are permitted in or on a system, system component, subsystem, or network.

security requirements — The types and levels of protection that are necessary for equipment, data, information, applications, and facilities to satisfy the security policy.

security requirements baseline — A description of minimum requirements necessary for a system to maintain an acceptable level of security.

security safeguards — The protective measures and controls that are prescribed to satisfy the security requirements specified for a system. Those safeguards can include (but are not necessarily limited to) the following: hardware and software security features, operating procedures, accountability procedures, access and distribution controls, management constraints, personnel security, and physical structures, areas, and devices. Also called safeguards.

security specifications — A detailed description of the safeguards required to protect a system.

Security Target (ST) — (1) In the Common Criteria, a list of the security claims for a particular IT security product. (2) A set of security functional and assurance requirements and specifications to be used as the basis for evaluating an identified product or system.

Security Test and Evaluation (ST&E) — Examination and analysis of the safeguards required to protect an IT system as they have been applied in an operational environment, to determine the security posture of that system.

security testing — A process used to determine whether the security features of a system are implemented as designed. This process includes hands-on functional testing, penetration testing, and verification.

sensitive information — Information that if lost, misused, modified, or accessed by unauthorized individuals could affect the national interest or the conduct of federal programs or the privacy to which individuals are entitled under Section 552a of Title 5, U.S. Code, but that has not been specifically authorized under criteria established by an executive order or an act of Congress, to be kept classified in the interest of national defense or foreign policy. The concept of sensitive information can apply to private-sector entities as well.

sensitivity label — A piece of information that represents the security level of an object. Sensitivity labels are used by the TCB as the basis for mandatory access control decisions.

serial interface — An interface to provide serial communications service.

Serial Line Internet Protocol (SLIP) — An Internet protocol used to run IP over serial lines and dial-up connections.

service migration — The process and capability to move applications or services among different cloud vendors.

Session Layer — One of the seven OSI model layers. Establishes, manages, and terminates sessions between applications.

shared key authentication — A type of authentication that assumes each station has received a secret shared key through a secure channel, independent from an 802.11 network. Stations authenticate through shared knowledge of the secret key. Use of shared key authentication requires implementation of the 802.11 Wired Equivalent Privacy (WEP) algorithm.

Simple Mail Transfer Protocol (SMTP) — The Internet e-mail protocol.

Simple Network Management Protocol (SNMP) — The network management protocol of choice for TCP/IP-based Internets. Widely implemented with 10BASE-T Ethernet. A network management protocol that defines information transfer among management information bases (MIBs).

single-user mode — An OS loaded without Security Front End.

single-level device — An automated information systems device that is used to process the data of a single security level at any one time.

slashdot effect — Also known as slash-dotting, this is the phenomenon of linking a popular website to a smaller site, causing the smaller site to slow down or even temporarily close due to the increased traffic.

SMS — Short (or small) message service.

SNR — Signal-to-noise ratio.

social engineering — Attacks targeting an organization's employees through the use of social skills to obtain sensitive information.

software engineering — The science and art of specifying, designing, implementing, and evolving programs, documentation, and operating procedures whereby computers can be made useful to humans.

software process — A set of activities, methods, and practices that are used to develop and maintain software and associated products.

software process capability — Describes the range of expected results that can be achieved by following a software process.

software process maturity — The extent to which a software process is defined, managed, measured, controlled, and effective.

software process performance — The result achieved by following a software process.

software security — General-purpose executive, utility, or software development tools and applications programs or routines that protect data handled by a system.

software system test and evaluation process — A process that plans, develops, and documents the quantitative demonstration of the fulfillment of all baseline functional performance and operational and interface requirements.

spoofing — An attempt to gain access to a system by posing as an authorized user. Synonymous with impersonating, masquerading, or mimicking.

SQL injection — The process of an attacker inserting SQL statements into a query by exploiting vulnerability for the purpose of sending commands to a web server database.

SSL — Secure Sockets Layer.

SSO — System security officer.

ST connector — An optical fiber connector that uses a bayonet plug and socket.

ST&E — See Security Test and Evaluation.

standalone (shared system) — A system that is physically and electrically isolated from all other systems and is intended for use by more than one person, either simultaneously (e.g., a system that has multiple terminals) or serially, with data belonging to one user remaining available to the system while another user uses the system (e.g., a personal computer that has nonremovable storage media, such as a hard disk).

standalone (single-user system) — A system that is physically and electrically isolated from all other systems and is intended for use by one person at a time, with no data belonging to other users remaining in the system (e.g., a personal computer that has removable storage media, such as a floppy disk).

star topology — A topology wherein each node is connected to a common central switch or hub.

state variable — A variable that represents either the state of the system or the state of some system resource.

storage object — An object that supports both read and write access.

Structured Query Language (SQL) — An international standard for defining and accessing relational databases.

subject — An active entity, generally in the form of a person, process, or device, that causes information to flow among objects or that changes the system state. Technically, a process/domain pair.

subject security level — A subject's security level is equal to the security level of the objects to which it has both read and write access. A subject's security level must always be dominated by the clearance of the user with whom the subject is associated.

superscalar processor — A processor that allows concurrent execution of instructions in the same pipelined stage. The term superscalar denotes multiple, concurrent operations performed on scalar values, as opposed to vectors or arrays that are used as objects of computation in array processors.

supervisor state — See executive state.

Switched Multimegabit Digital Service (SMDS) — A packet-switching connectionless data service for WANs.

symmetric (private) key encryption — Cryptographic system in which the sender and receiver both know a secret key that is used to encrypt and decrypt a message.

Synchronous Optical NETwork (SONET) — A fiber-optic transmission system for high-speed digital traffic. SONET is part of the B-ISDN standard.

Synchronous transmission — A type of communications data synchronization whereby frames are sent within defined time periods. It uses a clock to control the timing of bits being sent. See asynchronous transmission.

system — A set of interrelated components consisting of mission, environment, and architecture as a whole. Also, a data processing facility.

system development methodologies — Methodologies developed through software engineering to manage the complexity of system development. Development methodologies include software engineering aids and high-level design analysis tools.

system entity — A system subject (user or process) or object.

system high security mode — A system and all peripherals protected in accordance with (IAW) requirements for the highest security level of material in the system; personnel with access have security clearance but not a need-to-know. See modes of operation.

system integrity — A characteristic of a system when it performs its intended function in an unimpaired manner, free from deliberate or inadvertent unauthorized manipulation.

system low security mode — The lowest security level supported by a system at a particular time or in a particular environment.

system testing — A type of testing that verifies the installation of the entire network. Testers normally complete system testing in a simulated production environment, simulating actual users in order to ensure the network meets all stated requirements.

Systems Network Architecture (SNA) — IBM's proprietary network architecture.

T1 — A standard specifying a time division–multiplexing scheme for point-to-point transmission of digital signals at 1.544 Mbps.

tampering — Unauthorized modification that alters the proper functioning of equipment or a system in a manner that degrades the security or functionality it provides.

Target of Evaluation (TOE) — In the Common Criteria, TOE refers to the product to be tested.

TCB — See Trusted Computing Base.

technical attack — An attack that can be perpetrated by circumventing or nullifying hardware and software protection mechanisms, rather than by subverting system personnel or other users.

technical vulnerability — A hardware, firmware, communication, or software flaw that leaves a computer processing system open for potential exploitation, either externally or internally — resulting in a risk to the owner, user, or manager of the system.

TELNET — A virtual terminal protocol used in the Internet, enabling users to log in to a remote host. TELNET is defined as part of the TCP/IP protocol suite.

TEMPEST — Codename referring to the investigation, study, and control of spurious compromising emanations emitted by electrical equipment.

terminal identification — The means used to uniquely identify a terminal to a system.

test case — An executable test with a specific set of input values and a corresponding expected result.

threat — Any circumstance or event with the potential to cause harm to an IT system in the form of destruction, disclosure, adverse modification of data, and/or denial of service.

threat agent — A method that is used to exploit a vulnerability in a system, operation, or facility.

threat analysis — The examination of all actions and events that might adversely affect a system or operation.

threat assessment — Formal description and evaluation of threat to an IT system.

threat monitoring — The analysis, assessment, and review of audit trails and other data collected for the purpose of searching for system events that might constitute violations or attempted violations of system security.

ticket-oriented — A computer protection system in which each subject maintains a list of unforgeable bit patterns called *tickets*, one for each object the subject is authorized to access. Compare with list-oriented.

time-dependent password — A password that is valid only at a certain time of day or during a specified interval of time.

time-domain reflectometer (TDR) — Mechanism used to test the effectiveness of network cabling.

TLS — Transport Layer Security.

token bus — A network that uses a logical token-passing access method. Unlike a token-passing ring, permission to transmit is usually based on the node address, rather than the position in the network. A token bus network uses a common cable set, with all signals broadcast across the entire LAN.

token ring — A local area network (LAN) standard developed by IBM that uses tokens to control access to the communication medium. A token ring provides multiple access to a ring-type network. FDDI and IEEE 802.5 are token ring standards.

top-level specification — A nonprocedural description of system behavior at the most abstract level; typically, a functional specification that omits all implementation details.

topology — A description of the network's geographical layout of nodes and links.

traceroute — Software utility used to determine the path to a target computer.

tranquility — A security model rule stating that an object's security level cannot change while the object is being processed by an AIS.

transceiver — A device for transmitting and receiving packets between the computer and the medium.

Transmission Control Protocol (TCP) — A commonly used protocol for establishing and maintaining communications between applications on different computers. TCP provides full-duplex, acknowledged, and flow-controlled service to upper-layer protocols and applications.

Transmission Control Protocol/ Internet Protocol (TCP/IP) — A de facto, industry-standard protocol for interconnecting disparate networks. TCP/IP are standard protocols that define both the reliable full-duplex transport level and the connectionless, best effort unit of information passed across an internetwork.

Transport Layer — OSI model layer that provides mechanisms for the establishment, maintenance, and orderly termination of virtual circuits while shielding the higher layers from the network implementation details.

trapdoor — A hidden software or hardware mechanism that can be triggered to permit the circumvention of system protection mechanisms. It is activated in a manner that appears innocent — for example, a special "random" key sequence at a terminal. Software developers often introduce trapdoors in their code to enable them to reenter the system and perform certain functions. Synonymous with backdoor.

Trojan horse — A computer program that has an apparently or actually useful function but contains additional (hidden) functions that surreptitiously exploit the legitimate authorizations of the invoking process to the detriment of security or integrity.

trusted computer system — A system that employs sufficient hardware and software assurance measures to enable its use for simultaneous processing of a range of sensitive or classified information.

Trusted Computing Base (TCB) — The totality of protection mechanisms within a computer system, including hardware, firmware, and software, the combination of which is responsible for enforcing a security policy. A TCB consists of one or more components that together enforce a unified security policy over a product or system. The ability of a TCB to correctly enforce a unified security policy depends solely on the mechanisms within the TCB and on the correct input of parameters by system administrative personnel (e.g., a user's clearance level) related to the security policy.

trusted distribution — A trusted method for distributing the TCB hardware, software, and firmware components, both originals and updates, that provides methods for protecting the TCB from modification during distribution and for the detection of any changes to the TCB that might occur.

trusted identification forwarding — An identification method used in networks whereby the sending host can verify that an authorized user on its system is attempting a connection to another host. The sending host transmits the required user authentication information to the receiving host. The receiving host can then verify that the user is validated for access to its system. This operation might be transparent to the user.

trusted path — A mechanism by which a person at a terminal can communicate directly with the TCB. This mechanism can be activated only by the person or by the TCB; it cannot be imitated by untrusted software.

trusted process — A process whose incorrect or malicious execution is capable of violating system security policy.

trusted software — The software portion of the TCB.

twisted-pair wire — Type of medium using metallic-type conductors twisted together to provide a path for current flow. The wire in this medium is twisted in pairs to minimize the electromagnetic interference between one pair and another.

UART — Universal asynchronous receiver transmitter. A device that either converts parallel data into serial data for transmission or converts serial data into parallel data for receiving data.

untrusted process — A process that has not been evaluated or examined for adherence to the security policy. It might include incorrect or malicious code that attempts to circumvent the security mechanisms.

user — (1) A person or process that is accessing an AIS either by direct connections (e.g., via terminals), or by indirect connections (i.e., preparing input data or receiving output that is not reviewed for content or classification by a responsible individual) (2) A person or process authorized to access an IT system.

User Datagram Protocol — UDP uses the underlying Internet protocol (IP) to transport a message. This is an unreliable, connectionless delivery scheme. It does not use acknowledgments to ensure that messages arrive and does not provide feedback to control the rate of information flow. UDP messages can be lost, duplicated, or arrive out of order.

user ID — A unique symbol or character string that is used by a system to identify a specific user.

user profile — Patterns of a user's activity that can be used to detect changes in normal routines.

user representative — The individual or organization that represents the user or user community in the definition of information system requirements.

U.S. Federal Computer Incident Response Center (FedCIRC) — FedCIRC provides assistance and guidance in incident response and provides a centralized approach to incident handling across U.S. government agency boundaries.

U.S. Patriot Act of October 26, 2001 — A law that permits the following:

- Subpoena of electronic records
- Monitoring of Internet communications
- Search and seizure of information on live systems (including routers and servers), backups, and archives
- Reporting of cash and wire transfers of $10,000 or more

Under the Patriot Act, the government has extended powers to subpoena electronic records and to monitor Internet traffic. In monitoring information, the government can require the assistance of ISPs and network operators. This monitoring can even extend into individual organizations.

U.S. Uniform Computer Information Transactions Act (UCITA) of 1999 — A model act that is intended to apply uniform legislation to software licensing.

utility — An element of the DII providing information services to DoD users. Those services include Defense Information Systems Agency Mega-Centers, information processing, and wide-area network communications services.

utility computing — Utility computing is a model whereby computing resources are made available to a customer on a charge-for-usage basis.

V.21 — An ITU standard for asynchronous 0–300 bps full-duplex modems.

V.21FAX — An ITU standard for facsimile operations at 300 bps.

V.34 — An ITU standard for 28,800 bps modems.

validation (in DITSCAP) — Determination of the correct implementation in the completed IT system with the security requirements and approach agreed on by the users, acquisition authority, and DAA.

validation (in software engineering) — Establishment of the fitness or worth of a software product for its operational mission.

vaulting — Running mirrored data centers in separate locations.

vendor lock-in — Describes a scenario in which a cloud client finds it difficult to migrate cloud services from one cloud vendor to another.

verification — The process of determining compliance of the evolving IT system specification, design, or code with the security requirements and approach agreed on by the users, acquisition authority, and the DAA. Also, the process of comparing two levels of system specification for proper correspondence (e.g., a security policy model with top-level specification, top-level specification with source code, or source code with object code). This process might be automated.

vertical cloud — A cloud computing environment optimized for use in a particular industry or application use case.

very-long-instruction word (VLIW) processor — A processor in which multiple, concurrent operations are performed in a single instruction. The number of instructions is reduced relative to those in a scalar processor. However, for this approach to be feasible, the operations in each VLIW instruction must be independent of each other.

virtualization — Virtualization is the instantiation of a virtual version of a server, operating system, or other computational resource.

virtual machine — A software program that emulates a hardware system and is hosted on another environment. A VM is a software implementation of a machine (computer) that executes programs like a real machine, and can be used to execute the instruction set of a platform different from that of the host.

virtual private cloud (VPC) — Describes a concept that is similar to, and derived from, the familiar concept of a virtual private network (VPN), but applied to cloud computing. It is the notion of turning a public cloud into a virtual private cloud, particularly in terms of security and the ability to create a VPC across components that are both within the cloud and external to it.

virus — A self-propagating Trojan horse composed of a mission component, a trigger component, and a self-propagating component.

vulnerability — A weakness in system security procedures, system design, implementation, internal controls, and so on that could be exploited to violate system security policy.

vulnerability analysis — A measurement of vulnerability that includes the susceptibility of a particular system to a specific attack and the opportunities that are available to a threat agent to mount that attack.

vulnerability assessment — Systematic examination of an information system or product to determine the adequacy of security measures, identify security deficiencies, provide data from which to predict the effectiveness of proposed security measures, and confirm the adequacy of such measures after implementation.

WAP — Wireless Application Protocol. A standard commonly used for the development of applications for wireless Internet devices.

Whitebox test — Test in which the ethical hacking team has full knowledge of the target information system.

Whitehat hacker — An individual who conducts ethical hacking to help secure and protect an organization's information systems.

wide area network (WAN) — A network that interconnects users over a wide area, usually encompassing different metropolitan areas.

Wired Equivalency Privacy (WEP) — The algorithm of the 802.11 wireless LAN standard that is used to protect transmitted information from disclosure. WEP is designed to prevent violation of the confidentiality of data transmitted over the wireless LAN. WEP generates secret shared encryption keys that both source and destination stations use to alter frame bits to avoid disclosure to eavesdroppers.

wireless — Describes any computing device that can access a network without a wired connection.

wireless metropolitan area network (wireless MAN) — Provides communications links between buildings, avoiding the costly installation of cabling or leasing fees and the downtime associated with system failures.

WLAN — Wireless local area network.

work breakdown structure (WBS) — A diagram of the way a team will accomplish the project at hand by listing all tasks the team must perform and the products they must deliver.

work factor — An estimate of the effort or time needed by a potential intruder who has specified expertise and resources to overcome a protective measure.

work function (factor) — The difficulty in recovering plaintext from ciphertext, as measured by cost and/or time. The security of the system is directly proportional to the value of the work function. The work function need only be large enough to suffice for the intended application. If the message to be protected loses its value after a short period of time, the work function need only be large enough to ensure that the decryption would be highly infeasible in that period of time.

write — A fundamental operation that results in the flow of information only from a subject to an object.

write access — Permission to write to an object.

X.12 — An ITU standard for EDI.

X.121 — An ITU standard for international address numbering.

X.21 — An ITU standard for a circuit-switching network.

X.25 — An ITU standard for an interface between a terminal and a packet-switching network. X.25 was the first public packet-switching technology, developed by the CCITT and offered as a service during the 1970s. It is still available today. X.25 offers connection-oriented (virtual circuit) service; it operates at 64 Kbps, which is too slow for some high-speed applications.

X.400 — An ITU standard for OSI messaging.

X.500 — An ITU standard for OSI directory services.

X.509v3 — An ITU-T digital certificate that is an internationally recognized electronic document used to prove identity and public key ownership over a communications network. It contains the issuer's name, the user's identifying information, and the issuer's digital signature, as well as other possible extensions in version 3.

X.75 — An ITU standard for packet switching between public networks.

Zeroed — The degaussing, erasing, or overwriting of electronically stored data.

References

Armbrust, Michael, and Armando Fox, "Above the Clouds: A Berkley View of Cloud Computing," February 10, 2009.

Balding, Craig, "ITG2008 World Cloud Computing Summit," 2008, http://cloudsecurity.org.

BEinGRID Project, Gridipedia: GridDic — "The Grid Computing Glossary, 2009," www.gridipedia.eu/grid-computing-glossary.html.

Brodkin, Jon, "Seven Cloud-Computing Security Risks," 2008, www .networkworld.com/news/2008/070208-cloud.html.

Burton Group, "Attacking and Defending Virtual Environments," www .burtongroup.com/Guest/Srms/AttackingDefendingVirtual.aspx.

Cavoukian, Ann, "Privacy in the Clouds — A White Paper on Privacy and Digital Identity: Implications for the Internet" (Information and Privacy Commissioner of Ontario), www.ipc.on.ca/images/Resources/ privacyintheclouds.pdf.

Center for Internet Security (CIS), Benchmark for Xen 3.2 Version 1.0 May, 2008.

————. Virtual Machine Security Guidelines Version 1.0, September 2007.

————. "CIS Level 1 Benchmark for Virtual Machines," www.cisecurity .org/bench_vm.htm.

Chen, P. M., and B. D. Noble, " When Virtual Is Better Than Real," In HOTOS'01: Proceedings of the Eighth Workshop on Hot Topics in Operating Systems, pg. 133, Washington, DC: IEEE Computer Society, 2001.

Cloud Security Alliance, "Security Guidance for Critical Areas of Focus in Cloud Computing," April 2009, www.cloudsecurityalliance.org/guidance/csaguide.pdf.

Croll, Alistair, "Why Cloud Computing Needs Security," 2008 , http://gigaom.com/2008/06/10/the-amazon-outage-fortresses-in-the-clouds/.

Defense Information Systems Agency (DISA) Security Technical Implementation Guides (STIGS), http://iase.disa.mil/stigs/index.html.

Directive 95/46/EC of the European Parliament and of the Council of 24 October 1995 on the protection of individuals with regard to the processing of personal data and on the free movement of such data.

Dunlap, G. W., S. T. King, S. Cinar, M. A. Basrai, and P. M. Chen, "Revirt: Enabling Intrusion Analysis through Virtual-Machine Logging and Replay," SIGOPS Operating Systems, Rev., 36(SI):211–24, 2002.

Erickson, Jonothan, "Best Practices for Protecting Data in the Cloud," 2008, www.ddj.com/security/210602698.

ESX Server V1R1 DISA Field Security Operations, Developed by DISA for the DoD, 28 April 2008.

Foster, I., C. Kesselman, S. Tuecke, "The Anatomy of the Grid: Enabling Scalable Virtual Organizations," *International Journal of Supercomputer Applications*, 2001, www.globus.org/alliance/publications/papers/anatomy.pdf.

Garfinkel, T., and M. Rosenblum, "A Virtual Machine Introspection Based Architecture for Intrusion Detection," in Proceedings of the 2003 Network and Distributed System Symposium, 2003.

Gu, Yunhong, Robert L. Grossman, "Sector and Sphere: The Design and Implementation of a High Performance Data Cloud," UK, 2008.

Invisible Things Blog, http://theinvisiblethings.blogspot.com/2006/06/introducing-blue-pill.html.

Jaeger, Paul, Jimmy Lin, Justin Grimes, "Cloud Computing and Information Policy," *Journal of Information Technology and Politics*, Vol. 5, No. 3, Oct. 2008, pp. 269–83.

Jericho Forum, "Cloud Cube Model: Selecting Cloud Formations for Secure Collaboration," April 2009, www.opengroup.org/jericho/cloud_cube_model_v1.0.pdf.

Joshi, A., S. T. King, G. W. Dunlap, and P. M. Chen, "Detecting Past and Present Intrusions Through Vulnerability-Specific Predicates," in SOSP'05: Proceedings of the Twentieth ACM Symposium on Operating Systems Principles, pp. 91–104, New York, NY: ACM, 2005.

Lamb, John, *The Greening of IT*: *How Companies Can Make a Difference for the Environment*, IBM Press, 2009.

Miller, Michael, *Cloud Computing*: *Web-Based Applications that Change the Way You Work and Collaborate Online*, Que, 2008.

Mills, Elinor, "Cloud Computing Security Forecast: Clear Skies," 2009, http://news.zdnet.com/2100-9595_22-264312.html.

NIST Computer Resource Center, http://csrc.nist.gov.

Open Cloud Consortium, 2008, www.opencloudconsortium.org/index.html.

Open Grid Forum, "Web Services Agreement Specification (WS-Agreement)," www.ogf.org/documents/GFD.107.pdf.

Open Group, "TOGAF (The Open Group Architecture Framework)," www.opengroup.org/architecture.

Open Security Architecture, 2009, www.opensecurityarchitecture.org/cms/.

Ormandy, Tavis, "An Empirical Study into the Security Exposure to Hosts of Hostile Virtualized Environments," Google, Inc.

Payment Card Industry (PCI) Data Security Standard Requirements and Security Assessment Procedures, Version 1.2, October 2008.

Payne, B. D., M. Carbone, M. Sharif, and W. Lee. Lares, "An Architecture for Secure Active Monitoring Using Virtualization," IEEE Symposium on Security and Privacy, 0:233–47, 2008.

Payne, Bryan D., Martim Carbone, and Wenke Lee, "Secure and Flexible Monitoring of Virtual Machines," Computer Security Applications Conference, Annual, 0:385–97, 2007.

Perry, Geva, "How Cloud and Utility Computing Are Different," 2008, http://gigaom.com/2008/02/28/how-cloud-utility-computing-are-different.

Petriu, D. C., M. Woodside, "Some Requirements for Quantitative Annotations of Software Designs," in Workshop on MARTE, MoDELS Conference, 2005.

Provos, N., "Honeyd — A Virtual Honeypot Daemon," in 10th DFN-CERT Workshop, Hamburg, Germany, Feb. 2003.

Reese, George, *Cloud Application Architectures*, Sebastopol, California: O'Reilly Media, 2009.

Rhee, J., R. Riley, D. Xu, and X. Jiang, "Defeating Dynamic Data Kernel Rootkit Attacks via VMM-based Guest-Transparent Monitoring," in Proceedings of the ARES 2009 Conference, 2009.

Rittinghouse, John, "Cloud Computing: Implementation, Management, and Security," 2009.

Safeguarding Against and Responding to the Breach of Personally Identifiable Information From: Clay Johnson III, Deputy Director for Management (2007/5/22).

Schwartz, Ephraim, "Hybrid model brings security to the cloud," 2008, www .infoworld.com/d/cloud-computing/hybrid-model-brings-security-cloud-364.

Seshadri, A., M. Luk, N. Qu, and A. Perrig, "SecVisor: A Tiny Hypervisor to Provide Lifetime Kernel Code Integrity for Commodity Os's," in SOSP 07: Proceedings of the Twenty-First ACM SIGOPS Symposium on Operating Systems Principles, pp. 335–50, New York: ACM, 2007.

Theilmann, W., L. Baresi, "Multi-level SLAs for Harmonized Management in the Future Internet," in *Towards the Future Internet: A European Research Perspective*, IOS Press, May 2009, www.iospress.nl.

Theilmann, W., R. Yahyapour, J. Butler, "Multi-level SLA Management for Service-Oriented Infrastructures," in *Proceedings of ServiceWave 2008 Conference*, 10.12.–13.12.2008, Madrid, www.servicewave.eu.

U.S. Department of Defense Information Systems Agency, "Virtual Machine Security Technical Implementation Guide," http://iase.disa.mil/stigs/ stig/vm_stig_v2r2.pdf.

Weinberg, Neil, "Cloudy picture for cloud computing," 2008, www .networkworld.com/news/2008/043008-interop-cloud-computing. html?ap1=rcb.

Index

SYMBOLS AND NUMBERS

* (asterisk), passwords, 72
9126 standard, ISO, 87–89
27001 standard, ISO, 220–222
27002 standard, ISO, 222–223
27004 standard, ISO, 223
27005 standard, ISO, 223–224
27006 standard, ISO, 224
1973 U.S. Code of Fair Information, 132–133

A

Abicloud, 22
Abiquo, 22
AC erasure, 254
access control, 145–146, 210–213, 253
  authentication, 274
  controls, 210–211
access control lists (ACLs), 212
access control triple, 212
accountability, 66, 127, 146
accurateness, ISO 9126 standard, 87
ACLs. *See* access control lists
acquisition and implementation (AI), 85
Active Directory, penetration testing, 104
active eavesdropping, 143–144
adaptability, ISO 9126 standard, 89
Advanced Research Projects Agency Network (ARPANET), DoD, 1
advisory policies, 155
AFCERT. *See* Air Force Computer Emergency Response Team
AFIWC. *See* Air Force Information Warfare Center

age, information classification, 184
AH. *See* authentication header
AI. *See* acquisition and implementation
Air Force Computer Emergency Response Team (AFCERT), 245
Air Force Information Warfare Center (AFIWC), IDT, 245
AIRS. *See* Automated Incident Response System
Ajax. *See* asynchronous JavaScript and XML
ALU. *See* arithmetic logic unit
Amazon, 42
  EC2, 5, 7, 42
Amazon Web Services (AWS), 41
American National Standards Institute (ANSI), 89
American Registry of Internet Numbers (ARIN), 105
analyzability, ISO 9126 standard, 88
ANSI. *See* American National Standards Institute
anticipatory, autonomic computing, 214
Anti-Tamper/Software Protection Initiative, DoD, 248
API. *See* application programming interface
application programming interface (API), 20
  Beowulf, 12
  black box, 98
  PaaS, 41
  security, 192–193
  service monitoring data, 31
Application Security (Domain11), 61
Application-as-a-Service, 51
architecture, 33–60

network, 273
security, 177–216
ARIN. *See* American Registry of Internet Numbers
arithmetic logic unit (ALU), 203
ARPANET. *See* Advanced Research Projects Agency Network
ASIM. *See* Automated Security Incident Measurement
asynchronous JavaScript and XML (Ajax), 4
asynchronous tokens, challenge-response protocol, 207
ATM card, authentication, 205
attack surface, 169
attacks. *See specific attack types*
attainable, software security requirement, 75–76
audit trail, 65
auditing, 65–66, 83–85, 275
  VM, 169
authentication, 64, 82, 127, 205
  access control, 274
  encryption, 90
authentication header (AH), 196
authorization, 64–65, 82–83, 127
Automated Incident Response System (AIRS), 245
Automated Security Incident Measurement (ASIM), 245
automation, 31
  IDS, 244–245
  IT service management, 30
autonomic computing, 6, 15
  security, 213–216
availability, 64, 82, 126–127
  communications, 192
AWS. *See* Amazon Web Services
Azure Services Cloud Platform, Microsoft, 7

349